CW00933117

RESEARCH ETHICS IN CRIMINOLOGY

Ethical principles and concerns are at the heart of criminological research and can arise at the planning, implementation and reporting stages. It is vital that researchers are aware of the issues involved so that they can make informed decisions about the implications of certain choices. This cutting-edge book charts the changing topography of ethics, governance and accountability for social science research in criminology, contributes to the developing discourse on research ethics and demonstrates the importance as to why research ethics should be taken seriously. Bringing together a range of experts who consider both quantitative and qualitative methodologies, this book examines the key issues and challenges of ethical research. Topics covered include:

- the measures in place to ensure ethical research practice for social scientists;
- the relationship between state funding and research findings;
- the challenge of researching sensitive areas;
- the changing face of governance and accountability for academic criminology.

Research Ethics in Criminology is a comprehensive and accessible text that is ideal for students studying criminological research methods. Supplementary material includes key points, chapter summaries, critical thinking questions, key definitions, case examples and recommendations for further reading. This book will provide a thorough grounding in the ethical issues faced by researchers, as well as an understanding of the role and purpose of ethics committees.

Malcolm Cowburn is Emeritus Professor of Applied Social Science at Sheffield Hallam University.

Loraine Gelsthorpe is Professor of Criminology and Criminal Justice at the Institute of Criminology, University of Cambridge.

Azrini Wahidin is Associate Dean for Research and Innovation in the School of Social Sciences, Business and Law, Teesside University.

"*Research Ethics in Criminology* offers a comprehensive insight into the practicalities and difficulties confronted by students and academics conducting research into sensitive topic areas. Drawing on a wide range of expertise the book has been assembled with the needs of students, both undergraduate and postgraduate, foremost in mind and is, without doubt, an essential companion for those studying and researching within and around the discipline of criminology."

Samantha Weston, Lecturer in Criminology
Keele University, UK

"This edited collection is a timely and significant contribution to the field of criminology and to the praxis of criminological research. The essays in the collection stand as thought-provoking interventions in what is a challenging academic climate. Taken together, they are a 'must read' for students, researchers, and anyone else interested in the ethics and governance of social research."

Jaime Waters, Senior Lecturer in Criminology
Sheffield Hallam University, UK

RESEARCH ETHICS IN CRIMINOLOGY

Dilemmas, Issues and Solutions

Edited by Malcolm Cowburn,
Loraine Gelsthorpe and Azrini Wahidin

Routledge
Taylor & Francis Group

LONDON AND NEW YORK

First published 2017
by Routledge
2 Park Square, Milton Park, Abingdon, Oxon OX14 4RN

and by Routledge
711 Third Avenue, New York, NY 10017

Routledge is an imprint of the Taylor & Francis Group, an informa business

© 2017 Malcolm Cowburn, Loraine Gelsthorpe and Azrini Wahidin; individual chapters, the contributors

The right of the Malcolm Cowburn, Loraine Gelsthorpe and Azrini Wahidin to be identified as the authors of the editorial material, and of the authors for their individual chapters, has been asserted in accordance with sections 77 and 78 of the Copyright, Designs and Patents Act 1988.

All rights reserved. No part of this book may be reprinted or reproduced or utilised in any form or by any electronic, mechanical, or other means, now known or hereafter invented, including photocopying and recording, or in any information storage or retrieval system, without permission in writing from the publishers.

Trademark notice: Product or corporate names may be trademarks or registered trademarks, and are used only for identification and explanation without intent to infringe.

British Library Cataloguing-in-Publication Data
A catalogue record for this book is available from the British Library

Library of Congress Cataloging in Publication Data
Names: Cowburn, Malcolm, editor. | Gelsthorpe, Loraine, editor. | Wahidin, Azrini, 1972- editor.
Title: Research ethics in criminology : dilemmas, issues and solutions / edited by Malcolm Cowburn, Loraine Gelsthorpe and Azrini Wahidin.
Description: Abingdon, Oxon ; New York, NY : Routledge, 2017. | Includes bibliographical references and index.
Identifiers: LCCN 2016025440| ISBN 9781138803695 (hardback) | ISBN 9781138803701 (pbk.) | ISBN 9781315753553 (ebook)
Subjects: LCSH: Criminology--Research--Moral and ethical aspects.
Classification: LCC HV6024.5 .R469 2017 | DDC 174/.9364--dc23
LC record available at https://lccn.loc.gov/2016025440

ISBN: 978-1-138-80369-5 (hbk)
ISBN: 978-1-138-80370-1 (pbk)
ISBN: 978-1-315-75355-3 (ebk)

Typeset in Bembo
by Saxon Graphics Ltd, Derby

Printed and bound in Great Britain by
TJ International Ltd, Padstow, Cornwall

CONTENTS

ACKNOWLEDGEMENTS

This book has had an unusually long journey and we are most grateful to our fellow contributors for their patience. We are particularly grateful to Hannah Catterall, at Routledge, for her continuing faith that we would deliver the book at some point – such support is really important. Loraine and Azrini would like to thank Malcolm for graciously taking on the lion's share of the editorial burden towards the journey's end, and we all three would like to thank Joanne Garner for her practical help in the final stages of the book preparation.

CONTRIBUTORS

Avi Brisman is Assistant Professor of Justice Studies at Eastern Kentucky University, USA. He is co-editor, with Nigel South, of the *Routledge International Handbook of Green Criminology* (Routledge, 2013), co-editor, with Nigel South and Rob White, of *Environmental Crime and Social Conflict: Contemporary and Emerging Issues* (Ashgate, 2015) and co-author, with Nigel South, of *Green Cultural Criminology: Constructions of Environmental Harm, Consumerism, and Resistance to Ecocide* (Routledge, 2014).

Kirsten Campbell lectures in the Department of Sociology at Goldsmiths College, UK. She is currently the principal investigator of the ESRC-funded project, 'The Gender of Justice', which examines the prosecution of sexual violence in armed conflict through case studies of the International Criminal Tribunal for the former Yugoslavia and the Bosnian courts. This project builds on her recently completed study of subjectivity and sociality in international criminal law.

Malcolm Cowburn is an Emeritus Professor of Applied Social Science at Sheffield Hallam University, UK. His research has focused on three areas; sex crime and responding to sex offenders; the management of diversity in prisons; and applied research ethics in social science. He has published widely in these areas. He is co-author (with Steve Myers) of *Social Work with Sex Offenders: making a difference* (2016). He is currently Alternate Vice-Chair of the National Research Ethics Service (NRES) South-West Committee, and has also served on the Social Care Research Ethics Committee and University Faculty ethics committees.

Chris Fox is Professor of Evaluation at Manchester Metropolitan University, UK and Director of the Policy Evaluation and Research Unit. He has undertaken numerous criminal justice evaluations and written extensively on new approaches to financing and innovation in the criminal justice system. His most recent book examined the rise of the Justice Reinvestment movement in the US and UK. He is currently writing *An Introduction to Evaluation* (Sage Publishing, 2016).

Loraine Gelsthorpe is Professor of Criminology and Criminal Justice at the Institute of Criminology, University of Cambridge, UK. She is also Director of the Cambridge ESRC Doctoral Training Centre and Co-convenor of the Cambridge Migration Research Network (CAMMIGRES). Loraine has published widely on women, crime and criminal justice, youth justice and community penalties, as well as on more general criminal justice topics. One recent book is *A Restorative Justice Approach to Family Violence. Changing Tack* (co-edited by Anne Hayden, Loraine Gelsthorpe, Venezia King and Allison Morris). Loraine was made a Fellow of the Royal Society of Arts in 2009 for distinguished contribution to criminal justice, and a Fellow of the Academy of Social Sciences in 2013. She was President of the British Society of Criminology (July 2011–July 2015).

Evi Girling is Senior Lecturer in Criminology at Keele University, UK whose research has focused on fear of crime, young people and communities, and penal sensibilities. She has used innovating methodologies to explore people's responses to crime, their demands for order and attitudes towards punishment. She is an experienced ethnographer and qualitative researcher and has developed and delivered qualitative research training for postgraduate taught and PhD level degrees in the Social Sciences at Keele since 1998.

Simon Hackett is Professor of Applied Social Sciences and Principal of St Mary's College, Durham University, UK. Simon's research focuses on child maltreatment in its various forms and to professional responses designed to safeguard children, as well as adoption and children living in and out of home care. He has particular expertise in the problem of children and young people who present with harmful sexual behaviours and is Chair Elect of the National Organisation for the Treatment of Abusers (NOTA).

Mark Israel is Winthrop Professor of Law and Criminology at the University of Western Australia. He has published in the areas of research ethics and integrity, higher education and research policy, political exile and migration, criminology and socio-legal studies. Mark has won teaching and research prizes in Australia, the United Kingdom and the United States, including the Prime Minister's Award for Australian University Teacher of the Year in 2004.

Paul Knepper is Professor of Criminology in the Department of Law and Justice at Central Washington University and Visiting Professor of Criminology at the School of Crime Sciences, University of Lausanne. Recent books include *Writing the History of Crime* (Bloomsbury, 2015) and *The Oxford Handbook of the History of Crime and Criminal Justice* (OUP, 2016), edited with Anja Johansen.

Fiona Measham was appointed Professor of Criminology in the School of Applied Social Sciences at Durham University, UK in 2012. Fiona has conducted research for over two decades across a broad area of criminology and social policy, exploring changing trends in legal and illegal drugs; the night time economy and the sociocultural context of consumption; gender; the regulation and policing of intoxication; electronic music scenes and club cultures; issues of deterrence, displacement and desistance; and broader policy implications. A key feature of her research has been the development of *in-situ* methods of data collection in pubs, clubs and festivals, a working environment with which she is familiar, having spent her early adulthood working in bars and clubs across several continents in various guises.

Linda Moore is Senior Lecturer in Criminology in the School of Criminology, Politics and Social Policy at Ulster University. Her research interests include penology, youth justice and human rights. She is author, with Phil Scraton, of: *The Incarceration of Women: Punishing Bodies, Breaking Spirits* (Palgrave Macmilan, 2014). She is currently working on an ESRC-funded project on the criminalisation of abortion pills in Northern Ireland. Linda is an active member of her local UCU trade union association.

Peter Neyroud served for 30 years as a police officer in Hampshire, West Mercia, Thames Valley (as Chief Constable) and the National Policing Improvement Agency (as CEO). In 2010, he carried out the 'Review of Police Leadership and Training' which led to the establishment of the new 'National College of Policing' in 2012. Since 2010, he has been doing a PhD, managing a major research programme at Cambridge University, teaching senior police leaders and advising governments across the world. He is a Trustee Board Member of the Internet Watch Foundation. He was awarded the Queens Police Medal in 2004 and a CBE in the Queen's Birthday Honours List in 2011.

David Smith was a probation officer before being appointed to a lectureship at Lancaster University in 1976, where he has worked ever since. He was made Professor of Social Work in 1993, Professor of Criminology in 2001 and Emeritus Professor in 2012. He has researched and written on a range of criminological topics, including youth justice and probation policy and practice, as well as on problems of research in social work.

Nigel South is a Professor in the Department of Sociology, University of Essex, UK. In 2013 he received a Lifetime Achievement Award from the American Society of Criminology, Division on Critical Criminology. With Avi Brisman, he is co-editor of the *International Handbook of Green Criminology* (2013) and co-author of *Green Cultural Criminology* (2014), both published by Routledge.

Azrini Wahidin is Associate Dean for Research and Innovation in the School of Social Sciences, Business and Law, Teesside University. Azrini established the undergraduate criminology course at Queen's University Belfast and was an international visiting scholar at the University of Melbourne. Azrini has published widely on older offenders, women in prison and transitional justice. Her most recent book is *Ex-combatants, Gender and Peace in Northern Ireland: Women, Political Protest and the Prison Experience* (Palgrave). Azrini is the current Chair of the British Society of Criminology Ethics Committee.

Simon Winlow is the Co-Director of the Teesside Centre for Realist Criminology. He is the author of *Badfellas* (Berg, 2001), and the co-author of *Bouncers* (Oxford, 2003), *Violent Night* (Berg, 2006), *Criminal Identities and Consumer Culture* (Willan, 2006), Rethinking Social Exclusion (2013), *Riots and Political Protest* (Routledge, 2014) and *Revitalizing Criminological Theory* (Routledge, 2014).

INTRODUCTION

Malcolm Cowburn, Loraine Gelsthorpe and Azrini Wahidin

When we first conceived of this book we set out to explore the changing landscape of ethics regulation in the UK as it has impacted on criminology, and we wanted to alert readers to an ever-widening range of challenges. But we also wanted to outline some possible solutions, or at least to give examples of ways in which the challenges have been addressed. The subject of ethics in criminology and criminal justice has certainly gained prominence over the past two decades or so, as concerns about risk in higher education institutions, criminal justice agencies, other public authorities and individuals have prompted ethical questions and recognised the need to establish standards and provide guidance to those with whom they engage.

Thus the book aims to provide guidance to both novice and more experienced researchers on ethical issues that they are likely to face in the course of criminological research. The book charts the changing topography of ethics, governance and accountability for social science research in criminology. It brings together a series of cutting edge essays reflecting the contours of ethical debates and governance (in relation to specific research areas), examining the key issues and challenges of ethical research.

Governance, of course, is about power, and although we do not address this issue in a substantive chapter, we hope that the book will stimulate some thinking about power and knowledge within the academy, and during the process of academic research supervision as well. There is need to be mindful of the way in which there is potential for academics in academic institutions, learned societies and other scholarly activities to shape research directions, include, emphasise or exclude certain forms of knowledge and research methods in teaching the next generation of scholars and in inculcating a value base. A number of contributors to this book recognise the power relationship between the researcher and the researched. But even the power relationship between student and supervisor contributes to the shaping of knowledge and interpretation in a particular way. Indeed, there has been much less reflection on 'ethics from below' than on the implementation of 'ethical safeguards' from 'above' so to speak. The realities of empirical research and being in the field can involve a good deal of negotiating and 'ethical manoeuvring'; where is the supervisor to stand? Should the supervisor side with regulatory bodies and limit the research in order to protect the student, or trust the student to take whatever steps are necessary within the broad remit and values of the research, and with a broad understanding of 'ethics'. Lyng (1998: 222) has argued that '[m]any important empirical and theoretical problems taken up in the social sciences can be thoroughly and honestly studied only by placing oneself in situations that may compromise safety and security in a normative or corporeal sense'. Sticking strictly to 'safeguards' might thus result in 'failed fieldwork' if research is constrained by those safeguards. Yet importantly, universities have a duty of care to their students, and research organisations have a similar duty to researchers. Taking risks can provide a vista to the realities of research participants' lives, but this needs to be carefully balanced with knowledge of the field situation, experience, and trust in the researcher (Armstrong et al., 2014). Thus we hope that engagement with ethical dilemmas through this book will prompt some thinking about the need for balance; to protect researchers and the researched where protection is needed, but to also challenge new regimes of regulatory ethical control which impose unnecessary constraint. So a key aim of the book is to encourage further reflexivity at all levels, including: regulatory bodies, learned societies, institutions, departments, agencies, research teams, and supervisors and research students.

In each chapter authors have identified key points, key definitions and have provided a brief guide for further reading. Additionally, authors variously use empirical (case) material to illustrate and explore the points they develop. We also hope that the illustration of different ethical dilemmas and solutions within the book will remind readers to be alert to changes in the landscape of criminological research. Criminology does not stand still. Ethical considerations do not stand still.

References

Armstrong, R., Gelsthorpe, L. and Crewe, B. (2014) 'From Paper Ethics to Real-World Research: Supervising Ethical Reflexivity When Taking Risks in Research with 'the Risky', in K. Lumsden and A. Winter (Eds.) *Reflexivity in Criminological Research. Experiences with the Powerful and the Powerless.* Basingstoke: Palgrave Macmillan.

Lyng, S. (1998) 'Dangerous Methods: Risk Taking and the Research Process', in Ferrell, J., and M. S. Hamm (Eds.) *Ethnography at the Edge: Crime, Deviance, and Field Research.* Boston: Northeastern University Press.

PART I

Research methods
Issues and practice

Introduction to Part I

The first part of the book is rooted in empirical areas of criminological research. It opens with Chris Fox's exploration of the challenges of conducting evidence based policy research. Within increasing demands for 'intellectual rigour' and 'robust' research, it is fitting to start the book by raising questions of what may be concealed by political rhetoric or pragmatic manoeuvring. The political contestations of policy research perhaps, more clearly than other research highlight the implications of epistemological assumptions and methodological choices. Paul Knepper in his chapter suggests that 'historical criminology does not invite the same kind of ethical issues as social science research', and whilst this may be the case in relation to ethical issues related to the conduct of data collection with living people, we suggest that issues also highlighted by Knepper – 'the collection of historical evidence, the use of theory, the moral message of the story and the construction of memory' – are also of central importance to both the epistemological underpinning and ongoing conduct of criminological research. Archival research, as Knepper suggests, highlights the 'moral issues in how historical knowledge serves present interests'. Evi Girling suggests that research with children has been guided by professional codes of conduct that construe children and young people as a relatively homogenous and vulnerable group. She calls for greater sophistication in thinking ethically about this group; this requires active consideration of 'the "situational" realities and diversities of children and young people'. She does acknowledge that this level of complex consideration is 'relatively onerous', but goes on to suggest that such detailed attention should also be given to research with all people. Her chapter starts with consideration of theoretical issues and moves on to address practical issues such as the problems of gaining access, informed consent, autonomy, confidentiality; anonymity and protection. Linda Moore and Azrini

Wahidin's chapter is located in the practicalities and epistemological dilemmas of prisoner research; tensions related to allegiance ('whose side are you on?') and researcher safety are explored, along with sensitive issues concerning faithful reporting of the 'pains of imprisonment' whilst ensuring that all parties involved in the research remain safe and unharmed. Peter Neyroud considers the tensions and divided loyalties of 'insider' research of the police. His chapter is set in a very applied context of seeing research as a potential vehicle for cultural change within police forces – identifying obsolete practices and describing new possibilities. However, describing in detail a case study he discusses issues of consent, risk and harm assessment and the role of the researcher. In the final chapter of this section David Smith explores the ethics of researching social work in the criminal justice system, within this he acknowledges the ambivalent position of Probation, as a one-time criminal justice social work agency. His prime concerns are to assert a 'virtue-based approach to thinking about research ethics' and then explore issues of confidentiality in criminological research, including potential impacts of publishing results. His chapter concludes with consideration of issues relating to researching 'people of whom one disapproves'.

1

THE ETHICAL CHALLENGES OF EVIDENCE-BASED POLICY RESEARCH

Chris Fox

The concept of evidence-based policy (EBP) and the ethical challenges it poses are explored. First a 'standard' model of EBP is outlined and implicit assumptions it makes about the nature of evidence and the policy-making process are examined. Debates about how best to implement EBP in the criminal justice sector are investigated before various critiques of EBP are discussed. These start with methodological debates relating to the generation of empirical evidence and how to review evidence, but a set of ethical concerns soon emerge. These are not abstract, academic debates. Using the example of different approaches to offender rehabilitation the practical dimensions of such ethical concerns are demonstrated using offender rehabilitation as an example.

Key points

1. EBP is a well-developed concept in the UK criminal justice system.
2. In its 'traditional' form EBP gives precedence to experimental evaluation designs and the use of systematic reviews to interrogate the evidence base.
3. EBP draws heavily on the concept of evidence-based medicine but this raises questions about the transfer of ideas and methodologies to questions of social policy.
4. Ethical challenges to EBP often focus on the use of experimental research designs and whether 'scientific' approaches to social research are appropriate when addressing social issues.
5. A discussion of the relationship between evidence and practice in offender rehabilitation illustrates some of the questions that an overly 'scientific' approach to EBP raises.

What is evidence-based policy?

Defining evidence-based policy is not straightforward and definitions are contested. The UK government has defined evidence-based policy as being:

> based upon the best available evidence from a wide range of sources; all key stakeholders are involved at an early stage and throughout the policy's development. All relevant evidence, including that from specialists, is available in an accessible and meaningful form to policy makers.
>
> *(Cabinet Office 1999: 73)*

This approach is seen as integral to modern, professional policy making (Bullock et al. 2001). Davies suggests that it:

> helps people make well informed decisions about policies, programmes and projects by putting the best available evidence from research at the heart of policy development and implementation.
>
> *(Davies 1999 quoted in Davies 2004: 4)*

and contrasts it with opinion-based policy, which

> relies heavily on either the selective use of evidence (*e.g.* on single studies irrespective of quality) or on the untested views of individuals or groups, often inspired by ideological standpoints, prejudices, or speculative conjecture.
>
> *(Davies 2004)*

Straight away this presents us with a challenge because, inevitably, not all research is of the same quality and therefore we may not want to treat all research equally when using it to inform policy decisions (Davies 2004). If EBP is to be a reality it will require more systematic approaches to searching for and assessing the methodological quality of evidence so that policy-makers can achieve a balanced understanding of the research evidence and of its strengths and weaknesses (Davies 2004).

Thus, policy-makers with an interest in evidence-based decision-making have turned increasingly to systematic reviews of the results of previous inquiries in the relevant policy domain (Pawson 2002). Systematic reviews consider existing research literature on a topic based upon (Government Social Research Unit 2007a):

- comprehensive searching of print, electronic and unpublished sources;
- explicit search procedures for identifying the available literature;
- explicit criteria for distinguishing the quality of research studies; and
- presenting available evidence in a way that makes the quality of the evidence upon which the review is based transparent.

This systematic approach to reviewing the existing evidence is intended to overcome some of the problems inherent in traditional, 'narrative' literature reviews which typically suffer from several limitations such as 'selection bias' and 'publication bias', provide few details of the procedures by which the reviewed literature has been identified and appraised and are often unclear how the conclusions of narrative reviews follow from the evidence presented (ibid.).

Systematic reviews often include a meta-analysis. This is a statistical method for combining and summarising the results of studies in a systematic review. Once relevant studies have been identified, grouped together according to similar intervention characteristics and screened for methodological rigour the study outcomes are identified and effect sizes computed. Corrections are applied for small sample sizes and the mean effect of each class of intervention calculated (Government Social Research Unit 2007a).

Evidence-based medicine

To some extent the 'present fascination' with evidence-based policy was a response to contemporary interest in evidence-based medicine (Young 2011: 20) and the influence of evidence-based medicine is clear within experimental criminology (Sherman 2009). Over a number of decades there has been a growing awareness in the medical profession that medical professionals, despite acting on the best of intentions, do not always make good decisions (Evans et al. 2011). The history of medicine contains many examples of interventions that, at the time were thought to be effective, but turned out not to be or that were effective, but were used inappropriately. Well-known examples include the drug Thalidomide (Evans et al. 2011), the over-prescription of antibiotics and the advice to sleep babies on their fronts (Chalmers 2003).

In medicine the solution to these problems has been two-fold. First there is a need for a 'fair test' of the treatment, secondly, systematic reviews, normally including meta-analysis are required. In evidence-based medicine the 'fair test' is usually a randomised control trial (RCT). The RCT is not just the 'gold standard' for evaluating the effect of a treatment, it is the default design, and systematic reviews in medicine are heavily skewed towards evidence generated through RCTs. The design of an RCT is a relatively straightforward one. The simplest randomised experiment involves random allocation of units (these may be people, classrooms, neighbourhoods, etc.) to two different conditions and a post-test assessment of units. In the simplest experimental design the control group gets nothing. In a clinical trial this might involve giving one group of patients a treatment and the other group a 'placebo'. Often the outcome variable is measured before and after the intervention for both the intervention and control group. Shadish et al. (2002: 260) go as far as to suggest that in most cases the absence of a pre-test measure is 'risky' because it limits the opportunity for statistical analysis of pre-existing differences (Rossi et al. 2004). Pre-test can also help determine how much gain an intervention has made (Rossi et al. 2004).

In the pursuit of evidence-based medicine the systematic review has become a vital tool for policy-makers and practitioners and the creation of systematic reviews an important element of medical research, policy and practice, perhaps 'one of the most important innovations in medicine over the past 30 years' (Goldacre 2011: xi).

The scale and reach of this endeavour is perhaps clearest when one considers the Cochrane Collaboration – an international collaboration of more than 31,000 people across over 100 countries which has so far published over 6,000 systematic reviews (Cochrane Reviews) in an open-access, on-line library[1].

(Quasi) experimental-based policy

The model of evidence-based policy promoted by government tends to reflect the approach implied in evidence-based medicine. In this model experiments are the gold standard of evaluation and to some extent, the term 'evidence-based policy' has become understood to mean experimental-based policy (Sampson 2010). Thus, the Cabinet Office has consistently promoted the greater use of experiments in social policy making (see for instance, Government Social Research Unit 2007b) and in recent guidance on 'Developing Policy with Randomised Controlled Trials (RCT)' argued that:

RCTs are the best way of determining whether a policy is working (Haynes et al. 2012: 4).

Arguments for the superiority of RCTs are often found in the social and behavioural sciences (Weisburd et al. 2001; Lum and Yang, 2005). This is because, if implemented properly, they have the highest possible level of internal validity. Internal validity refers to 'the correctness of the key question about whether the intervention really did cause a change in the outcome' (Farrington 2003: 52 and described in detail in Shadish et al. 2002). As in medicine, the preference however, is not to rely on a single RCT, but to instead conduct systematic reviews and, where possible meta-analyses. As Sherman (2009) notes, a meta-analysis can sometimes be particularly illuminating in a social policy context where RCTs are often based on small samples and a meta-analysis can show the effect of an intervention when the effect was not apparent from looking at the results of individual, small studies. However, when compared to healthcare far fewer randomised field trials take place.

It is not always possible or desirable to implement an RCT and sometimes quasi-experiments provide a better solution. These have treatments, outcome measures and experimental units, but not random assignment so comparisons are between non-equivalent groups (Cook and Campbell 1979). In essence, as the design moves further away from the 'gold standard' of a social experiment, the less strong the internal validity assured by the design and the less certainty there is that any effects observed can be attributed to the intervention being studied.

There are a large number of quasi-experimental designs, too numerous, and, in some cases too complex to describe in detail here. Probably the most common quasi-experiment is the 'untreated control group design with dependent pre-test and post-test samples' often called the 'non-equivalent comparison group design' (Shadish et al. 2002). The design is based on an intervention and control group that are not created through random assignment, hence they are non-equivalent. Data is collected on the outcome measure (dependent variable) both before and after treatment for both groups. This design allows some of the threats to internal validity to be avoided. The Ministry of Justice currently runs a Justice Data Lab which uses a form of non-equivalent comparison group design. Specifically, the Lab favours a matched pairs design using Propensity Score Matching to match cases in the intervention and control groups.

Evidence-based policy in criminal justice

Within the criminal justice system the concept of evidence-based policy is now well-embedded. When New Labour came to power in 1997 it made a clear commitment to evidence-based policy making across government, summed up by Tony Blair when he declared 'what matters is what works'[2]. This was particularly apparent in crime and criminal justice through such initiatives as the £400 million Crime Reduction Programme, set up by the Home Office to fund crime reduction initiatives and in which evaluation and then the dissemination and use of research-based knowledge were intended to be central (Maguire 2004).

Since 1997, and mirroring developments in the US systematic reviews have become increasingly important in crime and criminal justice policy-making. A key milestone was the publication, in the US, of Sherman and colleagues (1998) review: *Preventing Crime: What Works, What Doesn't, What's Promising*. This extensive review of the evidence base for preventing crime was commissioned by the US Justice Department. Sherman and colleagues at the University of Maryland reviewed 500 evaluations that reported evidence of a programme's impact upon crime. It was not a systematic review. Welsh and Farrington (2006) class it as a 'Vote-Count Review Method', albeit a relatively sophisticated one. In addition to counting up the number of studies with statistically significant findings in favour of, and contrary to, the null hypothesis, Sherman and colleagues also developed the Scientific Methods Scale in which evaluation designs are ranked according to their level of internal validity (Sherman et al. 1998). RCTs are identified as the most rigorous evaluation design and quasi-experiments in which a comparison group is established as the 'next best thing'. Programmes were classed as 'working' if they had at least two Level 3 evaluations and the preponderance of all available evidence showing effectiveness. On the basis of this assessment Sherman et al. (1998) identified 15 programmes that worked, 23 that didn't and 30 that were promising. A similar approach has been used by the University of Colorado's Centre for the Study and Prevention of Violence, which is funded by the US Health Department[3] although the assessment criteria are more conservative.

Many systematic reviews have been undertaken in the fields of crime reduction and criminal justice. Particularly well-known and widely used include: Petrosino et al.'s (2000) review of Scared Straight; Welsh and Farrington's (2006) review of crime prevention; Lipsey et al.'s (2001) review of Cognitive Behavioural Therapy for offenders; Losel and Schmucker's (2005) review of treatment for sex offenders; Wilson et al.'s (2006) review of drug courts, to name but a few.

Mirroring the Cochrane Collaboration, the Campbell Collaboration was formed in 2000 to draw together and promote the use of systematic reviews in a number of social policy areas including 'crime and criminal justice'. At the time of writing the Crime and Criminal Justice Group listed 38 Campbell systematic reviews that had been published[4]. Over recent years the number of experiments undertaken within the criminal justice sector has been rising. For example, the number of experiments with offending outcomes published between 1982 and 2004, while still relatively small at 83, was a substantial increase on the 35 published between 1957 and 1981 (Farrington and Welsh 2005, Farrington 1983)[5].

There is currently a move to extend systematic reviews and meta-analysis to incorporate qualitative research although, as Thomas and Harden (2007: 4) note this strategy is contested, partly because methods are less developed, but more importantly because:

> the whole enterprise of synthesising qualitative research is itself hotly debated. Qualitative research, it is often proposed, is not generalisable and is specific to a particular context, participants and time. Thus, in bringing such research together, reviewers are open to the charge that they de-contextualise findings and wrongly assume that these are commensurable.

In the UK the commitment to evidence-based policy transcends party political boundaries. The Coalition government that came to power in 2010 established a 'What Works Network' of six What Works Centres to collate existing evidence on effective policies and practices, produce syntheses and systematic reviews of evidence where there are currently gaps and to disseminate this knowledge among policy-makers and practitioners. The Centres are based on the established National Institute for Health and Care Excellence (NICE) and the Educational Endowment Foundation. One of the others is the College of Policing What Works Centre for Crime Reduction[6].

Future directions?

Some influential criminologists would like the UK government to go further still. For example, Sherman (2009) puts forward a passionate argument for the greater use of experimental criminology in informing evidence-based policy and practice in the criminal justice sector. He argues both that more experiments and more meta-analysis are needed in order to provide a more influential evidence base for policy-makers and practitioners. Recognising the slow progress being made within experimental criminology Sherman suggests a strategy of 'prospective meta-analysis' to accelerate progress. This is a 'top-down' approach to generating evidence-based policy in which key policy questions are turned into testable hypotheses and many RCTs are conducted simultaneously, leading to a meta-analysis and hence the development of operational guidance for practitioners.

Critiquing evidence-based policy

Both 'evidence' and 'evidence-based policy' are contested concepts. First we look at the 'building blocks' of evidence-based policy: experimental and quasi-experimental evaluation designs and some of the criticisms that have been made of them. Then, we move on to look at whether some of the assumptions of evidence-based policy making hold up in the 'real world'.

Ethical concerns with randomised field trials

Some commentators have ethical objections to randomised field trials. A common ethical objection and one of the most compelling (Rossi et al. 2004) relates to the condition of the control group who might be deprived of either the benefit of a new intervention or an existing intervention. First, a point of clarification: normal practice in a social experiment is for the control group to receive the usual or conventional intervention and for the intervention group to receive a new intervention. Thus, the test is not between an intervention and nothing but between intervention as normal and a new intervention. However, returning to the basic objection, the counter argument made by supporters of experiments is that until we know that an intervention is effective it should not be given to people as a randomised field experiment, because of its high internal validity, is the best evaluation design for showing that an intervention is effective.

Supporters of experiments point to many examples of social interventions that were not only ineffective, but actually harmful and where it was only through an experimental evaluation design that the harm was revealed. Classic examples in the field of criminal justice include Scared Straight (Petrosino et al. 2000) and the Cambridge-Somerville study (McCord 2003). Therefore, given that a randomised field experiment is the impact evaluation design with the highest level of internal validity it could be argued that it is unethical to use an intervention *until* it has been tested using a randomised field experiment. In support of this counter argument Chalmers highlights what he sees as the double standard whereby many rigorous ethical processes are in place to regulate when and how RCTs are done and yet practitioners routinely use untested interventions without having to meet the same ethical standards (Chalmers 2003).

The scientific-realist critique of (quasi-) experiments

A different type of critique focuses on the methodological limitations of experimental designs. For example, Heckman and Smith (1995) argue that the 'black-box' of such experiments only allow researchers to answer the question of the mean effect of an intervention, while policy-makers are also interested in how effects vary between groups or which factors impact participation in the programme. That is, randomised experiments do not tell us *why* interventions succeed or fail. Furthermore, this lack of attention to theory may have implications for the generalizability of the findings of a RCT to other settings, populations and points in time.

To take this idea a little further, social processes may not just undermine the generalizability of the findings generated by RCTs, but they may also undermine the assumptions required to implement RCTs. Sampson (2010) identifies the requirement for RCTs to assume that outcomes are independent of treatment assignment; an assumption that he points out may be undermined by social processes. He illustrates this with the example of housing vouchers designed to support people to move away from poor areas. The way in which people use these vouchers will be impacted by the experience of others in receipt of vouchers if they know others in the treatment group. That is, outcomes are not independent of treatment assignment.

These critiques alert us to a more fundamental criticism of the 'scientific' approach to social research that underpins much of the evidence-based policy movement. In this vein, one of the most widely discussed critiques of recent years has come from Pawson and Tilley (1997) who argue that:

> For us, the experimental paradigm constitutes a heroic failure, promising so much and yet ending up in ironic anticlimax. The underlying logic … seems meticulous, clear-headed and militarily precise, and yet findings seem to emerge in a typically non-cumulative, low impact, prone-to-equivocation sort of way.
>
> *(Pawson and Tilley 1997: 8)*

For Pawson and Tilley this is because this seemingly 'scientific' and 'objective' approach to evaluation smuggles in a particular set of understandings about what interventions and programmes are and how they work (Pawson and Tilley 1994). The problem is that (quasi-) experimental evaluation designs reduce initiatives to a series of variables and 'the business of research is that of applying controls until we can be sure that all explanatory factors, save for the influence of the programme itself, are squeezed out' (Pawson and Tilley 1994: 294). But this is a misunderstanding of how the social world works:

> Programmes cannot be considered as some kind of external, impinging 'force' to which subjects 'respond'. Rather programmes 'work', *if subjects choose to make them work and are placed in the right conditions to enable them to do so.* This process of 'constrained choice' is at the heart of social and individual change to which all programmes aspire, and this mechanism is something which cannot be captured in evaluation which takes the form before-and-after, controlled comparison.
>
> *(Pawson and Tilley 1994: 294)*

Pawson and Tilly argue that instead of undertaking experiments and quasi-experiments, researchers should investigate *context–mechanism–outcome* configurations whereby interventions and programmes have successful outcomes only in so far as they introduce appropriate ideas and opportunities ('*mechanisms*') to groups in the appropriate social and cultural conditions ('*contexts*') (Pawson and Tilley 1997).

This scientific-realist critique extends to the meta-analyses that draw on (quasi-) experimental evaluation designs. For example, Pawson (2002) puts forward a number of objections relating to (a) the melding of programme mechanisms (the danger of grouping together interventions which are dissimilar), (b) oversimplifying programme outcomes (the outputs of a meta-analysis are expected outcomes of averages of means) and (c) the concealment of programme contexts (the danger of not taking sufficient account of subjects and situations).

Evidence-based policy or policy-based evidence?

The model of evidence-based policy promoted by government tends to reflect the approach implied in evidence-based medicine. This approach appears to be grounded in a positivist, or at least 'scientific'[7] understanding of research and the interplay between research and policy (Young 2011). It is assumed in this model that policy making is a rational process. The rational model suggests a logical and ordered sequence of policy-making phases – a linear process in which knowledge is apolitical and neutral (Stone et al. 2001). The underlying model of science hints strongly of positivism (Stone et al. 2001, Pawson 2002). However, many would argue that the reality of policy making is more complicated.

Clearly, policy-makers do not just rely on evidence generated from robust evaluations. They bring their own experience, expertise and judgement to the process (Davies 2004). Policy making also takes place within the context of finite resources and this influences decisions (ibid.). Policy-makers are also influenced by values (their own, that of politicians and of institutions) as well as the habits and traditions of institutions such as Parliament, civil servants and the judiciary (ibid.). Outside forces such as lobby groups, pressure groups and consultants are able to influence the policy-making process and the whole policy-making process is subject to pragmatics and contingencies such as parliamentary terms and timetables and the capacities of institutions (ibid.). Thus, many commentators prefer the phrase 'evidence-informed policy' (*e.g.* Treadwell Shine and Bartley 2011).

However, some would go further and question the extent to which evidence-based policy making actually takes place at all. Stone et al. (2001) set out alternative models of policy making where the role of evidence and of evaluators is either marginal (for example in a 'muddling through' model of policy making, premised on the notions of 'bounded rationality' and 'satisficing') or only influential at certain stages in the development of a 'policy paradigm'. By way of illustration, Stevens (2011: 238) describes working as 'a policy adviser for six months on a placement in a policy making section of the UK civil service', presumably the Home Office[8]. Stevens' ethnographic study describes civil servants' in the UK government using evidence selectively to build convincing narratives or 'create persuasive policy stories' (Stevens 2011: 237) and concludes that the use of evidence is 'ideological in that it supports systematically asymmetrical relations of power' (Stevens 2011: 237). This was something that was acknowledged in the report by the UK House of Commons Select Committee on Science and Technology into Scientific Advice, Risk and Evidence-Based Policy Making issued in October 2006. The committee stated:

> [Ministers] should certainly not seek selectively to pick pieces of evidence which support an already agreed policy, or even commission research in order to produce a justification for policy: so-called 'policy-based evidence making'. ... Where there is an absence of evidence, or even when the government is knowingly contradicting the evidence – maybe for very good reason – this should be openly acknowledged.
>
> *(House of Commons Science and Technology Committee 2006: para.89)*

Evidence-based policy and democracy

The analysis above suggests that the concept of evidence-based policy is not straightforward. Some commentators have gone further and questioned its place in a democratic system. For example, Young (2011) asks how a commitment to evidence-based policy can be reconciled with democracy. He is concerned with maintaining political equality if 'evidence' is privileged in decision-making. This is because, logically, those who are responsible for the production and interpretation of evidence will then have more political influence than other citizens. In particular, if hierarchies of evidence such as the Scientific Methods Scale (Sherman et al. 1998) are employed and a narrow concept of evidence is accepted then 'there will be a small percentage of the citizenry that possesses a degree of potential political influence that extend notably beyond that available to the remainder of their fellow citizens' (Young 2011: 23). The second, related difficulty is protecting the practice of a majority rule, which could pose a significant danger to the realisation of evidence-based policy (Young 2011).

Research paradigms and ethical practice

As the promise of a rational, scientific approach to policy making starts to break down the ethical dimensions of evidence-based policy become clearer. Questions start to emerge such as 'What is the status and role of evidence?' and 'What is the status and role of the researchers and evaluators?' To some extent these are philosophical questions. Rosenberg argues that:

> The positions scientists take on answers to philosophical questions determine the questions they consider answerable by science and choose to address, as well as the methods they employ to answer them.
>
> *(Rosenberg 2012: 3)*

The philosophical ideas that underpin evaluation and evidence-based policy change over time. Vedung (2010) describes four 'waves of evaluation diffusion' stretching from the 1960s into the new century. The first, 'scientific' wave, saw academics using experiments work out the best means to reach policy goals. After a subsequent 'dialogue-oriented' wave, followed by a 'neo-liberal' wave, Vedung detects, in the current 'evidence-based' wave a return to aspects of the scientific wave.

The 'scientific' approach that underpins the first and fourth waves has its foundations in positivist assumptions. Positivism is a broad set of ideas but positivist researchers in the social sciences have tended to subscribe to the same approach to science as that adopted in the natural sciences such as physics, chemistry and biology. The assumption therefore is that people are a part of nature – albeit a complex part. It is assumed that an objective account of the social world is possible and that social science is value free. The role of social scientists is to develop universal causal laws. The only test of a scientific law is whether hypotheses (predictions) that are based on it hold when empirically tested. This is the *hypothetico-deductive model* – a hypothesis is deduced from a theory and then tested against data.

Nevertheless, it would be wrong to characterise the scientific wave as a straightforward application of positivism. Cook and Campbell (1979) whose work, along with Stanley, during the 1960s and 1970s was extremely influential in the scientific wave are careful to distinguish their approach to quasi-experimentation and experimentation from aspects of positivism, particularly logical positivism. Instead they advocate a 'critical-realist philosophy of science' (Cook and Campbell 1979: 92), which, in keeping with positivism, assumes the possibility of an objective, scientific approach to social science using the methods of experiments and quasi-experiments 'shared *in part* with the physical sciences' (ibid.). However, they diverge from positivism in important respects including, for example, a 'looser' understanding of causation and adopting Popper's process of falsification. The result is to 'relinquish the hope for a simple social science' (Cook and Campbell 1979: 94) and to recognise that 'the social disciplines, pure or applied, are not truly successful as sciences' (ibid: 92). This epistemological position has some similarities with the scientific-realist understanding of knowledge and hence evaluation (Tilley 2000).

The key ethical challenge for evidence-based policy is therefore essentially the same as key ethical challenge for the social sciences. For Rosenberg the choice of methods that social scientists adopt is a gamble:

> When social scientists choose to employ methods as close as possible to those of natural science they commit themselves to the position that the question before them is one that empirical science can answer. When they spurn such

methods, they adopt the contrary view, that the question is different in some crucial way from those addressed in the physical or biological sciences. *Neither of these choices has yet been vindicated by success that is conspicuous enough to make the choice anything less than a gamble.*

(Rosenberg 2012: 4, emphasis added)

The same is true in evidence-based policy. The choice of methods and of underlying epistemology (philosophy of knowledge) carry with them assumptions about the role of moral questions in social science. Vedung (2010) suggests that the scientific wave of evaluation in the 1960s held out the possibility of an 'engineering model of public intervention' in which evaluation discoveries would be accepted as true and transformed into binding decisions. This is a value-neutral exercise. In the engineering model evaluative findings are used *instrumentally* in the sense that evaluators are not concerned about the *ends* of the policy, rather they provide neutral and objective evaluation discoveries about the most efficient *means* to achieve it (Vedung 2010).

However, the realist approach to science described by Cook and Campbell and Pawson and Tilley implies that evaluation knowledge and evaluation will fall short of engineering. As Pawson and Tilley describe:

> Realist evaluation begins with theory and ends with further theory. … The grand evaluation payoff is thus nothing other than improved theory, which can then be subjected to further testing and refinement, through implementation in the next program. And so the cycle continues.
>
> *(Pawson and Tilley 1998: 89–90)*

As we move further away from the 'scientific' approach to evidence-based policy and introduce a wider range of qualitative approaches, claims to value neutrality are also discarded and any claim the researcher may have for 'special status' in the process of evidence-based policy compared to all the other constituencies that try to influence policy be they think tanks, lobbyists, the media, etc. seems less defensible.

Case study: offender rehabilitation

In this section we consider how these issues apply to more practical questions of criminal justice policy and practice using debates about offender rehabilitation as an example.

Two models of rehabilitation are currently particularly influential: the Risk, Needs and Responsivity (RNR) model (Andrews and Bonta 2010) and the Good Lives Model (GLM) that draws on desistance theory (Ward and Maruna 2007, McNeil 2006). They are underpinned by different conceptions of evidence, and, these different understandings of evidence influence different understandings of offender rehabilitation and the interventions most likely to be effective in supporting rehabilitation.

One of the strengths of the RNR model is that it has a strong empirical base. It takes a 'scientific' approach to evidence and is based on random control trials, systematic reviews and meta-analysis (Bonta and Andrews 2007). Desistance studies have generally been relatively small-scale studies with more emphasis on qualitative research and the use of case studies (Maruna 2001 or Farrall 2002) and there are few evaluations of the GLM.

The focus of studies is also different with RNR studies concentrating on demonstrating causal links between interventions and reductions in re-offending and desistance studies trying to understand the process of desistance within the context of psychological and social processes rather than just within the narrow context of criminal justice 'programmes' (Ward and Maruna 2007). However, these differing approaches are also embodied in two very different types of criminal justice policy and practice.

The RNR model assumes that individuals are motivated by 'no more than a series of reward-cost contingencies' (Andrews et al. 2011: 101) and this implies that 'human beings are a function of reward-cost contingencies rather than acknowledging individuals as goal directed and self-determined'. By contrast the GLM 'Assumes that human behaviour at its highest level is intrinsically motivated and not the reflection of reward and cost' (Andrews et al. 2011: 739). Describing the 'good life' is necessarily a moral project (see Albertson and Fox 2014 for a fuller discussion), something that sits uncomfortably within the scientific tradition of social research. When social scientists start to consider what the most rational ends of social action are they move from describing what *is* to what *ought* to be. This carries with it an implied moral dimension to social enquiry. Social science theories based on substantive rationality assume that human needs can be objective and universal and therefore make judgements about the type of society in which we *should* live. These are moral judgements and at odds with the claim to value neutrality implied within the 'scientific' approach to social science research.

If offender rehabilitation is a moral project then a pragmatic application of 'what works' is not sufficient. Interpreting and applying what works is a moral exercise and hence probation practice must be seen partly in moral terms.

Summary

While the obvious ethical concern about evidence-based policy is its tendency to prefer experimental evaluation designs, a form of evidence generation that has attracted extensive ethical critique, our discussion has suggested more fundamental ethical challenges. These range from the difficulty of reconciling the scientific, rational approach to evidence-based policy making with social research that gives pre-eminence to understanding 'context' and that uses qualitative research methods to do this, to squaring EBP with democratic principles, to suggestions that if social scientists are to contribute to discussions about the 'good life' an ethical dimension to research and theory is inevitable.

In the criminal justice sector Sherman (2009) has argued for a more systematic approach to generating and adopting evidence-based approaches, however, following Rosenberg (2012) we can argue that subscribing to an essentially 'scientific' approach to evidence generation is a gamble. Our discussion of the relationship between evidence and practice in offender rehabilitation illustrates the importance of the moral dimension to offender rehabilitation and the difficulty of accounting for this is in an overly scientific approach to EBP. The Risk–Need–Responsivity model (Andrews et al. 2011) with its emphasis on experimental evaluation and systematic review seems to fit more comfortably in the scientific tradition of EBP. In comparison, approaches designed to achieve desistance that require an elaboration of the 'good life' which seem to elicit different assumptions about the nature of social research and the role of social scientists in creating knowledge and contributing to debates about policy.

Much progress has been made over recent years in establishing evidence-based policy making as the norm. But important questions about the nature and status of evidence have not been resolved. In recent years the debate between quantitative and qualitative versions of the social sciences have become less heated and the rise of 'mixed-method' or 'multi strategy' (Robson 2011) designs have arguably pushed some difficult epistemological debates about the nature of knowledge and the role of social scientists into the background. However, the concept of evidence-based policy brings these back into stark relief and emphasises that ethics can never be ignored in crime and criminal justice research.

Review questions

1. What are the key elements of EBP?
2. How is EBP applied in the criminal justice system?
3. What are the main ethical concerns raised by EBP?

Guide to further reading

For a clear description of EBP and a discussion of the case for EBP an excellent starting point is Davies (2004).

For an understanding of the evidence-based medicine a good starting point is Evans et al. (2011).

The definitive work on experimental and quasi-experimental methods in the social sciences is Shadish et al. (2002).

For the case for greater use of experiments and systematic reviews in the criminal justice system see Sherman (2009). A number of leading criminologists wrote responses to Sherman in subsequent editions of the same journal.

For a discussion of the ethical character of probation practice see McNeil and Farrall (2013).

Notes

1 Information taken from the Cochrane Collaboration website: www.cochrane.org (accessed 2nd November 2014).
2 Speech at the Corn Exchange, City of London, 7 April 1997.
3 The project's website is www.colorado.edu/cspv/blueprints/index.html.
4 www.campbellcollaboration.org/reviews_crime_justice/index.php.
5 Sherman (2009), notes that the far smaller number of experiments and systematic reviews undertaken in criminology, compared to health care does not reflect the difference in the number of questions to be answered. Rather it reflects the relative resources invested in research. Sherman cites figures from the US suggesting that the US National Institutes of Health spend about $28 billion a year on new evidence whereas the comparable amount given to the US National Institute of Justice is about $28 million.
6 Information taken from www.gov.uk/what-works-network (accessed 14 October 2014).
7 These terms are discussed below.
8 Given that, at the time of writing his account he was Professor of Criminal Justice and that his published research is mostly in the area of drugs and crime it is reasonable to assume that he was on a placement in the Home Office.

References

Albertson, K. and Fox, C. (2014). *Justice, with Reason: Rethinking the Economics of Crime and Justice*, Issues in Community and Criminal Justice, Monograph No.9.
Andrews, D.A. and Bonta, J. (2010). *The Psychology of Criminal Conduct* (5th Ed.) New Providence, NJ: Matthew Bender.
Andrews, D.A., Bonta, J. and Wormith, J.S. (2011). 'The Risk–Need–Responsivity (RNR) Model: Does Adding the Good Lives Model Contribute to Effective Crime Prevention?' *Criminal Justice and Behavior*, Vol. 38(7), pp. 735–755.
Bonta, J. and Andrews, D.A. (2007). *Risk-Need-Responsivity Model for Offender Assessment and Treatment* (User Report No. 2007–06). Ottawa, Ontario: Public Safety Canada.
Bullock, H., Mountford, J. and Stanley, R. (2001). *Better Policy Making*. London: Cabinet Office.
Cabinet Office (1999). *Professional Policy Making for the Twenty First Century*. London: Cabinet Office.
Chalmers, I. (2003). 'Trying to Do More Good than Harm in Policy and Practice: The Role of Rigorous, Transparent, Up-to-Date Evaluations', *The Annals of the American Academy of Political and Social Science*, Vol. 589, pp. 22–40.
Cook, T. and Campbell, D. (1979). *Quasi-experimental Design and Analysis Issues for Field Settings*. Boston: Houghton-Mifflin.
Davies, P. (2004). *Is Evidence-Based Government Possible?* Jerry Lee Lecture 2004 presented at the 4th Annual Campbell Collaboration Colloquium Washington DC, 19 February 2004.
Evans, I., Thornton, H., Chalmers, I. and Glasziou, P. (2011). *Testing Treatments: Better Research for Better Health Care*. London: Pinter & Martin Ltd.
Farrall, S. (2002). *Rethinking What Works with Offenders: Social Context, Probation Supervision and Desistance from Crime*. Cullompton: Willan Publishing.
Farrington, D. P. (1983). 'Randomized Experiments on Crime and Justice'. In Tonry, M. and Morris, N. (eds.), *Crime and Justice*, Vol. 4, pp. 257–308. Chicago: University of Chicago Press.

Farrington, D. P. (2003). 'Methodological Quality Standards for Evaluation Research', *The Annals of the American Academy of Political and Social Science* Vol. 587(1), pp. 49–68.

Farrington, D. P. and Welsh, B. C. (2005). 'Randomised Experiments in Criminology: What have we Learned in the Last Two Decades', *Journal of Experimental Criminology*, Vol.1(1), pp. 9–38.

Goldacre, B. (2011). 'Forward'. In Evans, I., Thornton, H., Chalmers, I. and Glasziou, P., *Testing Treatments: Better Research in Healthcare* (2nd Ed.). London: Pinter and Martin Ltd.

Government Social Research Unit (2007a). Background paper 2 – What do we already know? Harnessing existing research. London: Cabinet Office.

Government Social Research Unit (2007b). Background paper 7 – Why do social experiments? Experiments and quasi-experiments for evaluating government policies and programmes. London: Cabinet Office.

Haynes, L., Service, O., Goldacre, B. and Torgerson, D. (2012). *Test, Learn, Adapt: Developing Public Policy with Randomised Controlled Trials*. London: Cabinet Office.

Heckman, J. J. and Smith, J. A. (1995). 'Assessing the Case for Social Experiments', *Journal of Economic Perspectives,* Vol.9(2), pp. 85–110.

House of Commons Science and Technology Committee (2006). *Scientific Advice, Risk and Evidence Based Policy Making*, Seventh Report of Session 2005–6 Volume 1. London: House of Commons.

Lipsey, M. W., Chapman, G. and Landenberger, N. A. (2001). 'Cognitive-Behavioural Programs for Offenders', *The Annals of the American Academy of Political and Social Science,* Vol.576, pp. 144–157.

Losel, F. and Schmucker, M. (2005). The Effectiveness of Treatment for Sexual Offenders: A Comprehensive Meta-Analysis. *Journal of Experimental Criminology,* Vol.1(1), pp. 117–146.

Lum, C. and Yang, S. M. (2005). 'Why Do Evaluation Researchers in Crime and Justice Choose Non-experimental Methods?', *Journal of Experimental Criminology*, Vol.1, pp. 191–213.

Maguire, M. (2004). 'The Crime Reduction Programme in England and Wales: Reflections on the Vision and the Reality', *Criminal Justice*, Vol.4(3), pp. 213–237.

Maruna, S. (2001). *Making Good*. Washington, DC: American Psychological Association Books.

McCord, J. (2003). 'Cures that Harm: Unanticipated Outcomes of Crime Prevention Programs', *The Annals of the American Academy of Political and Social Sciences*, Vol.587, pp. 16–30.

McNeil, F. (2006). 'A Desistance Paradigm for Offender Management', *Criminology and Criminal Justice*, Vol.6(1), pp. 39–62.

McNeil, F. and Farrall, S. (2013). 'A Moral in the Story? Virtues, Values and Desistance from Crime'. In Cowburn, M., Duggan, M., Robinson, A and Senior, P. (eds.) *Values in Criminology and Community Justice*. Bristol: Policy Press.

Pawson, R. (2002). 'Evidence-based Policy: In Search of a Method', *Evaluation*, Vol 8(2), pp. 157–181.

Pawson, R. and Tilley, N. (1994). 'What Works in Evaluation Research?' *British Journal of Criminology,* Vol.34, pp. 291–306.

Pawson, R. and Tilley, N. (1997). *Realistic Evaluation*. London: Sage.

Pawson, R. and Tilley, N. (1998). 'Caring Communities, Paradigm Polemics, Design Debates', *Evaluation*, Vol.4, pp. 73–90.

Petrosino, A., Turpin-Petrosino, C. and Finckenauer, J. O. (2000). 'Well Meaning Programs Can Have Harmful Effects! Lessons from Experiments of Programs Such as Scared Straight', *Crime and Delinquency,* Vol.46, pp. 354–379.

Robson, C. (2011). *Real World Research*. Chichester: Wiley.

Rosenberg, A. (2012). *Philosophy of Social Science*. Boulder: Westview.

Rossi, P., Lipsey, M. and Freeman, H. (2004). *Evaluation: A Systematic Approach*. California: Sage Publications.

Sampson, R. J. (2010). 'Gold Standard Myths: Observations on the Experimental Turn in Quantitative Criminology', *Journal of Quantitative Criminology*, Vol.26(4), pp. 489–500.

Shadish, W. R., Cook, T. D. and Campbell, D. T. (2002). *Experimental and Quasi-experimental Designs for Generalized Causal Inference*. Boston: Houghton-Mifflin.

Sherman, L. (2009). 'Evidence and Liberty: The Promise of Experimental Criminology', *Criminology and Criminal Justice*, Vol.9(1), pp. 5–28.

Sherman, L. W., Gottfredson, D., MacKenzie, D., Eck, J., Reuter, P. and Bushway, S. (1998). 'Preventing Crime: What Works, What Doesn't, What's Promising', *National Institute of Justice Research in Brief*, Washington D.C.: National Institute of Justice.

Stevens, A. (2011). 'Telling Policy Stories: An Ethnographic Study of the Use of Evidence in Policy-making in the UK', *Journal of Social Policy*, Vol. 40(2), pp. 237–255.

Stone, D., Maxwell, S. and Keating, M. (2001). *Bridging Research and Policy*, Paper for an International Workshop funded by DfID at Warwick University 16–17 July 2001.

Thomas, J. and Harden, A. (2007). 'Methods for the Thematic Synthesis of Qualitative Research in Systematic Reviews', *ESRC National Centre for Research Methods Working Paper 10/07*, London: Evidence for Policy and Practice Information and Co-ordinating Centre.

Tilley, N. (2000). Realistic Evaluation: An Overview, Paper at the Founding Conference of the Danish Evaluation Society, September 2000.

Treadwell Shine, K. and Bartley, B (2011). Whose Evidence Base? The Dynamic Effects of Ownership, Receptivity and Values on Collaborative Evidence-informed Policy Making, *Evidence and Policy*, Vol.7(4), pp. 511–530.

Vedung, E. (2010). 'Four Waves of Evaluation Diffusion', *Evaluation*, Vol.16(3), pp. 263–77.

Ward, T. and Maruna, S. (2007). *Rehabilitation*. London: Routledge.

Weisburd, D., Lum, C. M. and Petrosino, A. (2001). 'Does Research Design Affect Study Outcomes in Criminal Justice?', *The Annals of the American Academy of Political and Social Science*, Vol.578, pp. 50–70.

Welsh, B. and Farrington, D. (2006). 'Evidence-Based Crime Prevention'. In Welsh, B. and Farrington, D. (eds.) *Preventing Crime: What Works for Children, Offenders, Victims and Places*. Dordrecht: Springer.

Wilson, D. B., Mitchell, O. and Mackenzie, D. L. (2006). 'A Systematic Review of Drug Court Effects on Recidivism', *Journal of Experimental Criminology*, Vol.2, pp. 459–487.

Young, S. P. (2011). 'Evidence of Democracy? The Relationship between Evidence-based Policy and Democratic Government', *Journal of Public Administration and Policy Research*, Vol.3(1), pp. 19–27.

2

CRIMINAL HISTORY

Uses of the past and the ethics of the archive

Paul Knepper

Historical criminology, even when based on no more than documents in an archive, does involve a series of ethical issues. These have to do with the collection of historical evidence, the use of theory, the moral message of the story and the construction of memory. To illustrate some of these issues, this chapter presents a recent case of fraud in historical research, reviews controversies between historians in writing history and discusses the aims of crime museums which have become popular in recent years.

Key points

1. Documents constitute important evidence for historical research and raise ethical issues even when limited to persons no longer living.
2. Theory is important to writing history, but must engage evidence and avoid partisanship.
3. 'Crime' and 'victim' are evocative words in history given their potential for encouraging social action in the present.
4. Crime museums present important issues about what and how we remember crime in the past.

Key definitions

Bottom up history: Attention to the experience of ordinary people in the past, especially those who might be considered victims of historical processes.

Construction of memory: Establishment of museums, monuments and memorials to shape views of the past.

Dark tourism: Visits to historical sites that involved death and suffering, often as a result of criminal action.

Historicism: building a view of the past from documents originating in the period of interest.

Partisanship: Commitment to a theory for reasons other than serious consideration of the evidence.

Introduction

Historical criminology does not invite the same kind of ethical issues as social science research. Generally, historical research involves working with documents of past events and (often) persons no longer living, so the familiar conventions of obtaining informed consent, anonymity in reporting results and managing security of data sets do not apply. But writing history does, nevertheless, present ethical issues. These involve not only collecting and interpreting evidence, but presenting the past. All historians are interested, consciously or unconsciously, in the present and there are moral issues in how historical knowledge serves present interests.

The crime novelist Tony Hillerman provides a good example of what is at stake in *Talking God*. The story begins with Catherine Morris Perry, a lawyer at the Smithsonian Museum in Washington DC, who receives a package from a mysterious source. Inside the box, she finds human bones, a newspaper clipping and a letter. The clipping has to do with the museum's decision to maintain its collection of American Indian bones despite requests from several Indian nations for them to be returned for traditional burial. The letter explains that the bones in the box are for display at the museum, but are not Indian bones; they were recently taken from graves at her family's cemetery. They are remains of her grandparents. Hillerman's imaginary story raises real questions about who owns the past and how it is used.

This chapter explores ethical issues arising in historical criminology, and specifically, the use of documents. We want to consider the ways in which the history of crime can become a 'criminal' form of history. Part 1 deals with the collection of historical evidence. Part 2 examines theory and partisanship. Part 3 the moral of the story, and part 4, the use construction of memory.

Use and abuse of evidence

The tradition of documentary research in history was established in Germany in the late nineteenth century. Leopold von Ranke taught historians to examine the documents of a particular period and to interpret them in the light of that period. Experience can only be understood in light of time and place, and consequently, can only be understood in light of historical contexts. Historians should avoid the lofty claims that history offered moral lessons; they should avoid invoking the past to justify future actions. Instead, historians should aim to find out *wie es eigentlich gewesen*, 'how things happened'. To do this, they would need to spend time in archives, examining the documentary evidence. Ranke's model spread across Europe and established the traditional method of professional, academic history (Warren 2010).

Historians working in this tradition obligate themselves to ethics of historical research. These include making a reasonable effort to find relevant documents and to fit them together to form an argument. It is common for historical arguments to be based on fragmentary or incomplete evidence and historians disagree about what to do about the missing evidence. But where the historical researcher comes across evidence contrary to the argument, this must be accounted for and explained. Further, the historian must report what appears in the documents, citing accurately so that others can see for themselves.

An example of historical research gone wrong took place in the 1990s. The case of Michael Bellesiles involved not only deliberate setting aside of evidence, but fabrication of documents that did not exist. In *Arming America* (2000), Bellesiles proposed that the United States did not have a 'gun culture' before the Civil War, but acquired one only since then. Before 1850, few Americans owned guns, or knew how to use, repair or preserve them. Guns were exceptional, not the norm; they were stored in armouries, not private homes; they were in poor condition, even when in private hands; and they were too expensive to be owned by most men. As a result, guns contributed little to murder. Murder rates were low everywhere, even in the South and on the Western Frontier. These patterns changed after the Mexican War and especially after the Civil War when gun use became widespread and many Americans began to acquire handguns. In the mid-nineteenth century, Samuel Colt created the romance of the gun with his marketing campaign for his revolver. With mass-production, guns became easier to load, more lethal, and more available, and this resulted in a tornado of gun-related homicides (Bellesiles 2000).

Bellesiles offered a bold thesis that appeared to be built on solid historical evidence. Initially, the book received praise. In 2001, Columbia University awarded the Bancroft Prize to the book, although by that time, suspicions had started to surface. Historians talked about egregious errors owing to comprehensive incompetence, biased selection or deliberate fabrication. To support his claims about low rates of gun ownership, Bellesiles cited several sources, but particularly calculations he obtained from probate records from several jurisdictions. When other historians examined these records, they found that his counts were incomplete or wrong. Contrary to what Bellesiles said, guns were more common than Bibles in estates of early American families. To arrive at his figures, Bellesiles repeatedly substituted women for men, classified 'old guns' as broken, and found guns in wills that did not exist. Historians did not find evidence to support what he had claimed, or rather, they could not find them because the documents simply did not exist. The records for San Francisco Bellesiles claimed to have analysed were destroyed in the fire brought about by the 1906 earthquake (Lindgren 2002).

To make his argument that the United States did not have a 'gun culture' before the late nineteenth century, Bellesiles not only claimed that rates of gun ownership were low, but that rates of murder were also low. This ran counter to the homicide evidence for the period. Randolph Roth pointed out that homicide rates for the seventeenth century were higher than in the early twenty-first century. Bellesiles claimed that homicide rates were low before the 1850s between European Americans everywhere, but this is not true. Roth showed that homicide was rare at some times and places, but that it was common at other times and places. To make his case, Bellesiles did not look for, or overlooked, important evidence. He confused the low number of homicides in surviving court records with low homicide rates. But homicide rates not only depend on the number of homicides, but also the population, which was also small (meaning the rate was higher relative to population). Further, the number of homicides cannot be estimated from surviving court records in this period, especially where law enforcement was weak. Again, Bellesiles resorted to inventing evidence. He cites a low number of homicides in Vermont from 1760–1790, citing records from the Vermont Superior Court. There has never been a Vermont Superior Court, and records for the Vermont Supreme Court for this period – if this is what he meant – have been missing for nearly a century (Roth 2002).

In the 1970s, Michel Foucault created a stir among historians with his approach to the past. Ostensibly, *Discipline and Punish* (1975) offered an account into the origins of the modern prison. It begins with a description of punishment under the monarchic, aristocratic regime that operated in France from the fifteenth to the eighteenth century. Foucault details the execution of Robert-François Damiens, who tried to kill King Louis XV in 1757, and the procedures of physical torture used to extract a confession. Foucault narrated the 'gloomy festival' of public punishment and the message intended for its audience, followed by the reforms of the Enlightenment and early experiments with incarceration. In the final part, he examined the legacy of the reformers as reflected in the systems of punishment they sought to introduce. To show the significance of prison discipline, he moved away from the legal realm to other institutions in society: the military, the factory and the school. He presented Jeremy Bentham's proposal for the panopticon, or 'the all-seeing eye', an architectural plan for a circular building enabling continuous and effortless surveillance. Punishment has shifted, not merely from the body to the mind, but to a new system that brought body and mind within a more pervasive regime of social control (Foucault 1979).

Historians criticised Foucault for being highly selective in his sources. Robert Nye (1978) complained that Foucault made his allegations stick only by ignoring the wider institutional setting within France at the time. To present a coherent narrative, Foucault overlooked conflicts among founders and points of disagreement among policymakers. It was contrived to put the criminal policy-making process of France between 1780 and 1850 mid-way on an imaginary continuum between simple-medieval and complex-modern policymaking processes. Centralisation and codification of secular law was an important element of medieval state-building, and ecclesiastical sanctions continued for some time after, 'making the task of combining the various corporate discourses into a synthetic national one virtually impossible' (Nye 1978: 5). Other historians pointed to mistakes of fact. Although Foucault had been to the archive, and retrieved documents for his history, he did not adhere to the conventions of historical scholarship and made amateurish mistakes. 'In his empirical statements, Foucault was often wrong' Eric Monkkonen (1986: 1153) said of *Discipline and Punish*; 'Any careful reader of Foucault realizes that Foucault's thesis has no relationship to empirical work, perhaps not even to reality'.

Essentially, Foucault built his narrative around a few documents that fit the ending he had in mind and ignored complications along the way. This would have made Foucault a very poor historian, even guilty of deliberate distortion, except that he did not claim to be an historian. He denounced the pursuit of 'scientific history'. Empirical evidence cannot be made to support any claim of recovering the past for what it really was. Foucault tried to identify the structures of thought without aligning himself with any of the starting assumptions familiar to historians. He resisted the idea that he followed a generalisable method. His method is 'counter-history' and 'social critique'. Although Foucault used narrative, his method subverted traditional presentation of history. He rearranged the evidence, denied its conclusions and appropriated its resources for his own purposes. He was a philosopher interested in the past, in pursuit of what would be called poststructuralism or postmodernism (Flynn 2005. 29, 33).

Foucault claimed to have invented a new way of using historical documents, what he would eventually refer to as a 'problematisation'. Whether he succeeded is open to question. In a thoughtful critique, Castel (1994) argues that no one who has not worked with primary sources and followed the rules of historical methodology has a right to claim to write a better interpretation of these materials than historians who have studied them. Foucault did not write a conventional social history of the prison. So the question can be put: By what right may one give a different reading to historical material, including what is written by historians, if one knows no more (and arguably less) than a conventional historian? (Castel 1994: 240). In choosing to ignore, or transcend, historical scholarship, Foucault assigned himself two Herculean tasks. The second makes clear why the first is so difficult. First, the problematisation approach must contribute something to what has already been achieved by conventional historical approach. He needs to say something more than what social history has said. Second, what a given problematisation contributes to our understanding must not come at the price of our knowledge of the past. In other words, a problematisation can be refuted if it contradicts historical knowledge, and only historians are the judges of that. 'The right to choose one's materials and to refocus them in light of a current issue, to place them in different categories – sociological categories, for example – is not permission to rewrite history' (Castel 1994: 252).

But the fact that Foucault was clear about what he was doing, in the sense that he rejected traditional historical research, means than his limited selection and imaginative interpretation of archival material is not unethical. He said he was not following the rules and he did not lie about this.

Theory and partisanship

Theory is an essential part of historical inquiry. The evidence is not left behind in an orderly fashion; it does not arrange itself into meaningful patterns. Rather, historians make use of theories to understand and read evidence in response to questions they have about the past. Fulbrook (2002: 4) explains the 'intrinsically theoretical nature of historical investigation'. Historians cannot limit themselves to 'the facts' (as von Ranke implied), but must construct their interpretation using unspoken assumptions and convictions about human beings, about politics and society. Historians use theories to extract meaning from evidence, and to suggest the kind of documents that represent evidence. Commitment to a theory can lead to a singular view of the past, to insist on an explanation despite plausible alternatives, although this is not necessarily unethical.

For more than 40 years, Pieter Spierenburg has remained committed to a single theory, the 'civilising process' of Norbert Elias. Spierenburg recalls that he met Elias in 1969, while he was a history student in Amsterdam and Elias lectured there. A month or so into Elias's history seminar, Spierenburg began reading *The Civilising Process*, which had been published in a new German-language edition the year before. He found it fascinating, and decided to write a PhD on the topic of violence and judicial sanctions the conceptual vocabulary Elias had formulated (Spierenburg 2013). Spierenburg's dissertation, *The Spectacle of Suffering* (1984), covers the rise and fall of public executions. He develops an explanation for the transformation of punishment: from pre-industrial Europe, where whipping, maiming and hanging were public events, to the twentieth century, in which the death sentence all but disappeared (and where it remains, takes place in secret). Spierenburg drew on court records from Amsterdam, supplemented with material from Germany, Netherlands, France and England. He covers the work of executioners, the aims of the authorities, the crowd of spectators and characteristics of the condemned. As Spierenburg explained, an original punitive attitude towards the suffering of convicts slowly gave way to a rising sensitivity, which reached a critical threshold in the nineteenth century, when executions disappeared from public life. These aspects of 'conscience formation' took place together with the rise of a network of states, and more specifically, the transformation from the early modern state to the modern nation-state (Spierenburg 1984).

In 2005, the *American Historical Review* asked Eric Monkkonen, Elizabeth Dale and Pieter Spierenburg why the United States had such a high rate of homicide over the past two hundred years compared to Europe. Monkkonen compared social attitudes, Dale examined legal culture and Spierenburg said it has to do with the civilising process. Homicide, Spierenburg theorised, was linked to the process of state formation and the European experience percolated over a longer period than the American experience. The North American continent moved into the modern world almost overnight, without having gone through the process surrounding the monopolisation of violence and civilising of honour as took place in European states. This truncated history of civilisation left the resolution of threats to honour as a contested area beyond the power of the state. For Spierenburg, 'there was no phase of centralisation before democratization set in. One might say that democracy came to America too early' (Spierenburg 2006: 109).

Although more than one historian has tried to lead Spierenburg away from the civilising process, he has remained devoted to Elias. I mention this to demonstrate that commitment to a theory is not illegitimate; I am quite sure that Spierenburg believes Elias to have furnished the best explanation of the evidence. The point is, Spierenburg continues to test theory against the evidence. Each time he has applied the civilising process to a new subject, he has engaged the evidence before him.

Where commitment to a theory blinds a historian to evidence is another matter. The application of evolution to history, or evolutionary psychology, furnishes an example of theory in history gone wrong. In recent years, historical studies by Steven Pinker (2011) and Martin Weiner (2004), among others, have explained patterns and trends in crime and violence with reference to biology. Essentially, the idea is that the explanation for patterns in the history of violence, such as the overrepresentation of young men, is found in biological characteristics. This biological propensity developed in the course of evolution. Both the source of crime and violence, and its regulation, are found in psycho-physiological machinery hardwired into the human brain, and fluctuations in levels of crime and violence have to do with a complex interaction between this biological machinery and cultural and social conditions. The advocates of this approach are keen to situate in their work in recent advances in science ('scientists tell us…') rather than previous work of historians, but the fact is evolution as a form of historical explanation has been around a long time.

In the 1920s, Harry Elmer Barnes used evolution as the framework for his history of prisons. Barnes, who at one time taught history at Columbia University, offered one of the most thorough elaborations of evolution in history in his historical penology. *The Evolution of Penology in Pennsylvania* (1927) presents Pennsylvania the foremost example of a modern, advanced system of punishment, the culmination of reform movements to have occurred over more than a century. 'Herbert Spencer's formula of evolution as a passage from a crude and undifferentiated homogeneity to a differentiated and specialized heterogeneity…' Barnes declared, 'admirably describes and summarises the course of development of the penal, reformatory and correctional institutions of Pennsylvania, as well as those in the country as a whole' (Barnes 1927: 3). Barnes regarded the establishment of a state prison in 1789 within Walnut Street Jail as the first step in a 'differentiated treatment of criminals'; the second step was a house of refuge for delinquents opened in Philadelphia in 1828. Further advances occurred in the creation of the hospital for insane at Harrisburg, the training school for 'feeble-minded children' at Elwyn, and in the 1920s, the implementation of non-institutional supervision through probation. Barnes concluded by saying that more progress had been made in the 'real scientific basis of criminology' in the past 40 years than had been achieved since the dawn of history, but that it could be successfully applied only after a 'persistent campaign of public education' (Barnes 1927: 406).

Barnes seems to be using evolution as a metaphor for history, but this is not so. He was a prolific writer who produced books of history, criminology and other topics. During the interwar period, he became enamoured with scientific criminology. Every form of human conduct, he decided, was determined by biological heredity and the social environment. Barnes made no credible effort to engage documentary evidence and devise a theory in relation to what he found. Nor did he start with a theory and look to evidence to confirm or disconfirm it. Rather, he started with a eugenicist's view of human nature and this informed his view of crime and history. Crime was not a legal issue, but a socio-medical problem to be dealt with through a comprehensive prevention scheme, founded on biological and eugenic provisions to ensure that future generations would contain more 'well born' and fewer 'defective' individuals. His views put him in ideological kinship with the eugenics programme of the National Socialists in Germany, and after the war, he became the American leader of Holocaust denial (Lipstadt 1993). In other words, Barnes committed himself to a form of partisanship so extreme as to accept Nazi propaganda concerning murder of European Jews.

The moral of the story

'Criminal' and 'victim' are evocative words in historical contexts. To suggest that a person or group committed an injustice, or that some person or group are victims of historical processes, is to address wider morality in the course of history. In historical criminology, a persistent theme has been to question, even reverse, the roles assigned at the time. That is, to situate the criminal act or legal proceeding in the context of a wider injustice.

George Wood, the chair of history at the University of Sydney, stated this theme clearly in his history of transportation to Australia. Most convicts sent to Australian colonies, he said, were victims of an unjust legal system which disproportionately represented the interests of the aristocracy. The convicts were 'more sinned against than sinning', condemned by 'blustering ruffians on the bench'. Conflicts arose in the colony, not because convicts were 'more immoral' than aristocrats and administrators, but because convicts disturbed the comfortable order. Wood justified the convicts' crimes as acts of rebellion or temporary solutions to poverty. Nothing the convicts did before transportation or after their arrival was as immoral as the decisions of judicial authorities and the system of punishment that sent them. 'The greatest English criminals', he emphasised, 'remained in England on the court benches and the House of Lords' (Wood 1922).

No one did more to make this part of historical criminology than the British Marxist historians. The British Marxist historians promoted the idea of 'history from the bottom up'. What became the known as the British Marxist historians group, started in the 1950s with the Communist Party Historians and the idea of writing a people's history of England. In 1972, at a gathering of labour history, Eric Hobsbawm, Edward Thompson, Douglas Hay and other developed the idea of 'social crime'. Owing to desperate conditions, common people engaged in activities that although violated the law, and officially criminal, were not regarded as such by their own communities. Hobsbawm, Thompson and the others found examples of social crime in studies of bandits, poachers, smugglers and arsonists (Hobsbawm 1960; Hay et al. 1975). Nothing these individuals did amounted to as serious a crime in the legal sense as what the ruling aristocracy did in a moral sense.

The bottom up approach to history has had enormous impact on the history of crime. Patricia O'Brien (1982) surveyed the development of prisons in France from 1810 to 1885, and by sifting through the wealth of archived materials, produced a history of the prison concerned with the individuals that shaped the new system. She concentrated on the experience of the imprisoned, separate from the ideals of those who administrated prisons, and arranged her history from the 'inside out' in the same way crowds had been studied from the 'bottom up'. She included a discussion of gender: differences in women and men prisoners, the causes of criminality for women and men, and the formation of institutions for women and men (O'Brien 1982). Anand A. Yang (1985) found inspiration in bottom up history for 'subaltern studies' of crime. His *Crime and Criminality in British India* (1987) includes studies on the increase of dacoity after colonial settlement in Bengal, on social banditry in western India in the nineteenth century and on the effects of criminal tribes legislation on the people designated as members. 'Turning things upside down', by looking for acts of social protest among violence and criminality, was necessary in order to reveal the 'judgmental process' in the extension of colonial legal order (Yang 1987: 12).

Siding with the 'victims of history' is a worthy goal of historical investigation, although the ethics of this when doing historical criminology are not as simple as they might be in other areas of social history. This can be seen in an exchange between Douglas Hay and John Langbein. In 'Property, Authority and the Criminal Law', Hay notes how the number of capital offences multiplied throughout the eighteenth century to some 200 by the early nineteenth century, although relatively few executions were actually carried out. He examined why the law remained on the books during a period in which the number of executions remained low or declined. He argued that the law had much to offer the ruling class. They regarded the introduction of a regular police force as distasteful and preferred to rely on the force of the law. For rulers as much concerned with protecting their authority as their property, courtroom procedures involved spectacle. They were careful to preserve the appearance that the law in England held everyone to account. 'The ideology of the law', Hay said, 'was crucial in sustaining the hegemony of the English ruling class' (Hay 1975: 56).

A few years after it appeared, John Langbein (1983) published his article 'Albion's Fatal Flaws', in which he questioned not only Hay's conclusions about the contours of law in the eighteenth century, but about where the history of crime should be located within wider history. Drawing on cases from sessions at the Old Bailey between 1754 and 1756, Langbein denied that the law had been administered by the ruling class to suit their interests. It was a mistake to romanticise criminal offences as a challenge to the elite. Most of the 'little crooks' at the Old

Bailey (shoplifters, pick-pockets and pilferers) were employed, but poor, and most of their victims were hardly better off, typically small shopkeepers, artisans and innkeepers. So, 'social crime' was less a reaction to the rich exploiting the poor than the poor victimising other poor. Hay had found his evidence by targeting the game law, although the larger problem was not selective use of the evidence but the interpretation. Hay had offered the 'legitimisation thesis' which interpreted cases in which the courts held the wealthy to account as part of the symbolic process of disguising the ruling-class conspiracy. Absorbing contrary evidence in this way meant that Hay's argument was 'not a thesis about the evidence' or even a 'thesis about history'. Rather, it was an essay about what Marx taught. 'The criminal law' Langbein concluded, 'is simply the wrong place to look for the active hand of the ruling classes' (Langbein 1983).

Peter Linebaugh (1985) chiselled away at Langbein's various points before sapping the foundations of the legal approach. By pursuing 'his brand of narrow legal scholarship', Langbein had missed the point. Hay and colleagues had turned to legal records because of what they revealed of 'history from below', about the lives of people who left few written records of their own. Hay had not pursued the methods of legal history, but brought together legal history and social history to reveal the lives of people who left few written records. Linebaugh argued that Langbein had visited the wrong archives and mismanaged what he found. He had not bothered to examine evidence from the countryside as Hay had done. Instead, Langbein looked at London, and missed seeing what was going on – 'even the most cursory historical investigation suggests a dynamic of class relations' (Linebaugh 1985: 225).

But the point Langbein makes about crime victims seems valid. Who were most of the victims of the criminals who came to court? If, as Langbein contends, they came from the same class as the criminals, surely they too are victims of history. We can understand prisoners, lawbreakers, etc. as victims in a general sense – recognise their humanity, sympathise with their circumstances, recognise injustice against them – but this should not keep us from acknowledging victims in the specific sense of those injured by theft, assault, threats and so on.

Construction of memory

In recent decades, crime museums have become popular sites for 'dark tourism'. Visitors have been attracted to museums of crime, which feature recreations of crime scenes, forensic items and artwork of prisoners. There are numerous police and prison museums as well, located in buildings that formerly housed police organisations or built as national penitentiaries. These contain collections of uniforms and firearms, communications equipment, and newspaper clippings and photographs. The museums spotlight ethical issues, not merely concerning the exhibits themselves, but within the history of crime more generally.

There must be a reason for displays of criminality and victimisation other than amusement. Vienna's Kriminalmuseum contains exhibit rooms of crimes in the city from the eighteenth to the twentieth century. The displays include illustrations of sensational murders, and artefacts of these events. These include axes, hammers, ropes, knives and guns selected by murderers, and pictures of skulls and wounds illustrating the injuries sustained by their victims. Throughout the museum, visitors see the repeated display of the murdered human body. The *lustmord* ('lustmurder') section offers crime scene photographs that reveal victims in death. Visitors gaze at women's bodies, their faces containing a reminder of their former humanity, their naked bodies revealing in horrific detail the extent of their injuries. According to its curators, the museum aims to provide an alternative history of Vienna and educates visitors about Austrian criminal justice (Huey 2011).

The museum initiated by Cesare Lombroso housed at the Institute for Medical Jurisprudence at Turin contains display cases and cupboards, boxes, glass containers, wax models and human bones. There are photographs depicting criminals, psychiatric patients and prostitutes; objects made by inmates of prisons and asylums; brains and complete heads suspended in liquid; tools used for crime and photographs of criminals with their tools; plaster masks of fugitives, plaster moulds of ears and hands, preserved slices of tattooed skin, and many skeletons and skulls. As Regener (2003) explains, in the nineteenth century, the authorities retained such material for its scientific value. Collections were meant for research into criminal anatomy, and instruction in forensic techniques (Regener 2003).

The museum, closed at the time of Regener's (2003) analysis, reopened in 2009, on the hundredth anniversary of Lombroso's death. The curator, Silvano Montaldo (2013), explains how Lombroso's collection survived over the years and how it became the public museum. The exhibitions aim to present the 'science' of criminal anthropology in the context of the wider social and cultural history of the period. He emphasises that most visitors surveyed reported their visit to be a positive experience. Although, it is not clear what aspects of the museum they had in mind. Montaldo (2013: 108) notes the controversy surrounding the museum by those who associate Lombroso with a 'racist vision towards those from the south of Italy'.

Per J. Ystehede explains how in 2010, shortly after the Lombroso Museum opened to the public, a large group of protestors gathered outside and shouted *Lombroso razzista, Mazzini terrorista*, 'Lombroso was a racist, Mazzini was a terrorist'. The protestors' objection recalled the formation of the Italian state in the nineteenth century led by the Piedmontese army. As the protestors saw it, Lombroso had supported Piedmont's invasion and occupation of the south of Italy. His science legitimised murder, oppression and violence against Southern Italians. Some of the protestors believed the remains of their ancestors were found among the skulls and bones on display. Further, the protest was animated by the longstanding grievance of the South against the North. By opening the museum, the Italian state reaffirmed its oppression of the South. The protestors wanted to assert for Southern Italians the identity of a persecuted group in Italy similar to Jews or Roma. As Ystehede explains, the protestors' knowledge of Lombroso and his role in history is rather inaccurate. He was not a loyal supporter of Piedmontese politics and had no contempt for the South (Ystehede 2016).

The Lombroso Museum is not the only such site to provoke controversy. Jean Comaroff and Joel Comaroff discuss the South African police museum in Pretoria. The museum began in the 1960s as a haphazard collection of relics from criminal cases: murder weapons, photographs of mutilated bodies, effects of a notorious female poisoner. The museum had been allowed to display artefacts from cases that ended in convictions: it catalogued the triumph of law and order over the enemies of the state. The displays organised around apprehension of spectacular criminals and protection of the 'national security' against the threat of terrorism. But the museum was housed at the national police headquarters, a building from the 1930s where the infamous national security service had made interrogations. By the 1990s, in post-Apartheid South Africa, the site had become abhorrent. The museum directors added fresh exhibits to the museum, offering the possibility of different readings of history. The museum, under the jurisdiction of an ANC-administered Ministry of Safety and Security, became the space of contest and argument as never before. The museum closed because of its own contradictions (Comaroff and Comaroff 2004).

Jacqueline Z. Wilson raises an important question about such sites in her study of decommissioned prisons in Australia converted into tourist sites. Australians have a special relationship with prisons – 'the country having been founded as a jail' – especially where prison history involves convicts. Whose story is the site meant to tell? Or, more precisely, whose story is left out? She suggests that for more than one reason, the museums supply an 'established' or 'official view' of the prison, as dominated by the voices of custodial staff, policymakers and media. What gets left out are the views of those confined. She aimed to recover the lost narratives, those of the inmates 'othered' by society at the time but also by public history since then. She challenged the 'established' view, based on interviews with tourists, curators, managers and former prison staff, and anthropological reading of the site, including physical sources of architecture and graffiti (Wilson 2008).

Wilson makes an important point about the official message. Police and prison museums arrange displays to chronicle their organisation and justify their existence to a public prepared to doubt their effectiveness. After the Second World War, many police museums were not maintained, their collections destroyed. Within the last decade or so, many have reopened by organisations anxious to promote good community relations. These tend to feature the history of the organisation, with uniforms, weapons and equipment on display (Regener 2003). This may be an underlying message in museums with scenes depicting horrific crimes: the need for government authority in a world where such horrible things have happened. What the state wants to tell and what visitors understand is not necessarily the same thing.

Bronfman (2012) emphasises that the diverse items at the Museum of Legal Medicine at the University of Havana fit awkwardly together. They reveal the failure of the institution to incorporate all the objects into a coherent system of thought. There is no unifying logic. Some items, such as 'tattooed mulatto skin', the efforts of criminological science to grasp criminality; other items, a flying donkey constructed of bread crumbs, the effort to make the mind of the dangerous visible, the linking of insane and criminal, a chamber-of-horrors approach intended to reveal tangible products of criminal mind. Bronfman says that the collections – strange combinations of grotesque, banal and sinister – display no hidden logic of power, but survive as places of the illogical, places where coherence falls apart. The material culture of criminality is not displayed with a clear narrative, whether triumph of police or success of criminological science, but the opposite; the failure to contain, the inability to categorise and catalogue (Bronfman 2012).

Who owns the material culture of past crime? Should it be displayed? For what purpose? These questions relate to crime history more generally, even history based on documents, because they have to do with the construction of memory.

Summary

The imaginary story of the museum employee who confronts the display of bones of her own family members for the education and entertainment of visitors seems not so remote. Historical criminology aims to learn from crimes, injustice, victimisation in the past and there are ethical and unethical ways of going about this. In this chapter, we have explored the use of documentary evidence, theoretical interpretation and partisanship, understanding the meaning of 'victims', and the construction of memory in museums.

Review questions

1. What is the relationship between evidence and theory in the writing of history?
2. In what sense should historical writing about crime contain a moral message?
3. What is an appropriate purpose for a museum of crime? What sort of objects should be displayed?

Guide to further reading

Evans, R. (2000) *In Defence of History*. London: Granta. Evans responds to the challenge to history presented by poststructualism and the implication that there is no difference between fact and fiction in accounts of the past.

Evans, R. (2001) *Lying about Hitler: History, Holocaust, and the David Irving Trial*. New York: Basic Books. Detailed examination of the 2000 London court verdict against Holocaust denier David Irving to demonstrate the difference between legitimate historical research and falsification of the historical record.

Hobsbawm, E. (2005) *On History*. London: Abacus. Essays by Hobsbawm on the writing of history. The essays offer insight into the Marxist approach that had such an important role in the emergence of historical criminology.

Knepper, P. (2015) *Writing the History of Crime*. London: Bloomsbury. Surveys methods and theories used in historical study of crime. Provides an overview of major traditions in historiography and explains controversies over interpretation of evidence

Lawrence, P. (2012) 'History, criminology and the "use" of the past' *Theoretical Criminology* 16: 313–328. Considers the interaction between history and criminology. Lawrence argues for greater cooperation between the two while acknowledging the different purposes.

Macmillan, M. (2009) *The Uses and Abuses of History*. London: Profile Books. A wide-ranging discussion about who makes claims about the past and the motivations for them.

References

Barnes, H. E. (1927). *The Evolution of Penology in Pennsylvania*. Indianapolis: Bobbs-Merrill.

Bellesiles, M. (2000). *Arming America: The Origins of a National Gun Culture*. New York: Alfred Knopf.

Bronfman, A. B. (2012). 'The Fantastic Flying Donkey and the Tattoo' *Radical History Review* 113: 134–142.

Castel, R. (1994). '"Problematization" as a mode of reading history' in Jan Goldstein, ed, *Foucault and the Writing of History*. Oxford: Blackwell, pp. 237–252.

Comaroff, J. and Comaroff, J. (2004). 'Criminal obsessions, after Foucault: Postcoloniality, policing, and the metaphysics of disorder' *Critical Inquiry* 30: 800–824.

Foucault, M. (1979) *Discipline and Punish: The Birth of the Prison*. Vintage: New York.

Flynn, T. (2005). 'Foucault's mapping of history' in G. Gutting, ed, *The Cambridge Companion to Foucault*. Cambridge: Cambridge University Press, pp. 29–48.

Fulbrook, M. (2002). *Historical Theory*. London: Routledge.

Hay, D. (1975). 'Property, authority and the criminal law' in D. Hay, P. Linebaugh, J. G. Rule, and C. Winslow, eds, *Albion's Fatal Tree: Crime and Society in Eighteenth Century England*. London: Allen Lane.

Hay, D, P. Linebaugh, J. G. Rule, and C. Winslow, eds, (1975). *Albion's Fatal Tree: Crime and Society in Eighteenth Century England*. London: Allen Lane.

Hobsbawm, E. (1969). *Bandits*. London: Weidenfeld and Nicolson.

Huey, L. (2011). 'Crime behind the glass: Exploring the sublime in crime and the Vienna Kriminalmuseum' *Theoretical Criminology* 15: 381–399.

Langbein, J. H. (1983). 'Albion's fatal flaws' *Past and Present* 98: 96–120.

Lindgren, J. (2002). 'Falling from grace: *Arming America* and the Bellesiles scandal' *Yale Law Journal* 111: 2195–2249.

Linebaugh, P. (1985). '(Marxist) social history and (conservative) legal history: A reply to Professor Langbein' *New York University Law Review* 60: 212–243.

Lipstadt, D. (1993). *Denying the Holocaust: The Growing Assault on Truth and Memory*. London: Penguin.

Monkkonen, E. (1986). 'The dangers of synthesis' *American Historical Review* 91: 1153.

Montaldo, S. (2013). 'The Lombroso Museum from its origins to the present day' in P. Knepper and P. J. Ystehede, eds, *The Cesare Lombroso Handbook*. London: Routledge, pp. 98–112.

Nye, R. A. (1978). 'Crime in modern societies: Some research strategies for historians' *Journal of Social History* 11: 491–507.

Pinker, S. (2011). *The Better Angels of Our Nature: The Decline of Violence in History and its Causes*. London: Allen Lane.

O'Brien, P. (1982). *The Promise of Punishment: Prisons in Nineteenth-Century France*. Princeton: Princeton University Press.

Regener, S. (2003). 'Criminological museums and the visualization of evil' *Crime, History and Societies* 7: 2–13.

Roth, R. (2002). 'Guns, gun culture, and homicide: the relationship between firearms, the uses of firearms, and interpersonal violence' *William and Mary Quarterly* 59: 223–240.

Spierenburg, P. (1984). *The Spectacle of Suffering: Executions and the Evolution of Repression: From a Preindustrial Metropolis to the European Experience*. Cambridge: Cambridge University Press.

Spierenburg, P. (2006). 'Democracy came too early: a tentative explanation for the problem of American homicide' *American Historical Review* 104–114.

Spierenburg, P. (2013). 'A personal recollection of Norbert Elias and how I became a crime historian' in Pieter Spierenburg, ed, *Violence and Punishment: Civilizing the Body Through Time*. Cambridge: Polity Press, pp. 174–180.

Warren, J. (2010). 'The Rankean tradition in British historiography, 1840–1950' in Stefan Berger, Heiko Feldner and Kevin Passmore, eds, *Writing History: Theory and Practice*. London: Bloomsbury, pp. 22–39.

Weiner, M. (2004). *Men of Blood: Violence, Manliness and Criminal Justice in Victorian England*. Cambridge: Cambridge University Press.

Wilson, J. Z. (2008). *Prison: Cultural Memory and Dark Tourism*. New York: Peter Lang.

Wood, G. A. (1922). 'Convicts' *Royal Australian Historical Society Journal and Proceedings* 8:177–208.

Yang, A. A. (1987). *Crime and Criminality in British India*. Tucson: University of Arizona Press.

Ystehede, P. J. (2016) 'Contested spaces – on crime museums, monuments and memorials' in P. Knepper and Johansen, A. eds, *The Oxford Handbook of the History of Crime and Criminal Justice*. Oxford: Oxford University Press, pp. 338–352.

3

ETHICAL CHALLENGES

Doing research with children

Evi Girling

Most of the guidance on researching children within ethical frameworks presumes children to be an 'identifiable, knowable constituency whose members share particular characteristics that distinguish them from others' (Halsey and Honey, 2005: 2144). Yet the constructions and discourses of childhood posit a distinct challenge to their knowability and characteristics other than in relation to adults. This relational definition or understanding of childhood permeates dominant cultural, legal and political constructions of childhood through paradigms of dependence, vulnerability, immaturity (moral/physical/cognitive) (Morrow and Richards, 1996) and in turn have shaped the ethical frameworks of social research with children which will be discussed below.

Key definitions

Child: According to the United Nations Convention on the Rights of the Child (1989) children include all those under the age of 18.
Assent: Acquiescence (as opposed to informed consent, which requires more active agreement).

Introduction: the ethical burden of researching children (and adults)

Research with children is often perceived by researchers as risky and unpredictable in all its stages and for all concerned. Children 'are being seen to inhabit risky spaces' (Farrell, 2005: 3) and research with children is viewed as a 'risky enterprise' (p3) and governed as such. The key ethical principles and debates appear to be similar to those concerning adults as they have been discussed elsewhere in this volume: informed consent, protecting participants from harm (beneficence and non-maleficence), confidentiality and privacy and the requirements, negotiations and implications of the role of gatekeepers to participants and research settings. Yet the scope of the debates appears to be markedly different:

- raising questions about the very feasibility of informed consent from children and the very adequacy of traditional methods of ensuring it;
- considering whether any research with children should have a higher burden to demonstrate a greater extent of benefit to children before it can take place given concerns about informed consent and concerns about the abject vulnerability of children to adult interventions;
- wondering whether informed consent is possible/desirable or whether positive informed consent should be replaced by 'assent' – acquiescence as a more practical and realistic alternative;
- considering the challenge of privacy and confidentiality not only in terms of legal requirements of disclosure of abuse and risk of harm but also in the context of the institutional and family settings in which such research takes place.

Research with children is often presented as 'burdensome' on a number of levels:

1. logistically (e.g. difficulty in gaining access and negotiating with gatekeepers who are perceived to present substantial barriers to children's participation);
2. methodologically (e.g. in the need to respond to and address calls for appropriate and less familiar methods to reflect the research settings and the participants and the demand for responsive and thereby somewhat unpredictable research designs that such approaches entail);
3. in terms of ethical compliance before, during and after the research (meeting legal requirements, attending to the demands of institutional management of risks of such research and the more rigorous process of ethical review it entails).

Researchers would need to consider whether these disincentives foreclose areas of research with children in general and discourage research designs which demand more sustained and predictable engagement with research participants. Furthermore, these disincentives raise more acute questions about the extent to which this has a disproportionate impact on the most vulnerable and least adult-like of children (see Carter, 2009) encouraging research to be about them but silencing their experience in theory and policy. This latter point can have important implications for criminological research as it can dovetail with more punitive and actuarial approaches to youth justice described below. One of the first questions to consider is not only whether it is possible given ethical considerations to carry out particular research with children but also the ethical implications of NOT conducting the research or reframing research questions.

The governance of research ethics with respect to children reflects Rose's (1989: 121) observation that 'childhood is the most intensively governed sector of personal existence'. Navigating the ethical maze of researching children requires:

- Awareness and compliance with law, the definition and safeguarding of children in particular jurisdictions as well as the spirit of international conventions and specifically the United Nations Convention on the Rights of the Child (UNCRC) (Masson, 2000). According to the UNCRC (1989) children include all those under the age of 18. A key area of the convention in terms of research ethics is its protection of the right to express one's views and the right of the child to express his or her views in all matters affecting his or her life (UNCRC Article 12). Assuring the 'child who is capable of forming his or her own views the rights to express those views freely in all matters affecting the child, the views of the child being given due weight in accordance with the age and maturity of the child' (UNCRC Article 12).
- Awareness and compliance with codes of ethics of professional bodies, which provide general guidance on research ethics in particular disciplinary research areas and specific guidance in relation to children.
- Compliance with a culture and practice of research ethics governance which, in addition to providing peer scrutiny and representing participant and institutional interests in the research, manages institutional risks of any proposed research with children and may be 'risk averse' in such decision-making (Israel and Hay, 2006).

Yet this panoply of law, codification and risk management can be inadequate in the face of the complexity and diversity of the day to day planning and the carrying out of research with children.

Before going on to discuss the ways in which research with children seem to require more intensive ethics governance and more ethical reflexivity compared to that of research with adults, it is important to ponder on the terms of that difference. Even though the principles that guide research with children are similar to the ones outlined for adults in most research guidelines, research with children brings some of the thorniest debates in terms of research ethics (such as consent for example) into a sharp focus. The ethical conduct of research with children requires the researcher to be sensitised not only to the processes of ensuring ethical conduct but to the spirit, aims and rationale of those frameworks that govern the relationship between researchers and participants. In practice a research design involving children in its implementation of ethical frameworks can feel very different to a corresponding one for adults (Tisdall et al., 2009). Researchers conducting research with children have argued for an appreciation of the ethical conduct of research as an ongoing process (e.g. Alderson and Morrow, 2011).

Whilst acknowledging common ethical principles governing research with children and adults, professional codes of ethics (for example those of the British Sociological Association, the British Society of Criminology and the ESRC Research Ethics Framework), situate children in a more general category of vulnerable groups. They urge awareness of the legal framework surrounding consent and the safeguarding of children or the requirement for the researcher to take extra care in applying the general principles to research with children. The involvement of children in research in terms of guidance is often to be found in lists of vulnerable groups or sensitive topics which require more sustained scrutiny and reflection in terms of ethics.

One of the arguments about the special status of childhood as a category in terms of research is that it covers a diverse range of experiences and capacities (Christensen and James, 2008). Yet the category of adulthood also encompasses a diversity of experiences and interests. The task of thinking about the application of general ethical principles and values in the 'situational' realities and diversities of children and young people is, as I discuss below, a relatively onerous task, but then so should the task of applying them in the situational reality for adult participants and particularly adult social groups 'experiencing social exclusion' (Christensen and Prout, 2002: 481). We should not consider discussions about ethics and children as a 'case of exceptionalism' but we need to explore the relevance of that burden for other vulnerable or hard to reach groups.

Children and young people who are asked to participate in criminological research can have multiple vulnerabilities, their structural vulnerabilities as part of a group experiencing social exclusion may be further compounded both by age and by the special gaze of a criminal justice system that intensively governs and collects evidence on children as current and future offenders (see below). Arguably whatever is true of the challenges of criminological research generally is even more true in criminological research with children. However we should be mindful of the need to avoid the ghettoisation of ethical concerns in doing research with young people as a special case; the ethical sensitisation culture of research with children would do well to permeate research ethics with all groups more generally.

Childhood in the sociological imagination and its methodological implications

The understanding and practice of ethics in research with children needs to be set against particular historical, sociological and popular constructions of children and childhood. The ontological and epistemological assumptions of the researcher regarding children will not only influence the research questions and research design but may also ultimately determine the ethical positions and sensibilities of the research.

What is often presented as a legal precipice between childhood and adulthood in various jurisdictions masks the 'tortuous path' (Prout and James, 1997) of what sociologists and historians of childhood have shown to be an elusive and shifting concept (ibid; Hendrick, 1997). In the 1980s and 1990s a 'new' sociology of childhood developed a well articulated critique of existing theories and research on and with children as premised on a construction of children as 'less than fully human, unfinished or incomplete' (Jenks, 1996: 10) and as 'human becomings' rather than human beings' (Qvortrup, 1994: 2).

The paradigm shift of these reconceptualisations of childhood and children augured an ontological, epistemological and methodological revolution in social science research. These developments have led to research agendas and designs which aim to capture children's voices and experiences, respecting their right to participate or refuse to take part and facilitating the unencumbered expression of their views. The emphasis has been to recast children at the epicentre of research questions, research designs and data collection methods. Thus privileging children's and young people's voices and experiences which would on the one hand recast

---

BOX 3.1 Christensen and Prout (2002: 480–481). Four patterns in the conceptualisation of children in research designs and some of their attendant ethical dilemmas.

Child as object: Even though in terms of academic discourse this approach is discredited it is still common and researchers should actively reflect the extent to which their research design sets up the child as an object (not as an actor). It draws from narratives of children's dependency on others and as Christensen and Prout suggest their lives and welfare are 'investigated from the perspectives of the adults, obtaining accounts of parents, teachers and others involved in the care of the child' (2002: 480). Adults (in their personal or professional relationship to the child) make judgment on children's participation based on their assessment of the child's best interest and welfare (ibid).

The 'child-centred' perspective: Research designs tend to recognize the child as a person with subjectivity whose involvement in research is important but this position is tempered and 'conditioned by judgements about cognitive abilities and social competencies' (ibid). The maturity and development of participants comes under scrutiny and the researchers use age-based criteria as well as their own assessments of competence/capacity for inclusion or exclusion of children in different research activities.

Children as subjects rather than objects in research: Similar to the child-centred approach but children are viewed as autonomous, not merely dependent on institutions and families. In that respect there is no difference between research with adults and research with children. The same methodological attentiveness that informs and animates research with adults is also extended to children.

Children as active participants and co-researchers in the research process: This reflects the tenets of the UN Convention on the Rights of the Child (UNCRC) which emphasise children's participation and citizenship rights and seems to support new social science methodologies which see knowledge as a co-production between the researcher and the participant and breaks down the boundaries between the researcher and the researched and encourages involvement of participants as co-researchers.

children and young people as research participants and on the other encourage the development of appropriate methodologies which reflexively facilitate meaningful participation of children in research (Tisdall and Punch, 2012). Research with children has since explicitly acknowledged the importance of an appreciation of the social construction of childhood for researcher reflexivity.

Most discussions of research ethics with children place particular onus on the researcher to actively acknowledge the cultural and political constructions of childhood and of the assumptions s/he is making about the capacities, autonomy and subjectivities of children (Phelan and Kinsella, 2013). This active acknowledgment involves examining and questioning our 'own positionality, what brings us to the project, and what we really think about children' (Nutbrown (2010:11, cited in Phelan and Kinsella, 2013) and their capacities and possible contributions to the research (ibid).

Vignette: the politics of research with children in Youth Justice

The theorisation of childhood described above challenges natural or universalistic approaches (James and Prout, 1997; Jenks, 1996) and demands the appreciation of contingent and situated constructions of childhood. This is particularly resonant for criminological research which takes place in a context in which 'childhood identities [are] framed in accordance with particular political traditions, social and economic conditions, normative conventions and cultural contexts' (Goldson 2013: 111). This has two implications:

1. The politics and ethics of researching childhood need to be situated in the normative and cultural contexts of research settings and fields.
2. Researchers need to reflect on the political context of the research and of the categorical and individual vulnerabilities of children to the uses of research and of the research process.

This short section explores the implications of the normative and cultural context of Youth Justice in England and Wales and its implications for the politics of research with children and young people.

The 'crisis of childhood' (Aitken, 2001), which has invited (and continues to invite) the recasting of legal and criminological subjectivity of the child acts as a backdrop to both research with children and to our discussions about research ethics. Childhood and youth continues to be apprehended in penal policy and popular imagination as par exemplar a relational category demanding opposition and contrast – children are defined by what they are not and on the basis of what they are in the process (or at risk) of becoming and through their relationships with others (parents, guardians) (see Jenks, 1996). Much of the voluminous academic work on developments in Youth Justice since the late 1990s reflected on the construction of childhood and the problem of children in criminal justice in these terms. The backdrop of a childhood in crisis, a period of transition pregnant with risk and possibility of change recast it as a time and place of work for criminal justice, a site of research and site of intervention to fix individual and dystopian futures, for children, their families, their communities and the state. Research in this context seeks to identify and understand pathways of change and explores them forensically for all possible insights and sites for intervention in terms of crime and criminal justice.

Different legal systems espouse different views on children's moral and legal subjectivities and indeed on the balance between welfare and justice that they invite (deserve) in their interactions with criminal justice system. It is important to understand the intersections and tensions between these political cartographies of childhood, responsibility and the tensions with the broad definition of childhood and its attendant rights under UNCRC. The minimum age of criminal responsibility assumes the attainment of sufficient emotional, mental and moral maturity for criminal accountability for their actions and varies widely from country to country (from 6 to 18 years of age). Until the age of 18 young people are usually afforded special provisions as part of criminal justice arrangements that recognise that young people and children are different from adults. Researchers should reflect and acknowledge the ways in which these intersecting (and occasionally conflicting) moral geographies of age, maturity, rights and responsibilities drive particular policy research agendas in criminology in relation to children and young children.

Goldson (2013) has recently argued the adultification of children aged 10 years in criminal justice in England and Wales 'is a mutation of justice' (2013: 126) and the 'corrosive politicization of juvenile crime' (ibid) which both socially constructs them as undeserving dangerous others (both in their presents and in their biographical futures) and 'fatally obstructs the application of knowledge and evidence to the processes of legislative reform, policy formation and practice development' (ibid). More importantly, for our purposes it privileges certain types of empirical knowledge production which as I discuss below sets the parameters and gatekeeping of criminological research with children in the early twenty-first century.

Recent developments in Youth Justice in England and Wales have been driven by 'neoliberal correctionalism', which sees and seeks to correct/address offending (current and future) as the outcome of deficiencies either in the individual or in their immediate environment (family and community) (Muncie, 2008; Haines and Case, 2014). Children are responsibilised for their offending (e.g. Muncie, 2008). This neoliberal correctionalism is empirically sustained by 'a what works agenda' or 'evidence led' discourse which invites an avalanche of evaluation research which makes up a substantial sector of research with young people in the criminal justice system in terms of funding streams. According to Case and Haines (2014) the *Risk Factor Prevention Paradigm* of these approaches 'privilege the quantified assessment of risk (of offending/reoffending/reconviction) and (target) intervention to address identified risk, foster a homogenised, retrospective, deficit-focused, reductionist view of children and their (offending) behaviour' (2014: 3). As such, it stands in sharp contrast to the ontological basis of the new sociology of childhood described above.

There has been a rigorous academic critique of the politics of Youth Justice in England and Wales and its attendant research paradigms (see Muncie, 2006 and 2008, Goldson, 2010); an empirical response has also been emerging over the last decade. There are optimistic signs that empirical criminological research is responding to the ethical challenge of reimagining children in criminal justice research. For example recent research by Phoenix and Kelly (2013) explores the subjective situated meanings of responsibilisation discourses for young people. Gray's (2013) longitudinal study of young persistent offenders as the first recipients of Intensive Supervision and Surveillance Programmes (ISSPs) explores the long-term impact of intensive supervision on their lives through a cross-methodological research design that seeks to be reflexive about the politics of representation of both serious young offenders and the politics of evaluation research.

Yet the challenge is that there exists an abundance of official research 'on young lawbreakers and youth justice that is narrowly focused and excludes questions outside the framework of specific policy or practice innovations' (Phoenix, 2009:73). In a perverse way the ethical governance and hierarchy of gatekeepers of research may mean that young lawbreakers become simultaneously over-researched (within the narrow remit of policy and practice innovations) and under-researched for knowledge production beyond the realm of government objectives.

BOX 3.2 Managing the ethical volatility and complexity of researching (with) children: ethical symmetry, ethical mindfulness and ethical reflexivity.

New Sociology of Childhood and the hotspots of ethical and methodological debates

1. Considering the differences between research with children and research with adults.
2. Detailed consideration of ethical issues in researching children with sharing of researcher experiences (e.g. informed consent; gatekeepers).
3. Considering the demands and challenges of innovative methods of data collection.
4. The political imperative of engaging children and young people as active participants in the research process.

(Tidsall and Punch 2012: 251)

In considering the general application of codes of ethics in research with children Morrow (2008) suggests that a number of considerations are relevant:

a. Competency and capacity (as both a categorical, individual and contextual characteristic). Morrow and other researchers refer explicitly to competency of the child researcher but in the spirit of many of the discussions of competency – the competency of the researcher to understand, value and respond to the competencies of children and young people is equally important.
b. Vulnerability to adults generally and gatekeepers in particular (as both a categorical and individual characteristic).
c. Power of the researcher (as an adult and a researcher), especially the power to define the meaning of the situation (both in situ but also in the analysis of interpretation).
d. Gatekeeper control of the research participants and settings in which most research with children takes place.

Each of these considerations can present ongoing logistical and ethical challenges for the researcher. The literature reflects on how best to address the ethical unpredictability and the ethical responsiveness required of the researcher. A number of researchers have suggested that codification and risk management can be inadequate in the face of complexity and diversity in the day to day planning and carrying out of research with children and suggest what may be called 'dispositions' to enable them to recognise and respond to what some have called ethically important moments in research with children.

A number of terms have been used to describe these dispositions: 'thinking ethically' (Williams, 2006), developing 'strategic values' (Christensen and Prout, 2002), 'practising ethical symmetry' (ibid), 'ethical mindfulness' (Warin, 2011) and ethical reflexivity (Renold et al., 2008). These strategies reflect concerns within social science research with children that ethics cannot simply be reduced to codified principles and bureaucratic regulation (see Gallagher, 2009) but that in order to ensure ethically sound research the ethical process should be an 'an ongoing process of questioning, acting and reflecting, rather than straightforward application of general rules of conduct' (Gallagher, 2009: 26).

How should researchers approach the planning and conduct of ethical research with children? In the expansive literature which considers the ethical implications of research with children much of the discussion focuses on the ambiguity, complexity and unpredictability of the settings and participants. For example:

*   that it may be much more difficult for a child to communicate withdrawal of consent and even if they did it is possible that the researcher may not interpret it as such;
*   that the limits of promises of confidentiality and anonymity may be harder to communicate to young children;
*   that promises of confidentiality and anonymity may be challenging to fulfil within the educational or other institutional arrangements through which access to the children and young people was secured in the first place;

- that gatekeepers and their natural surveillance of settings in which research takes place creates a difficulty in ensuring 'safe places' vis a vis disclosure, privacy and confidentiality.

The complexities described above become more urgent in the drive for methodological innovation that has accompanied research with children in the last twenty years which calls for methodological innovation promoting data collection strategies which build and sustain relationships with participant children and young people and encourage children as active participants in the research process. These developments emphasise the need for responsive in situ ethical decision making.

Even though inevitably there may be some broad parameters of decisions about the competence and capacity of children according to age at the research design and ethical scrutiny stage, such decisions about the capacities/competency need to be contextualised across individual children during the lifetime of a research project.

It has been argued that even though research with children benefits from the existence of ethical codes, this codification can sometimes present a challenge. Yet codification of ethical practice can lead to a routinisation which in turn can 'act as a fig leaf for the instrumental determination to get the research done at any cost [and] a substitute for the active engagement ... with ethical issues' (Christensen and Prout, 2002: 491). Codification tends to create an ethical architecture in which emphasis is placed on certain features and certain periods of the research process; gaining access, recruitment, negotiating with gatekeepers, securing consent, legal compliance and auditing practices, anonymity and confidentiality (ibid).

Researching with children demands ongoing ethical reflexivity and relies to some extent on the researcher's ability to appreciate and respond in situ to the variability and complexity of children's capacities, vulnerabilities, interests and wishes of children (Christensen and Prout, 2002). The nature of the interactions facilitated or deemed appropriate by the research design may actually inhibit responsiveness or creativity and therefore research traditions with fixed research designs may not be best placed to respond or develop a situated understanding of the children's experiences and vulnerabilities during the research project. Research designs which encourage longer, more immersive interactions and sustained engagement with children and young people (qualitative/ ethnographic) allows researchers to 'better address ethical dilemmas as they arise' according to the needs of the situation (Eder and Corsaro, 1999: 528). Christensen and Prout (2002) suggest that researchers seeking to work with children should develop 'strategic values' to anchor the tactics required in their everyday practice' and that the research community should be engaged in a dialogue with its members and with children as participants in the research process (ibid). Reflexivity is sometimes presented as sensitisation an alertness and ability to recognise the 'microethical dimensions of research practice' and 'prepared for ways of dealing with the ethical tensions that arise' (Guillemin and Gillam, 2004: 278).

BOX 3.3 Same but different: practising ethical symmetry in situ.

'The understanding of children as social actors and participants is best founded on an a priori assumption of [...] "ethical symmetry" between adults and children.... The researcher takes as his or her starting point the view that the ethical relationship between researcher and informant is the same whether he or she conducts research with adults or with children' (Christensen and Prout, 2002: 482). Ethical principles are common to research with children or adults and that each of these principles and considerations also has 'its counterpart for children' (ibid).

This has a number of implications:

1. Symmetry of principles: 'The researcher employs the same ethical principles whether they are researching children or adults' (ibid).
2. Symmetry of rights and considerations: 'Each right and ethical consideration in relation to adults in the research process has its counterpart for children' (ibid).
3. Threats to symmetry: Presumptions and assumptions about differences need to be considered in 'the concrete situations involving children and cannot be assumed in advance' (ibid).

BOX 3.4 Practising ethical mindfulness in research with children and young people (Warin, 2011: 822 (*adapted with some additions*)).

An alertness/sensitivity to relational aspects of the research process. Ethical mindfulness and reflexivity are interdependent.

Recognise 'the complexity of consent (in terms of communication, architecture of ethics governance and forms)' (ibid).

Reframe consent as an ongoing process (The time frame either in the micro scale of the research/participant interaction or in the more complex relationship of longitudinal research) (ibid).

Reframe the distinction between necessary and sufficient levels of consent. Whilst the consent of gatekeepers is a prerequisite in research and in some cases it is a necessary condition (ibid) for research with children, it is never a sufficient condition and attempts to gain, maintain and recognise the consent of children/young people is essential.

Respond to disparities between gatekeeper consent and children's consent/ assent by recognising competing agendas and managing them both in the seeking of consent and in negotiating the day to day dilemmas of research with children in adult settings (ibid).

Recognise and respond to the experience of children in research (meaningful and enjoyable) (ibid).

Recognise that ethical dilemmas can appear and what may appear mundane for you may be important to children/young people (ibid).

Recognise ethically important moments and make them part of your analysis (ibid).

Recognise and reflect on yourself as the other (child) and on the other as yourself – 'work the hyphen' (ibid).

Appreciating the scope and scale of the ethical challenges

Case study: the dilemmas of informed consent and gatekeeping in research with children

Gaining consent for a child or young person to participate in research is often a more complex procedure when compared to gaining consent from other populations. Research Ethics Committees (which have the power to stop research in an organisational setting) and parents/guardians are likely to feature in most ethical and logistical deliberations of research with children.

The legal framework surrounding informed consent in research with children relates to concerns about competence/capacity (Masson, 2000, 2005; Alderson and Morrow, 2011). It varies from jurisdiction to jurisdiction and researchers are advised to familiarise themselves with the legal provisions of the state in which the research will be conducted. In England and Wales those under 16 can only be presumed to be legally competent to give consent if an assessment is made that they have sufficient understanding of what participation in research entails; here, parental consent is not necessary. There are two problems with this – how do we assess children's competence and what are the risks of making the wrong call on assessment. This is an assessment which relies very much on the individual researcher and their interpretation of what constitutes 'sufficient understanding'. Such decisions would be made at the risk of legal proceedings if the child suffered a harm as a result of their involvement (Masson, 2000, 2005). The outcome of any legal proceedings would be unclear because there have been no legal precedents for social research (ibid). The judgement that needs to be made by the researcher is therefore one in which an assessment of the risks of such research is twofold, assessing the risk of harm and the risk of not seeking parental concern. Gatekeepers assess the risks entailed in children's participation in research and balance and consider both the risk to the child if they participate versus the possible benefits but additionally they need to decide to take a positive action to engage with those risks in order to provide access. This is the case in both institutional settings but also as parents/guardians. Given the discourses of protection that surround childhood and increasing concerns about safeguarding children such research may appear to create an unnecessary level of risk and may be construed to be not in the best interest of the child or posit an institutional or personal risk to the adults who are legally responsible for safeguarding the child.

Researchers tend to adopt variations of the belt and braces approach when it comes to consent seeking consent from both children under 16 and their parents. Different strategies may be used which on the one hand protects the researcher from risk but also signals the symbolic significance of children's autonomy or other concerns about gatekeeping of research by concerned parents. For example a common approach in researching school children was used by Carroll-Lind et al. (2006) who sought passive 'opt-out' parental consent in her study of school children about children and violence. Unless parents responded to a written invitation to withdraw their child then parental consent was presumed and the children were then able to make their own decision.

Some criminological research may present challenges in identifying appropriate gatekeepers who present or increase risk of harm to a child. For example in research about domestic violence identifying appropriate processes of informed consent and gatekeepers 'becomes reliant on understanding children's care and protection, not only in the research process, but more broadly in a child's life. This context will influence where and how the research sample is selected, who are the possible gate-keepers (Campbell, 2008) and what dangers might be present' (Morris, Hegarty and Humphreys, 2012: 128).

Informed consent demands that participants must comprehend and voluntarily agree to the nature of the research and of their own role and contribution to it (Israel and Hay, 2006: 61). In research with children researchers must therefore consider a child's freedom to decide about participation (voluntariness), the child's capacity to make decisions (capacity) and the format, clarity and nature of the information provided to individuals to enable them to make such a decision. Especially in the case of research with children, the process of satisfying institutional requirements that the researcher has done enough to obtain informed consent and the process of obtaining informed consent by participants) may not always align (ibid: 60) or indeed ensure informed consent in practice.

The 'architecture' of ethics forms which in most instances have come to involve the signing of consent forms and the provision of a written Information Sheet to participants has meant that this may be an 'artificial and culturally inappropriate process' (Israel, 2004: vii) for children and young people. Given the specific difficulty of ascertaining what is material information for different children the seeking of consent should be an ongoing process between the researcher and the participant which encourages and facilitates the participant's exploration of what may be material information (Israel, 2004).

Traditional and institutionally encouraged means of securing and documenting the process of information provision to ensure informed consent tend to rely on information sheets which may assume levels of literacy and linguistic ability that render them ineffective. This is particularly important in researching the views of children and young people. Researchers have adopted alternative methods and contexts of providing information about research to children which place less emphasis on written information and more emphasis on other processes of communication (pictures, images, videos) which aspire to provide information in such a way that respects their level of 'capacity' and information demands (Alderson and Morrow, 2011; Christensen and Prout, 2002).

Assessing the perceived degrees of freedom to withdraw by young people and children is an essential part of fulfilling the voluntariness requirement of informed consent. Due to the logistical and gatekeeper requirements some settings of research may be what can be perceived by our research participants as part of wider coercive disciplinary institutions (schools/youth justice settings and so on). In settings where there is ongoing relationship with the participants it may be possible to establish relationships of trust where the participant will begin to believe in their autonomy and in the ways in which they can communicate decisions to withdraw. This is particularly important for some of the 'over-researched' groups in youth justice such as persistent young offenders where previous interactions with researchers (in the context of evaluation research) may have been part and parcel of their sentence (see Gray, 2013).

Overall, the conduct of the research in its adherence to autonomy and the principle of informed consent will present a more complex logistical challenge. Ensuring informed consent with children will always require identification and negotiation with gatekeepers. Parents/guardians, teachers, social workers and their personal, professional and vested interests will be an integral part of any project involving children (e.g. Tisdall, Davis and Gallagher, 2009). To some extent this posits not only a logistical problem but also the ethical challenge of questioning the very way in which children's participation is constructed and facilitated. Paradoxically children are ubiquitous but they are also a hard to reach group in its own terms, not because they are invisible or because they want to remain hidden but because of the architecture of gatekeeping, surveillance and control that governs their everyday and institutional lives.

Summary: harm, benefit and the ethics of risk

Research with children needs to strike a balance between protecting children from potential harms of taking part or outcomes from the research with potential (hoped-for) benefits and respecting children's autonomy and rights. As with adults, the risks of participation may be 'distress and anxiety, embarrassment and loss of self esteem' (Alderson and Morrow, 2011: 27) but given the structural vulnerabilities of childhood research may also result in physical harm to children especially where the very conduct of the research makes them vulnerable to those entrusted with their care (either gatekeepers or indeed the researcher themselves).

Assumptions about (im)maturity and (in)competence permeate conceptual-isations of childhood, constructing children as 'at risk and vulnerable to exploitation in the research process and therefore in need of protection' (Graham and Fitzgerald, 2010: 141). The imprecise act of balancing the general abundant discourses of risk surrounding childhood (Farrell, 2005: 1–4) and specific risks from participation with some distant-hoped-for benefits has to be carried out time and again by each link in the chain of gatekeepers that controls access to children and young people. It is further complicated by the gatekeeper's assessment of the personal and professional risks to themselves.

The 'ethics of risk' which seem to underpin research with children (Graham and Fitzgerald, 2010; Farrell, 2005) means that such research is now the subject of increasing surveillance and regulation. The unintended consequence of an ethics of risk is that it could be 'gate-keeping children out of research purely on the basis of potential risk to them' (Graham and Fitzgerald, 2010: 141).

For criminological research on young people and children this is an urgent political question as well as an academic and logistical one. The struggle to maintain an empirically supported knowledge base about young people in the criminal justice system in order to challenge the 'rupture' between knowledge and policy in a Youth Justice context is an ongoing and a difficult one (see Goldson, 2010).

Review questions

1. To what extent are the principles and practices governing the ethical conduct of research with children different to those of research with adults?
2. How can reflexivity contribute to the ethical conduct of research?
3. What is ethical burden of researching children in criminological research?
4. What are the guidelines and pitfalls regarding informed consent with children in research?

Guide to further reading

Alderson, P. and Morrow, V. (2011). *The Ethics of Research with Children and Young People*, London: Sage. A practical handbook (first published in the 1990s) providing a fairly comprehensive account. Many useful checklists of questions to consider for researchers embarking on research with children for the first time. Both authors have contributed extensively to the new sociology of childhood in general and to discussions of ethics in particular.

Farrell, A. (2005). *Ethical research with children*. Berkshire: Open University Press. An excellent edited collection which covers a comprehensive range of issues. It is aimed at experienced as well as novice researchers and it moves beyond the 'how to' to set discussions about research ethics and children within wider sociological debates.

Christensen, P. and Prout, A. (2002). 'Working with ethical symmetry in social research with children' *Childhood* 9(4): 477–497. A short but illuminating discussion of ethical symmetry by two leading contributors in the sociology of childhood.

Eder, D. and W.A. Corsaro (1999). 'Ethnographic Studies of Children and Youth: Theoretical and Ethical Issues' *Journal of Contemporary Ethnographic Studies* 28(5): 520–31.
It provides a useful discussion on the challenges of ethnographic research with children which is needed given the emphasis on more immersive and participatory methods in research with children.

Skelton, T. (2008). 'Research with children and young people: Exploring the tensions between ethics, competence and participation' *Children's Geographies* 6(1): 21–36.
This paper tackles the central issue of competence/capacity.

References

Aitken, S. C. (2001). 'Global crises of childhood: Rights, justice and the unchildlike child' *Area* 33: 119–127.

Alderson, P., and Morrow, V. (2011). *The Ethics of Research with Children and Young People: A Practical Handbook*. London: Sage.

Campbell, A. (2008). 'For their own good' *Childhood* 15(1): 30–49.

Carroll-Lind, J., Chapman, J., Gregory, J. and Maxwell, G. (2006). 'The key to the gatekeepers: Passive consent and other ethical issues surrounding the rights of children to speak on issues that concern them' *Child Abuse and Neglect* 30: 979–989.

Carter, B. (2009). 'Tick box for child? The ethical positioning of children as vulnerable, researchers as barbarians and reviewers as overly cautious' *International Journal of Nursing Studies* 46: 858–864.

Christensen, P. and James, A. (2008). 'Childhood diversity and commonality'. In: A. James and P. Christensen (eds.) *Research With Children: Perspectives and Practices*. London, New York: Routledge, pp. 160–178.

Christensen, P. and Prout, A. (2002). 'Working with ethical symmetry in social research with children' *Childhood* 9(4): 477–497.

Eder, D. and Corsaro, W. A. (1999). 'Ethnographic studies of children and youth: Theoretical and ethical issues' *Journal of Contemporary Ethnographic Studies* 28(5): 520–531.

Farrell, A. (2005). *Ethical Research with Children*. Berkshire: Open University Press.

Gallagher, M. (2009). 'Ethics'. In E.K. Tisdall, J. Davis and M. Gallagher (eds.) *Researching with Children and Young People: Research Design, Method and Analysis*. London: Sage.

Goldson, B. (2010). 'The sleep of (criminological) reason: Knowledge – policy rupture and New Labour's youth justice legacy' *Criminology and Criminal Justice* 10(2): 155–178.

Goldson, B. (2013). '"Unsafe, unjust and harmful to wider society": Grounds for raising the minimum age of criminal responsibility in England and Wales' *Youth Justice* 13(2): 111–130.

Graham, A. and Fitzgerald, R. (2010). 'Children's participation in research: Some possibilities and constraints in the current Australian research environment' *Journal of Sociology* 46: 133–147.

Gray, E. (2013). What happens to persistent and serious young offenders when they grow up: A follow-up study of the first recipients of intensive supervision and surveillance. London: Youth Justice Board.

Guillemin, M. and Gillam, L. (2004) 'Ethics, reflexivity and ethically important moments in research' *Qualitative Inquiry* 10: 261–283.

Haines, K. and Case, S. (2014). 'The rhetoric and reality of the "Risk Factor Prevention Paradigm" approach to preventing and reducing youth offending' *Youth Justice* 8(1): 5–20.

Halsey, C. and Honey, A. (2005). 'Unravelling ethics: illuminating the moral dilemmas of research ethics', *Signs: Journal of Women in Culture and Society* 30(4): 2141–2162.

Hendrick, H. (1997). *Children, Childhood and English Society, 1880–1990*. Cambridge: Cambridge University Press.

Israel, M. (2004). *Ethics and the Governance of Criminological Research in Australia*. Sydney: New South Wales Bureau of Crime Statistics and Research.

Israel, M. and Hay, I. (2006). *Research ethics for social scientists*. London: Sage.

James, A. and Prout, A. (eds.) (1997). *Constructing and Reconstructing Childhood*. London: Falmer Press.

Jenks, C. (1996). *Childhood*. London: Routledge.

Masson, J. (2000). 'Researching children's perspectives: legal issues'. In A. Lewis and G. Lindsay (eds.) *Researching Children's Perspectives*. Buckingham: Open University Press.

Masson, J. (2005). 'Researching children's perspectives: legal issues'. In K. Sheehy, M. Nind, J. Rix & K. Simmons (eds.) *Ethics and Research in Inclusive Education: Values into Practice*. London: Routledge.

Morris, A., Hegarty, K., and Humphreys, C. (2012). 'Ethical and safe: Research with children about domestic violence' *Research Ethics* 8(2): 125–139.

Morrow, V. (2008). 'Ethical dilemmas in research with children and young people about their social environments' *Children's Geographies* 6(1): 49–61.

Morrow, V. and Richards, M. (1996). 'The ethics of social research with children: An overview' *Children and Society* 10(2): 90–105.

Muncie, J. (2006). 'Governing young people: Coherence and contradiction in contemporary youth justice' *Critical Social Policy* 26(4): 770–793.

Muncie, J. (2008). 'The punitive turn in juvenile justice: Cultures of control and rights compliance in Western Europe and the USA' *Youth Justice* 8(2): 107–121.

Nutbrown, C. (2010). 'Naked by the pool? Blurring the image? Ethical issues in the portrayal of young children in arts-based educational research' *Qualitative Inquiry* 17: 3–14.

Phelan, S. K. and Kinsella, E. A. (2013). 'Picture this... safety, dignity, and voice – Ethical research with children practical considerations for the reflexive researcher' *Qualitative Inquiry* 19(2): 81–90.

Phoenix, J. (2009). 'Whose account counts? Politics and research in youth justice'. In W. Taylor, R. Earle and R. Hester (eds.) *Youth Justice Handbook: Theory, Policy and Practice*. Cullumpton, Devon: Willan Publishing, pp. 73–82.

Phoenix, J. and Kelly, L. (2013). 'You have to do it for yourself': responsibilization in youth justice and young people's situated knowledge of youth justice practice' *British Journal of Criminology* 53(3): 419–437.

Prout, A. and James, A. (1997). 'A new paradigm for the sociology of childhood? Provenance, promise and problems'. In A. James and A. Prout (eds.) *Constructing and Reconstructing Childhood*. London: Falmer Press, pp. 7–33.

Qvortrup, J. (1994). 'Childhood matters: An introduction'. In: J. Qvortrup, M. Bardy, G. Sgritta and H. Wintersberger (eds.) *Childhood matters: Social Theory, Practice and Politics*. Aldershot: Avebury, pp. 1–24.

Renold, E., Holland, S., Ross, N. J. and Hillman, A. (2008). '"Becoming participant": Problematizing informed consent in participatory research with young people in care' *Qualitative Social Work* 7(4): 427–447.

Rose, N. (1989). *Governing the Soul: The Shaping of the Private Self*. London: Routledge.

Tisdall, E., Davis, J. M. and Gallagher, M. (2009). *Research with Children and Young People: Research Design, Methods and Analysis*. London: Sage.

Tisdall, K. and Punch, S. (2012). '"Not So 'New"? Looking Critically at Childhood Studies' *Children's Geographies* 10(3): 249–264.

United Nations (1989). United Nations Convention on the Rights of the Child (UNCRC). Geneva: United Nations.

Warin, J. (2011). 'Ethical mindfulness and reflexivity: Managing a research relationship with children and young people in a 14-year qualitative longitudinal research (QLR) study' *Qualitative Inquiry* 17: 805–814.

Williams, B. (2006). 'Meaningful consent to participate in social research on the part of people under the age of eighteen' *Research Ethics Review* 2(1): 19–24.

4

THE ROLE OF ETHICS IN PRISONER RESEARCH

Linda Moore and Azrini Wahidin

The aim of this chapter is to examine the role of ethics in prisoner research drawing on the authors' own experience of conducting research in prison. The chapter will begin by historically contextualising the role of ethics, and examining the troubling historical context within which ethical codes and regulatory mechanisms emerged, the role of ethical governance and the ethical dilemmas that as prison researchers we have encountered.

This chapter:

1. outlines the development and content of contemporary ethical codes;
2. presents competing philosophical and methodological approaches to ethics;
3. explores typical ethical dilemmas which researchers face in the penal context, based on the authors' and other researchers' experiences;
4. highlights the value of adopting an ethical approach to prison research.

'Whether the 'truth' sets you free is neither here nor there. The choice is between 'troubling recognitions' that are escapable (we can live with them) and those that are inescapable. This is not the 'positive freedom' of liberation, but the negative freedom of being given this choice. This means making more troubling information available to more people' (Cohen, 2001: 296).

Key definitions

Beneficence: Means to do good or benefit others. In terms of social science research the principle of beneficence is to ensure the maximum benefit of the research whilst minimising the risk of potential and actual harm. In fact, most codes and statements of ethics state that the goal of research is to promote the welfare, understanding and protection of the individuals and groups under study.

Confidentiality: Pertains to the treatment of information that an individual has disclosed in and with the expectation that it will not be divulged to others without permission in ways that are inconsistent with the understanding of the original disclosure. For example, in relation to prison research, confidentiality is conditional on the grounds of minimising harm to the individual, harm to other agents and be cognisant of possible harms or breaches in security to the organisation.

    During the informed consent process, if applicable, subjects must be informed of the precautions that will be taken to protect the confidentiality of the data and be informed of the parties who will or may have access to the data. This will allow subjects to decide about the adequacy of the protections and the acceptability of the possible release of private information to the interested parties.

Ethics: In the words of Beauchamp and Childress (1994: 4), is 'a generic term of various ways of understanding and examining the moral life'. It is concerned with perspectives on right and proper conduct.

Ethics committee: A research ethics committee is a group of people appointed to review research proposals to assess formally if the research is ethical. This means the research must conform to recognised ethical standards, which includes respecting the dignity, rights, safety and well being of the people who take part. The aim of the ethics committee is to promote expectations for good ethical practice in the conduct of research. It provides an over-arching framework of ethical principles and a clear understanding of the internal structures that the organisation has in place to review its practices and activities in relation to research ethics. The policy applies to all those conducting research within, or on behalf of, an organisation.

Informed consent: For consent to be given, it must be voluntary and informed, and the person consenting must have the capacity to make the decision.

Reflexivity: A process whereby the researcher considers their own characteristics and subjectivities and the impact of these on the research.

Respect for persons: Individuals should be treated as autonomous agents able to exercise their autonomy to the fullest extent possible, including the right to privacy and the right to have private information remain confidential.

Introduction

Prisons are largely hidden institutions: prisoner and staff worlds (Goffman, 1961) shielded behind fences and walls. Through documenting and critically analysing conditions and regimes, independent research plays a crucial role in enabling 'outsiders' to better understand prison life and in exposing the 'pains of confinement' (Sykes, 1958). As expressed so powerfully by Cohen (2001: 296), critical researchers have a responsibility to make 'troubling information' more widely available, no more so than in the case of prisons which operate primarily away from public scrutiny. Ethical adherence has particular significance within penal environments. Considering their vulnerable situation, and the harms to which prisoners are routinely exposed, it is imperative that researchers do not compound this suffering, even unintentionally. Ethics, in the words of Beauchamp and Childress (1994: 4), is 'a generic term for various ways of understanding and examining moral life'. Concerned in essence with perspectives on right and proper conduct, ethical issues confront us individually and collectively in our daily lives. With regards to research, ethical decisions impact on every aspect of the process: from the choice of topic and aim and objectives of the study, through to funding arrangements, ways of acquiring access, methods used, treatment of participants, fellow researchers and ourselves, maintaining independence, data, analysis and writing and publication of results.

Codes of practice aim to guide researchers through complex ethical choices. An understanding of how contemporary guidelines were arrived at must be based on a recognition of the historical and social context of research on and involving prisoners; a history which has included much unethical practice. This chapter therefore opens with an overview of the harmful 'scientific' research practices that necessitated the development of protective codes. The principles central to contemporary governance frameworks are then presented, with reflection on the continuum of philosophical perspectives regarding adherence to ethical codes. There follows a discussion of the type of moral dilemmas faced by prison researchers. These issues are explored with reference to our own and other authors' fieldwork experiences, highlighting areas of particular complexity or challenge.

Of course, even with the most meticulous preparation, unplanned issues may arise. As noted by Genders and Player (1995: 42): 'the unpredictable nature of fieldwork ensures that unwelcome and unsolicited materials can be generated as instantaneously and as inexplicably as a rabbit from a magician's hat'. In acknowledging that not every dilemma can be anticipated, and that research within prisons creates particularly complex challenges, we argue in favour of critical research based on principles of independence, integrity and respect for participants, and involving continuous reflection and reflexivity to facilitate ethical decision-making.

Captive subjects: the history of unethical prison research

The history of research in prisons reveals many examples of unethical practice, which have resulted in severe distress and damage and it is within this context that formal codes of practice for research governance have been established. All too often, prisoners have been treated as the 'objects' of research, rather than as participants who should be afforded dignity and respect. Prison-based studies have included criminological, medical and psychological research as well as commercial product development and testing. In each of these strands, prisoners have been used as captive research subjects giving rise to significant harm.

With the emergence of the scientific 'professions' in the nineteenth century, criminologists and medics tended to view prisoners as a suitable and convenient group on which to conduct experimentation (along with children, soldiers and patients in mental health institutions). Photographs of convicts, autopsies of executed individuals and studies of tattoos on prisoners' skin all provided primary research material for Italian physician Cesare Lombroso (Gibson, 2006). Criminological research on the bodies of confined individuals continued into the twentieth century: Charles Goring's research on the physiology of English prisoners and William Sheldon's study of offender 'body-types' both represented attempts to determine the physical characteristics of criminality. Students who were unwitting subjects of Sheldon's research subsequently raised complaints about their treatment (Vertinsky, 2007). From 1913 until 1951, experimental medical procedures, including sterilisation and transplantation, were tested on prisoners in San Quentin, without their consent (Suckow and Yates, 2015).

The use of prisoners of war as research subjects throughout World War II brought even greater horror. Unit 731 of the Imperial Japanese Army conducted research on prisoners of war that included live vivisection, surgical experimentations, exposure to frostbite and to potentially fatal bacterial infection. An immunity arrangement with the United States, in exchange for data, meant that most of those responsible never faced trial (Tsuchiya, 2008). Physicians in Nazi concentration camps also conducted 'unparalleled medical atrocities' on 'inferiors' (Weindling, 2008: 18) that included the deliberate introduction of poisons and serious infections, drowning, intentional freezing and amputations. Children were among those used for dangerous and cruel experiments, including the notorious twin research used to study the role of genetics.

The brutal and cruel nature of Nazi 'research' definitively exposed the need to create a set of ethical principles and codes. Following the end of World War II, a series of international human rights instruments were developed aimed at ensuring that in future all research be conducted ethically. The Nuremburg Code (1947) established 10 principles for research on human subjects. Although specifically addressing medical experimentation, the Code's principles have since been developed to guide social science research. Its requirements include voluntary, informed consent from participants, that a study's benefits to humanity outweigh any potential risks to participants and that researchers avoid creating unnecessary suffering. The Universal Declaration of Human Rights (1948) confirmed in international law the principle of informed consent. From 1964, the Declaration of Helsinki added requirements for independent review of research protocols and that research only be conducted by appropriately qualified individuals.

Despite Nuremburg, in the following decades 'scientific' experimentation continued to breach ethical principles, some of the most notable examples occurring within the prison setting. As part of their defence at the Nuremburg trials, German doctors cited experiments in Statesville Penitentiary in America during the 1940s when prisoners had been intentionally exposed to malaria, albeit that participants had apparently 'volunteered' for the study (Comfort, 2009). From 1946 until 1948, American researchers deliberately infected thousands of Guatemalan people, including prisoners, with sexually transmitted infections to test the efficacy of penicillin: in 2010 US President Barack Obama apologised on the nation's behalf (Rodriguez and Garcia, 2013). Experimentation expanded significantly during the 1960s and 1970s, with drugs companies setting up laboratories close to prisons for ease of access (Petryna, 2009). In Holmesburg Prison (USA) cosmetics and chemical war agents were among the products tested on poorly remunerated 'volunteers', resulting in serious mental and physical injuries (Hornblum, 1998).

In the 1970s, the American public learnt of the state-sponsored Tuskegee Syphilis Study, on-going from the 1930s, which involved the deliberate withholding of treatment from 400 African American men with syphilis, through a process of official deception. Unaware of, and untreated for, the disease, the men were told they were being offered experimental treatment for 'bad blood'. President Clinton apologised in 2004 (Baker et al., 2005). The Tuskegee episode was significant in exposing the need for increased research controls. Following media coverage of the scandal, the National Research Act, passed in 1974, created the National Commission for the Protection of Human Subjects of Biomedical and Behavioral Research, the report of which (Belmont Report, 1979) identified three core principles: respect for subjects, beneficence (doing no harm, minimising risk and maximising potential benefits) and justice (treating participants fairly and equitably). These remain central to the conduct of research involving people.

Contemporary ethical expectations and processes

A range of contemporary codes and guidance are available to inform criminological research practice. The British Society of Criminology (BSC) Statement of Ethics for Researchers 2015 provides a 'framework of principles'. 'Aspirational' rather than 'prescriptive', it aims to guide researchers in their decision-making (BSC, 2015, preamble). The American Society of Criminology does not have a dedicated code of ethics but refers criminologists to analogous professional codes, whereas the Australian and New Zealand Society of Criminology code is based around similar principles to those followed in Britain.

The BSC Statement establishes researchers' responsibilities towards colleagues, participants, sponsors and the discipline of criminology. It requires researchers to be appropriately trained, knowledgeable and make no false claims about themselves or their research. Responsibilities to the discipline of criminology include the duty to promote and disseminate knowledge, to avoid 'contractual conditions that limit or compromise research integrity' and to present findings for peer analysis (Section 2). Senior researchers must avoid exploiting more junior colleagues; ensure the recognition of colleagues' contributions and avoid discriminatory practices (Section 3). Responsibilities to participants involve the avoidance of physical or emotional harm and respect for dignity and autonomy, and there is a corresponding duty to minimise the risk of harm to researchers themselves. Significantly, where studies expose harms such as 'corruption, violence or pollution', researchers are under no obligation to 'minimise harm to the corporate or institutional entities responsible for the damage' (Section 4, paragraph 1). Nonetheless, they are encouraged to have sympathy for organisational constraints, for example time considerations. Participants' involvement must be founded on voluntary, informed consent except in exceptional circumstances (due to the importance of the issue being researched). In such cases, covert research may be permissible 'where the ends might be thought to justify the means' (Section 4, paragraph 6). Confidentiality must be respected except in particular circumstances, for example to ensure child protection, and if possible in such cases individuals should be informed of the potential breach of confidence (Section 4, paragraph 12). Regarding sponsors and funders, there is an onus to check potential obligations and avoid arrangements which 'emphasise speed and economy at the expense of good quality research' or the appropriate dissemination of findings (Section 5, paragraph iii). Researchers should be professional and so far as possible preserve good relations with funders (Section 5).

Further guidance is available through the Respect project, established to develop a 'voluntary code of practice' for socio-economic research across the European Union (Dench et al., 2004). This guidance affirms the core principles discussed above, but also explores in more depth researchers' responsibilities towards society and the need for awareness of equality, social and economic power differentials along with the importance of ensuring that marginalised social groups are not excluded from research, but also that findings do not cause further marginalisation or stigmatization (Dench et al., 2004, p.26). In addition to professional and national codes, university researchers and those working for criminal justice agencies are generally subject to institutional research governance systems, for example in the United Kingdom the Economic and Social Research Council (ESRC) Research Ethics Framework (updated January 2015) requires research it funds to comply with ethical expectations. For health-related research, there are separate arrangements for different United Kingdom (UK) jurisdictions (see Department of Health, 2011).

The extent to which researchers are prepared to abide by relevant ethical codes and guidance derives from their philosophical perspective (although sometimes of course conformity with the codes is a requirement of the institution or of a funding body). Fletcher (1966: 17) identifies three broad positions: the *legalistic,* the *antinomian* and the *situational.* The *legalists,* at one extreme, strictly adhere to codes and regulations treating these as '*directives* to be followed', rather than as advisory [emphasis in original]. For the legalist, ready-made answers to ethical dilemmas may be accessed in the pages of books (p.17). At the other end of the spectrum, *antinomians* reject all such strictures. Suspicious of codes and rulebooks, the antinomian relies largely on instinct in ethical decision-making: in each 'unique situation', 'one must rely upon the situation of itself, *there and then* to provide its ethical solution' (Fletcher, 1966: 22). Between these polarised positions are an increasing number of accounts from practising field-workers that stress the complexity of ethical decision-making (see Punch, 1986; Holdaway, 1983; Fielding, 1982). Fletcher (1966: 31) describes how the *situationalist* 'is willing to make full and respectful use of principles' but views these as 'maxims' and not 'as laws or precepts'. Situational research therefore requires the researcher to address and respond reflectively and reflexively to ethical dilemmas as they arise. Reflexivity in this context involves ongoing consideration of the status, role and impact of the researcher themselves on the research process; the aim of the research and its potential audiences; and the power dynamics inherent in the research process.

The concept of situational-responsiveness has potential benefits in navigating the terrain between the requirements of formal ethical regulation and the realities of research practice, as discussed in the sections which follow.

Prison research and the governance role of ethics committees

As discussed above, the troubling historical context within which ethical codes and regulatory mechanisms emerged provides evidence in support of the need for accountability processes. Ethics committees play an important role in ensuring that research is well designed, and that potential risks to participants and researchers are identified and mitigated against. Our own experience is that the process of completing ethical forms and having these peer reviewed can be helpful in considering ethical dilemmas from different perspectives. Yet the expansion of bureaucratic ethics procedures has also presented difficulties, for individual researchers and for social science research in general.

An unnamed Vice Chancellor is anecdotally quoted in Iphofen (2009: 143) as complaining that researchers are 'always thinking that these review committees are about ethics…this has nothing to do with ethics – it's about management'. The proliferation of ethics committees, while a positive development in the light of past malpractice, cannot be separated from the general burgeoning of bureaucratic processes within the higher education sector, which emphasise uniformity and quantitative measurement of 'quality' through mechanisms such as the National Student Survey and various league tables which rank universities according to research and teaching among other criteria. University ethics committees share some of the characteristics of this trend, for example through the requirement that researchers complete generic application forms, based upon standard questions prior to conducting research, and that they regularly report back on progress, seeking permission for any amendments to the methodology. Unlike some administrative mechanisms, ethics panels tend to be comprised of academics reviewing applications from their students and peers, which offers a degree of collegiality and some protection from the managerial constrictions. Nonetheless, critics have portrayed the spread of institutional arrangements as a threat to independent research and to academic freedom. Describing the proliferation of formal review processes as 'mission creep' and 'ethics creep' (Gunsalus et al., 2006, Whitney et al., 2008), Haggerty (2004: 393) suggests that a focus on rules and regulation has failed to achieve enhanced morality in practice. Rather, they argue that a situation has been created where ethical oversight has come to be understood as a 'pro-forma compliance as opposed to [a] review of fundamental ethical issues' (Gunsalus et al., 2006: 373).

The prioritisation of 'risk reduction' within ethical processes has also been condemned as routinely stigmatising marginalised communities as potentially dangerous with consequent restrictions on the type of research which may be 'safely' conducted (Wilson, 2011) or the venues in which research may take place. This is particularly pertinent in a situation where panel members may have little experience of prisons or prisoners, and consequently suspect that incarcerated people may be dangerous *en masse*. A further inhibiting factor is identified by Caulfield and Hill (2014: 33) who argue that absolute compliance with the principle of informed consent would effectively rule out covert research. With this in mind, it is sobering to realise that Goffman's (1961) classic study of asylums, in which most staff and patients were unaware of his research role, would probably not be approved by contemporary ethics committees.

The phrase 'ethics creep' implies over-regard for ethical principles, yet the problem is not too much attention to morality, but that in an increasingly risk-averse environment, the spread of institutional ethics bodies may be more reflective of a desire to protect institutions from reputational or legal harm, than to promote the rights of participants. While protection of participants must remain paramount, we concur with Caulfield and Hill (2014) regarding the need to protect independent research from erosion through rigid restrictions on research topics and methods, and ultimately a safe balance must be struck. In contrast to the more objective physical harms that can be produced by the medical sciences, predicting the level of harm is notoriously difficult within social science research (McNally, 2003). In this context, guidance and codes offer a 'framework', rather than definitive answers, and ethical decision-making 'still involves addressing a series of dilemmas' (Dench et al., 2004: vii). Armstrong, Gelsthorpe and Crewe (2014) demonstrate how a situationally flexible, reflective and humanitarian approach may be adopted in the context of research with ex-prisoners. Noting the gap between 'paper ethics' drawn up in advance of fieldwork, and the 'real world research' which subsequently transpires, these authors note that pre-conceived protocols may not measure up to the complex decisions faced in research involving people, especially where emotions and relationships are involved. Instead they argue for a transparent, supportive approach which allows for honest conversations about the difficult dilemmas that confront individual researchers in the course of their studies.

When considering the role of ethical review processes, it is important to bear in mind that the institutional ethics system is not a one-way affair and researchers facing difficult circumstances should be able to rely upon the support of their institutions. The events which occurred at Boston College when recordings and transcripts of interviews with former loyalist and republican paramilitary combatants were disclosed to the Police Service of Northern Ireland in response to a subpoena, despite promises of confidentiality to participants, shows all too clearly the risks when institutional management and researchers do not have a shared understanding of the research process (Palys and Lowman, 2012). The discussion below identifies key challenges in the practice of prison-based research, providing support for a situational perspective, informed by critical, reflective and reflexive practice.

Ethical dilemmas in the practice of prisoner research

Prison research throws up particularly acute moral quandaries with potentially serious consequences for participants. Adopting the BSC Statement (2015) as a benchmark, we present here the type of dilemmas that may occur during the planning, conduct and presentation of prison-based research, citing our own and other criminologists' experiences to explore the challenges of preserving independence and integrity; achieving non-maleficence (doing no harm) and beneficence (social good), within what is an 'inherently harmful context' (Scott and Codd, 2010, p.15).

Ethical dilemmas: the challenges to research independence and integrity

The BSC Statement (2015) emphasises the importance of research independence and integrity at all stages of the process from planning through to publication and dissemination. The concept of integrity relates to honesty of approach, reliability of research findings and openness to critique. Positivism has tended to link reliability with objectivity and 'neutrality' however this has been challenged within critical criminology. Some scholars believe 'neutrality' to be the most ethical approach with the researcher playing the role of non-partisan observer in the pursuit of knowledge (see for example Hammersley, 2015). Yet supposedly non-ideological approaches may in reality represent support for the *status quo* and uncritical acceptance of dominant ideas. As stated by Howard Becker (1967: 239) 'the question is not whether we should take sides, as we inevitably will, but rather whose side we are on'. Setting out our stall therefore, we approach our research from a feminist and critical stance, and intend our work to promote the rights of incarcerated people and their families. Taking a critical position however should not involve the distortion of findings to suit our own perspective; honesty in analysis and reporting is important both to preserve research integrity and also because inaccurate research is more easily challenged and dismissed.

C. Wright Mills' advice regarding the role of powerful elites in shaping the research agenda was: 'Above all, do not give up your moral and political autonomy' (1959: 226). This can be difficult to achieve as threats to research independence may occur at each point of the process from conception through to publication of results and beyond. Sometimes attempts to shape or silence research are externally applied, but researchers may also be tempted towards self-censorship or manipulation of findings in order to gain official approval. For prison researchers the problem of access is particularly stark, as control over entry to the establishment, and to those detained within it, is tightly restricted. Haggerty (2004) notes an increasing tendency for criminal justice agencies to vet research proposals through their own procedures and to insist on prior sight of findings, sometimes even demanding a right to approve these before publication. Throughout the research process therefore a high degree of reflexivity and personal honesty is needed to ensure that independence and integrity is maintained.

Where research is commissioned and paid for by state agencies (or private companies) the remit, methods and dissemination may especially be open to interference. As Piacentini (2007: 154) states 'the principal question prison researchers confront ... is whether government-funded research is "strings-attached" research'. King and Liebling (2007: 433) note that the gatekeeping and funding role of the Home Office gives it 'considerable control over what is published and when'. Acknowledging that in state-commissioned research 'real power' rests 'largely in the hands of officialdom' (p.433) and that access is frequently achieved through the cultivation of contacts, they nevertheless maintain it is possible to resist the adoption of official narratives. Stating that with 'diplomacy, care and consideration', 'otherwise unpalatable truths' can be expressed, King and Liebling (2007: 441) nonetheless advise 'it would be folly to take a publish-and-be-damned attitude if one wanted to gain future research contracts'. Moore and Scraton (2014: 59) however warn against co-option, arguing that researchers must continually question the 'management and manipulation of the research process by official bodies' (p.vii).

Scraton and Moore (2007) dealt with a ban on entry to Hydebank Wood by interviewing recently released women, prisoners' legal representatives and family members. Access was subsequently granted when a new Director General took up post, indicating the significance of local controls. For Convery and Moore (2006) the power of the institutional gatekeeper became evident during their research on the rights of children in custody, conducted for the Northern Ireland Human Rights Commission. Access was negotiated with the Director of the Juvenile Justice Centre, however the Northern Ireland Office overturned this agreement and barred them from entry to the Centre on arrival to commence fieldwork. Fortunately, the Commission was able to challenge the obstruction through threat of legal action, and the research proceeded.

The significance of independence relates not only to individual projects and their management, but also presents challenges for the discipline as a whole: including what is the role and impact of our research, and on whose behalf are we working? This theme is taken up by Hillyard et al. (2004) who argue that the dominance of the Home Office in shaping the criminological research agenda has resulted in a surfeit of desistance or 'what works' studies, coupled with a marginalisation of research on rights–abuse, state and corporate crime. Scraton (2007: 11) concurs that administrative criminology, with its ties to police and penal institutions, has become a lucrative business and within such an environment, 'pressure is exerted on departments, universities, learned societies and independent research bodies to reconfigure their work'. Calling for a boycott of Home Office and Scottish Executive finance, Reece Walters (2008: 19) condemns some academics as being like 'field mice scurrying around a python, to appease university obsession with income generation and with the misguided belief that they will change or influence policy'.

The challenge to independence and integrity does not only come from within the criminal justice system, but also from increased pressure on researchers to obtain large-scale research funding from academically respected sources (Olssen and Peters, 2005). Within the context of the United Kingdom, the Research Excellence Framework (REF) has placed additional pressure on university researchers to conduct and publish their work within particular confines, a situation which many scholars consider poses challenges to academic freedom (UCU, 2013). In delivering unpalatable truths to criminal justice managers, researchers may risk alienating the very people they will later have to approach for references as to their research impact. In all of this, while individuals have a responsibility to uphold independence and integrity, university leaders also have a role to play in protecting their academic staff and students from internal and external oppressive influence.

Ethical dilemmas: protecting participants from harm

The requirement to 'do no harm' has particular significance given the well-documented vulnerability of prisoners, both through the fact of their incarceration and also because a high proportion have experiences of social exclusion, mental and physical health difficulties, trauma, bereavement and abuse. Thus, prisoners are identified as a 'vulnerable' group requiring special consideration when applying for ethical approval to conduct research. For researchers with little or no prior experience of the prison environment, it may be difficult to envisage what harms may occur either to participants or to themselves and the advice of more experienced researchers should be sought in preparing ethical approval applications. Researchers will also benefit from reading accounts based on other penal scholars' experiences in the 'field' (see for example, the thought-provoking collection of reflective accounts in Drake et al., 2015). The material below relates primarily to the prospect of harm to prisoners, given their particular vulnerability. However, key principles including informed consent, privacy and protection from harm apply also to prison officers who participate in research, although in circumstances where malpractice is involved the researcher has a duty to expose harm.

In selecting a focus for investigation, the researcher should be reflexive in considering their own motives for choosing imprisonment as an area for study and must take care to avoid research aims that voyeuristically view prisoners as the objects of study, or which have the potential to further marginalise or stigmatise them. Research design also involves ethical choices. Critical and feminist criminologists have been drawn to qualitative methods as having greatest potential to reduce power differentials between researcher and participant and to bring marginalised voices to the fore, semi-structured and unstructured interviews providing space for participants to shape the discussion, in comparison with more closed survey questions. Noaks and Wincup (2004) make a convincing case however for triangulating qualitative methods with quantitative investigation to strengthen findings. Feminist studies have also used personal reflexivity to emphasise the shared humanity of researcher and participants, as in Baldwin's (2015: 19) powerful study of motherhood in prison where she discusses her own experiences of young motherhood in the community: 'I remember all too well being a "teenage mum", trying to escape a past whilst at the same time trying to forge a future – a future in which no-one expected me to succeed. As with all of us there are aspects of our pasts that inform and shape our futures, we all have our story'.

Turning to the conduct of research fieldwork, there are immense challenges in guaranteeing the dignity of research participants within total institutions such as prisons, in which individuals are debased, humiliated and 'stripped of self' (Goffman, 1961). There is a growing, and very welcome, body of research conducted by prisoners and ex-prisoners (see for example the *Journal of Prisoners on Prisons*), however the first experience many researchers will have of a penal establishment is a staff-led tour of the institution. Wacquant (2002: 381–382) notes feelings of 'embarrassment' and 'dirtiness' when visitors (himself included) observe prisoners much as 'one might the occupants of a zoo'. Along with fellow researchers, we have found ourselves embarrassed as officers throw open cell doors without the occupants' consent; normally we have politely declined to look inside. Moreover, prison tours are normally highly choreographed affairs and the researcher is challenged to see beyond the official veneer. From the outset therefore in conducting prison research one should attempt to become familiar with the environment; the process of 'hanging around' to gain understanding of the nuances of prison life enabled Wahidin (2005) to obviate some of the difficulties that Riessman (1987) experienced in struggling to understand Puerto Rican women prisoners who participated in her research. Such lack of familiarity with the environment may cause unintentional harm to vulnerable people. Wahidin became a familiar sight in the prison developing a level of rapport with the women and demonstrating to both the women and prison staff that she was prepared to commit the time required to gain awareness of the nature and pains of the prison environment.

In the emotionally fraught environment of the prison, where prisoners have limited opportunity to exercise choices, issues of consent raise particular difficulties and researchers need to consider how best to provide potential participants with information. Wahidin (2005) used posters to advertise her research on older women prisoners. Scraton and Moore (2014) had the freedom to visit prison landings to distribute leaflets about their research for the Northern Ireland Human Rights Commission and to talk to women about possible involvement. Personal dissemination of information is preferable, however permission for this is not always granted and in such circumstances researchers should take special care to ascertain that there is no element of coercion in the recruitment process.

The issue of whether to use consent forms in closed institutions raises particular complexities. In the formal interview setting consent forms provide an opportunity for researchers to ensure that participants have understood the purpose of the study and are actively signing up to involvement. However, as Ibphofen (2009: 66) notes formal, written consent procedures may 'alienate some potential participants who might fear the researcher is a representative of "officialdom" and who might be wary of such engagements'. Thus, the 'giving of oral consent' may be less threatening to participants and 'more consistent with the ethos of qualitative enquiry' (Ibphofen, 2009: 1). As Roberts and Indermaur (2003) argue, written consent forms may be especially inappropriate in penal settings as, among other reasons, some prisoners may mistrust official-looking forms, and may fear institutional reprisal should their participation in research be made known. Scraton and Moore (2014) used oral consent for their research based on extended periods of observation over several years in Maghaberry and Hydebank Wood prisons, concerned that a written procedure would have mitigated against optimal participation, and may have left women feeling anxious about reprisals. Interviews were conducted in highly restrictive regimes, involving extensive lock-up, often resulting in snatched opportunities talk in confidence to women. Consider the following example:

> When we arrived at the gate to the Punishment Block [in Mourne House unit, HMP Maghaberry] there was a woman out of her cell mopping what appeared to be an already clean corridor. Ellie is one of two women held on punishment... The officer opened the gate and we went with Ellie to her cell.
>
> *(Scraton's field notes cited in Moore and Scraton, 2014: 34)*

Ellie (not her real name) was 'able and willing to hold a conversation', but was 'in poor mental and physical health' (Moore and Scraton, 2014: 34). She had been sent to the punishment/isolation block for allegedly throwing the contents of her colostomy bag at officers who had refused her cigarettes and who had, she claimed, tormented her by blowing smoke under her cell door. Scraton and Moore explained the research and their role and did not doubt Ellie's ability to consent to an interview. In such circumstances, the priority was to give voice to a vulnerable woman's experiences of an oppressive regime, and the requirement to sign a consent form would risk creating anxiety and would shorten the already brief opportunity to talk. Within the prison environment, therefore, while informed consent is imperative, written consent may not always be the most ethical option.

The preservation of confidentiality and anonymity also presents practical and ethical dilemmas. Researchers must alert participants to the limits on confidentiality particularly where there are concerns about safety. The prison can be a difficult environment to find a safe, private space to conduct research and to protect privacy interviews should be conducted out of earshot and, where appropriate, out of eyeshot of prison officers. Anonymity is also difficult to achieve within an institutional environment and prisoners should be alerted to the risk that although every effort will be taken to anonymise information, they may be identifiable especially to staff and professionals working in the prison. Using pseudonyms is a device generally used to ensure anonymity, yet as Iphofen (2009) notes this may render some participants feeling disempowered. To obviate this problem, Wahidin (2005), asked women to create their own pseudonym thus ensuring their active participation.

Prisoners' vulnerability requires that researchers adopt a sensitive approach. To protect prisoners' privacy and dignity, we adopt a position of never asking a prisoner about their alleged offence, unless this information is central to the research aims. Participants' well-being must be given priority; Gelsthorpe recalls that 'we frequently abandoned formal interviews altogether in the face of someone's distress or concern to express a particular point' (1990: 98). Participants may wish to continue with an interview, even when distressed, particularly if they view the subject matter as having the potential to improve the situation for others, however the researcher must as a minimum check whether they wish to continue, and are in a fit state to do so. Information about sources of independent support should be provided to participants, and within the institution researchers must take care to confirm that participants will be able to utilise such support in practice (for example, there is little point in giving someone telephone numbers of support organisations if they cannot access a telephone).

Respect and dignity are watchwords for ethical research yet, even with the best intentions, these can be difficult to achieve in environments where individuals are routinely exposed to 'mortification of self' (Goffman, 1961) and which Scott (2015. 40) describes as 'immoral spaces'. Scraton and Moore's (2007) research is illustrative of the lack of respect shown to prisoners:

> Observations of the regime over several weeks showed a wide disparity in attitudes in the way officers carried out their locking up duties. Some simply informed women that it was time for lock-up and gave them a short amount of time to gather their belongings together or quickly finish their meal. Others abruptly interrupted conversations the women were having and several shouted instructions. One officer sang 'You're so happy, happy, happy', as she locked women in their cells.
>
> *(p.56)*

During an evaluation of a befriending programme in a male high security prison, Convery, Moore and Wahidin (2014) were all too aware that interviews constituted a break from the monotony of prison life and that some interviewees would be returned to their cell as soon as the discussion ended. Sometimes researchers find themselves caught up in the intricacies of punitive regimes. During Convery and Moore's (2006) fieldwork, a teenage boy was threatened with physical restraint for refusing to go to bed unless he was allowed to pour himself a glass of orange squash. Staff refused this on the basis that it was past bedtime and a stand off ensued. Feeling responsible, Convery and Moore intervened to say that it was as a consequence of their interview that the boy was up late. Fortunately, the issue was resolved without restraint being used, but the researchers felt anxious and somewhat compromised by the event.

The carrying of keys is illustrative of the challenge of ethical negotiation of power relationships within prison research and the need for reflexivity on the part of individual researchers. Goffman (1961) chose not to hold keys feeling that this would contaminate the research relationship. Fleischer (1989: 97) vividly illustrates how prisoners distrusted him due to his key carrying: 'When you carry them keys on your hip, I don't care who the fuck you say you are, you're one of them'. Wahidin (2005) declined the offer of keys in her research with older women in prison: for her the chain and keys signified institutional power and authority and wearing the key would risk 'elders' in the study feeling they were 'objects' to be exploited rather than active participants in the process. This decision was informed by knowledge of the prisoners' attitude towards the wearers of keys, which is quite different to their view of a researcher who does not symbolically represent the institution. The point here is that even seemingly innocuous actions within the prison environment may have significant ramifications. Ultimately researchers must take decisions based on their own conscience and informed judgement but must take into account the particular power relations involved in any decision within the penal environment.

As noted above, researchers are required to report any safety concerns, usually to the prison authorities. Yet the process of imprisonment itself creates and exacerbates harm. For example, prison inspectors in the Northern Ireland context observed that female prisoners worried that if they disclosed mental health difficulties they might be 'taken over to the observation cells in the healthcare centre in the main [male] prison or to the punishment unit' (2002 inspection cited in HMCIP and CICJ in Northern Ireland, 2003: para MH.36). Concerns about safety must always be appropriately acted upon, yet prison is an inherently unsafe environment and reporting an issue does not necessarily mean that it will be appropriately resolved. As well as reporting concerns about safety, researchers need to consider what action (if any) they will take when they witness harm. King and Liebling (2007) advise researchers to intervene only in extreme circumstances, yet prisoners experience significant harm on a routine basis. Scraton and Moore (2014) intervened in a variety of harmful situations during their research in women's prisons. Both gave evidence at inquests into prisoner deaths, and Scraton participated in a judicial review regarding the conditions in which a 17 year old girl was being held in an adult prison. Kept in an isolation cell, 23 hours a day, dressed in an 'anti suicide' gown, refused underwear or possessions, and with a child's potty for a toilet, the girl said (2014: 133) 'I shouldn't be down here. There's nothing to do. It's worse in the night. I hear voices and see things. But no-one helps me'. On leaving the prison, Scraton and Moore immediately contacted the child's solicitor and Scraton's evidence helped to highlight her situation to the court. Because of the routine harm involved in imprisonment, it can be difficult to know when the line has been passed requiring intervention. Convery and Moore's research (2006) reported an individual staff members' alleged mistreatment of a child through the child protection process at the Juvenile Justice Centre, however they were later (justifiably) upbraided by the director for having failed to report handcuff marks on a child's arm. While highlighting concerns about the use of handcuffs in their findings, in the context of routine institutional harm Convery and Moore had not thought to raise the incident through the child protection process.

As well as avoiding harms to prisoners, the impact on researchers of working in this difficult environment must also be considered. Risks to physical safety should be assessed as part of the ethical review process and subsequent concerns addressed: as Iphofen (2009: 85) notes 'the safety both of participants and field researchers has to be monitored since there may be some mutual dependence'. Prison is 'not a comfortable place to live, to work, or to carry out ... research' (Dammer, 1994: 1). As Jewkes observes (Drake et al., 2015: xi) prison research is 'difficult, stressful and time-consuming, and many scholars leave the field early in their careers (often following completion of their PhD), never to return'. Piacentini (2007: 152) reports being asked: 'You do what? Prison research? Why do you do prison research? I mean, they are really horrible places. There must be far less difficult types of research, and less depressing too'. Prison research is challenging emotionally and physically and we have a responsibility to minimise harm to oneself and fellow researchers. Access to good sources of support is crucial, whether from supervisors, fellow researchers, friends or family. Yet ultimately it is prisoners and their families who feel the true pains of confinement. Moreover, we have often felt privileged to witness the dignity and strength shown by incarcerated people and to hear their personal stories.

Ethical dilemmas: the challenges of beneficence

As Marx wrote: 'Philosophers have only interpreted the world in different ways. The point is, however, to change it' (1885, thesis XI). In this vein, critical criminologists continue to view research not as an abstract occupation but as a contribution to understanding *and* transforming the world. In selecting the focus of study, in planning, conducting and publishing research an important consideration for critical scholars is the promotion of social good. Ethical codes direct us to the importance of beneficence, of making a contribution to society and challenging marginalisation and right-abuses. In 'The State of the Prisons' published in 1777, penal reformer John Howard, explaining why he had undertaken the arduous task of documenting the appalling conditions within jails in Britain and throughout Europe, stated that the travels were not undertaken for his own or his readers' entertainment but rather 'for the perusal of those who have it in their power to give redress to the sufferers' (p.6). Howard mused that if his work were to have any impact in 'alleviating the distresses' of prisoners, he would consider himself 'abundantly repaid' for the 'pains' taken, time spent and 'hazards' undergone (p.489). The ethical researcher must consider how best their study may promote social justice. Active dissemination of research findings and recommendations and openness to critique is an important part of this process. Where possible researchers should aim to disseminate the findings to participants and to bring the reality of the incarceration process to a broader audience and lobbying those in authority for change, including criminal justice agencies and political and policy decision-makers.

Paradoxically however critics argue that in the quest to inspire improvements in prison conditions, research may have the unintended effect of facilitating the management of punishment. As Carlen (2002) argues the reformist agenda may be 'clawed back' by the carceral machine to allow the prison to reinvent itself as an instrument of beneficence, and one must not forget that prison, in short, is the symbol of the state's power to punish. Hence the risk of becoming a cog in the machinery of punishment, as recognised by Foucault (1977) in describing the role of scientific 'experts' in processes of assessment, treatment and 'correction'. From this perspective it may be argued that criminology has become increasingly bound up with the punitive apparatus of the state. As Hillyard et al. (2004: 12) observe:

> The fact that we live within a society that has amassed the highest per capita prison population in Western Europe, while, at the same time, economic inequalities continue to rise at the fastest rate in Western Europe, cannot be disconnected from our working in an academic discipline which provides the intellectual resources to support the government apparatuses overseeing those trends.

Critical social analysis, by contrast, has an 'oppositional agenda' which 'seeks out, records and champions the "view from below" ensuring that the voices and experiences of those marginalised by institutionalised state practices are heard and represented' (Scraton, 2004: 180). As Carlton (2006: 32) states the 'challenges and responsibilities faced by critical researchers to confront and make visible the arbitrary and abusive exercise of power are greater than ever'.

Summary

The history of malpractice within prison-based research, demonstrates the need for ethical accountability. In recent years a plethora of research ethics guidelines have emerged along with a proliferation of professional and institutional ethics boards with growing regulatory scope and reach. The practice of drawing up research risk assessments and protocols provide the opportunity to consider issues, and to get peer advice prior to the conduct of research, to use guidance from the committees as a tool during fieldwork, and to have a period of reflection following completion of the study. Guidance and codes provide a framework, yet researchers in all disciplines encounter unexpected challenges during the course of fieldwork, which sometimes require immediate decisions to be made. Knowledge and understanding of the core principles of ethical practice, and sound preparation including consideration of the dilemmas faced by fellow researchers, will help the researcher to make morally sound decisions when required. Our aim in this chapter has not been to offer prescriptive solutions but rather to pose and reflect on some of the ethical challenges involved in prison research. We argue for a more responsive and reflexive approach where 'ethics in practice' complement 'procedural ethics' to minimise potential harms and maximise potential benefits of the research. To echo Gelsthorpe's work (1990: 101) 'in seeking to make the research relevant and responsive to those involved, [we were] not wearing a specific [feminist/prison abolitionist hat], merely a hat which told [us] this was "good practice"'. It is only by opening up a space to debate 'ethics in practice', that we can transform conventional and taken for granted research practices and move towards a more ethical criminology.

As Haggerty (2004, p.410) notes ethical relationships are 'characterized by an on-going interrogation of the types of responsibilities that we might owe to others, and 'cannot be reduced to a simple exercise in rule following'. Codes of practice fail if researchers conform not in order to conduct their research ethically but because they fear for reputations and careers. Moreover, an unintended consequence of the spread of bureaucratic procedures in the research process is that researchers may be reluctant to employ innovative research methods or may be refused permission to do so by their local ethics committees. The discipline is potentially lessened as a result of such constrictions. Ethical practice therefore is significant not only for individual researchers or research teams but also for the discipline. Pressures to secure funding and to publish results in highly rated journals, coupled with the difficulties in gaining access to closed institutions, increase the influence and power of statutory gatekeepers in shaping the nature of penological research. As indicated by the quote from Cohen (2001) with which we introduced this chapter, critical criminologists have a responsibility to resist official narratives, expose the damaging consequences of imprisonment and promote strategies based on equality and social justice.

Review questions

1. Is it possible to conduct ethical research in prison? Issues to consider include preservation of independence, minimising harm, protection of confidentiality and anonymity, respect for the dignity of participants.
2. How closely should the researcher stick to ethical codes and guidance? What room is there for flexibility?
3. How can researchers ensure optimum participation and power for respondents within prison research?
4. What can personal reflexivity add to the research process?

Guide to further reading

Israel, M. (2015). *Research Ethics and Integrity for Social Scientists: Beyond Regulatory Compliance*, 2nd edn, London, Sage. Updated edition of an excellent introduction to research ethics (previously co-authored with Iain Hay), this study demonstrates the importance of thinking systematically about ethical practice in social science research. The book explains the role of governance frameworks and the debates that emerged between researchers and the regulators of research.

The British Society of Criminology Statement of Ethics (2015) provides a framework to assist the choices which have to be made to reflect the principles, values and interests of all those involved in conducting research. The aim of the statement of ethics is to raise awareness of ethical issues. Overall, the guidance seeks to provide a critical appreciation of ethical practice in relation to research within the broader field of criminology (see http://britsoccrim.org/new/?q=node/22).

Caulfield, L. and Hill, J. (2014). *Criminological Research for Beginners: A Student's Guide*, Oxon, Routledge. Clear, accessible introductory text which includes a chapter on the ethical conduct of criminological research which recognises the complexities and contradictions within the process.

Drake, D., Earle, R. and Sloan, J. (eds) (2015). *The Palgrave Handbook of Prison Ethnography*, Basingstoke, Palgrave Macmillan. A thought-provoking collection of pieces by experienced prison researchers, including exploration of the theoretical, practical and ethical issues associated with conducting qualitative research within the prison environment. Available in e-book form.

References

Armstrong, R., Gelsthorpe, L. and Crewe, B. (2014). 'From paper ethics to real world research: supervising risk in research with the 'risky'', in Karen Lumsden and Aaron Winter (eds), *Reflexivity in Criminological Research: Experiences with the Powerful and the Powerless*, London: Palgrave.

Baker, S. M., Brawley, O.W. and Marks, L. S. (2005). 'Effects of untreated syphilis in the negro male, 1932 to 1972: a closure comes to the Tuskegee study, 2004', *Urology,* 65(6): 1259–1262.

Baldwin, L. (2015). *Mothering Justice: Working with Mothers in Criminal and Social Justice Settings*, Hampshire: Waterside Press.

Beauchamp, T. L. and Childress, J. F. (1994). *Principles of Biomedical Ethics*, 4th edn, New York: Oxford University Press.

Becker, H. (1967). 'Whose side are we on', *Social Problems,* 14(3): 239–247.

Belmont Report (1979). *Ethical Principles and Guidelines for the Protection of Human Subjects of Research*, National Commission for the Protection of Human Subjects of Biomedical and Behavioural Research.

Carlen, P. (2002). *Women and Punishment: The Struggle for Justice*, Cullompton: Willan.

Carlton, B. (2006). From H. Division to Abu Ghraib: regimes of justification and the historical proliferation of state-inflicted terror and violence in maximum security, *Social Justice,* 33(4): 15–36.

Caulfield, L. and Hill, J. (2014). *Criminological Research for Beginners: A Student's Guide*, Oxon: Routledge.

Cohen, S. (2001). *States of Denial: Knowing about Atrocities and Suffering*, London: Wiley.

Comfort, N. (2009). 'The prisoner as model organism: malaria research at Stateville Penitentiary', *Studies in History and Philosophy of Science: Part C*, 40(3): 190–203.

Convery, U. and Moore, L. (2006). *Still in Our Care: Protecting the Rights of Children in Custody*, Belfast: Northern Ireland Human Rights Commission.

Convery, U., Moore, L. and Wahidin, A. (2014). *Evaluation of Quaker Connections' Befriending Project*, Belfast: Quaker Service.

Dammer, H. (1994). The Problems of Conducting Ethnographic Research in American Prisons, Presented at Prison 2000 Conference: Leicester: England. (Unpublished Paper).

Dench, S., Iphofen, R. and Huws, U. (2004). *An EU Code of Ethics for Socio-Economic Research*, Brighton. http://www.respectproject.org/ethics/412ethics.pdf

Department of Health (2011). *Governance Arrangement for Research Ethics Committees: a harmonised edition*, London: DoH.

Drake, D., Earle, R. and Sloan, J. (eds) (2015). *The Palgrave Handbook of Prison Ethnography*, Basingstoke: Palgrave Macmillan.

Fielding, N. (1982). 'Observational research on the National Front', in M. Bulmer (ed) *Social Research Ethics*, London: Macmillan.

Fleischer, M. (1989). *Warehousing Violence*, London: Sage.

Fletcher, J. (1966). *Situational Ethics: The New Morality*, London: John Knox Press.

Foucault, M. (1977). *Discipline and Punish – The Birth of the Prison*, London: Allen Lane.

Gelsthorpe, L. (1990). 'Feminist methodologies in criminology: A new approach or old wine in new bottles?', in L. Gelsthorpe and A. Morris (eds), *Feminist Perspectives in Criminology*, Milton Keynes: Open University Press.

Genders, E. and Player, E. (1995). *Grendon: A study of a therapeutic prison*, Clarendon Press: Oxford.

Gibson, M. S. (2006). 'Cesare Lombroso and Italian criminology: theory and politics', in P. Becker and R. F. Wetzell, R. F. (eds), *Criminals and their Scientists: the History of Criminology in International Perspective*, Washington D.C. and Cambridge: Cambridge University Press and German Historical Institute.

Goffman, E. (1961). *Asylums – Essays on the Social Situation of Mental Patients And Other Inmates*, New York: Doubleday.

Gunsalus, C. K., Bruner, E. M., Burbules, N. C., Dash, L., Goldberg, J. P., Greenough, W. T., Miller, G. A. and Pratt, M. G. (2006). *The Illinois White Paper: Improving the System for Protecting Human Subjects: Counteracting IRB 'mission creep'*, Illinois: The Centre for Advanced Study.

Haggerty, K. (2004). 'Ethics creep: governing social science research in the name of ethics', *Qualitative Sociology*, 24(Winter): 391–414.

Hammersley, M. (2015). 'Research "inside" viewed from "outside": reflections on prison ethnography', in D. Drake, R. Earle and J. Sloan (eds), *The Palgrave Handbook of Prison Ethnography*, Basingstoke: Palgrave Macmillan.

Hillyard, P., Sim, J., Tombs, S. and Whyte, D. (2004). 'Leaving a "stain upon the silence": contemporary criminology and the politics of dissent', *British Journal of Criminology*, 369.

HM Chief Inspector of Prisons (HMCIP) and the Chief Inspector of Criminal Justice (CICJ) in Northern Ireland (2003). 'Report of a Full announced Inspection of HMP Maghaberry 13–17 May 2002 by HM Chief Inspector of Prisons'. London: Her Majesty's Stationery Office.

Holdaway, S. (1983). *Inside the British Police: A Force at Work*, Oxford, Blackwell.

Hornblum, A. M. (1998) *Acres of Skin: Human Experiments at Holmesburg Prison: A Story of Abuse and Exploitation in the Name of Medical Science*, London: Psychology Press.

Iphofen, E. (2009). *Ethical Decision-Making in Social Research*, Basingstoke: Palgrave Macmillan.

Israel, M. (2015). *Research Ethics and Integrity for Social Scientists: Beyond Regulatory Compliance* (2nd edn), London: Sage.

King, R. and Liebling, A. (2007). 'Doing research in prisons', in R. King and E. Wincup (eds), *Doing Research on Crime and Justice* (2nd edn), Oxford: Oxford University Press, chapter 15.

McNally, R. J. (2003). *Remembering Trauma*, Cambridge, MA: Harvard University Press.

Moore, L. and Scraton, P. (2014). *The Incarceration of Women: Punishing Bodies, Breaking Spirits*, Basingstoke: Palgrave Macmillan.

Noaks, L. and Wincup, E. (2004). *Criminological Research: Understanding Qualitative Methods*, London: Sage.

Olssen, M. and Peters, M. (2005). 'Neoliberalism, higher education and the knowledge economy: from the free market to knowledge capitalism', *Journal of Education Policy*, 20(3): 313–345.

Palys, T. and Lowman, J. (2012). 'Defending research confidentiality "to the extent the law allows": lessons from the Boston College subpoenas', *Journal of Academic Ethics*, 10(4): 271–297.

Petryna, A. (2009). *When Experiments Travel: Clinical Trials and the Global Search for Human Subjects*, Princeton: Princeton University Press.

Piacentini, L. (2007). 'Researching Russian prisons: a consideration of new and established methodologies in prison research', in Y. Jewkes (ed) *Handbook on Prisons*, Cullompton: Willan.

Punch, M. (1986). *The Politics and Ethics of Fieldwork*, London: Sage.

Riessman, C. K. (1987). 'When gender is not enough: women interviewing women', *Gender and Society*, 1(2): 172–207.

Roberts, L. and Indermaur, D. (2003). *Signed Consent Forms in Criminological Research: Protection for Researchers and Ethics Committees but a Threat to Research Participants?* Paper presented at the Evaluation in Crime and Justice: Trends and Methods Conference, Australian Institute of Criminology and Australian Bureau of Statistics, Canberra, March 2003. Available at: http://www.aic.gov.au/media_library/conferences/evaluation/roberts.pdf

Rodriguez, M. and Garcia, R. (2013). 'First do no harm: the US sexually transmitted disease experiments in Guatemala', *American Journal of Public Health*, 103(12): 2122–2126.

Scott, D. (2015). 'Walking amongst the graves of the living: reflections about doing prison research from an abolitionist perspective', in D. Drake, R. Earle and J. Sloan (eds), *The Palgrave Handbook of Prison Ethnography*, Basingstoke: Palgrave Macmillan, p. 40–58..

Scott, D. and Codd, H. (2010). *Controversial Issues in Prisons*, Maidenhead: Open University Press.

Scraton, P. (2004). 'Speaking truth to power: experiencing critical research', in Smyth, M. and Williamson, E. (eds), *Researchers and their 'Subjects': Ethics, Power, Knowledge and Consent*, The Policy Press: Bristol, p. 177-196.

Scraton, P. (2007). *Power, Conflict and Criminalisation*, Oxon: Routledge.

Scraton, P. and Moore, L. (2007). *The Prison Within: The Imprisonment of Women at Hydebank Wood 2004–06*. Belfast: Northern Ireland Human Rights Commission.

Suckow, M. and Yates, B. (eds) (2015). *Research Regulatory Compliance*, London: Elsevier.

Sykes, G. (1958). *Society of Captives: A Study of a Maximum Security Prison* (2007 edition), Princetown: Princetown University Press.

Tsuchiya, T. (2008). 'The Imperial Japanese experiments in China', in Ezekiel J. Emanuel, Christine C. Grady, Robert A. Crouch, Reidar K. Lie, Franklin G. Miller, David D. Wendler (eds), *The Oxford Textbook of Clinical Research Ethics*, Oxford: Oxford University Press.

University and College Union (UCU) (2013). *Research Excellence Framework (REF): UCU Survey Report*, London: UCU.

Vertinsky, P. (2007). 'Physique as destiny: William H. Sheldon, Barbara Honeyman Heath and the struggle for hegemony in the science of somatotyping', *Canadian Bulletin of Medical History*, 24(2): 291–316.

Wacquant, L. (2002). 'From slavery to mass incarceration', *New Left Review*, 13-40: 382.

Wahidin, A. (2005). *Older Women in the Criminal Justice System: Running Out of Time*, London: Jessica Kingsley.

Walters, R. (2008). 'Government crime policy and moral contamination', *Criminal Justice Matters*, 72(1): 65–71.

Weindling, P. (2008). 'The Nazi medical experiments', in Ezekiel J. Emanuel, Christine C. Grady, Robert A. Crouch, Reidar K. Lie, Franklin G. Miller, David D. Wendler (eds) *The Oxford Textbook of Clinical Research Ethics*, Oxford: Oxford University Press.

Whitney, S. N., Alcser, K., Schneider, C. E., McCullough, L. B., McGuire, A. L. and Volk, R. J. (2008). Principal Investigator Views of the IRB System, *International Journal of Medical Sciences*, (5): 68–72.

Wilson, A. (2011). 'Research ethics and the "iron cage" of bureaucratic rationality', *Addiction, Research and Theory*, (19)5: 391–393.

5

THE ETHICS OF LEARNING BY TESTING

The police, professionalism and researching the police

Peter Neyroud

A renewed approach to professionalising the police has produced new institutions and a shift towards professional ownership of research about policing. Research into policing has long been a contested area and the chapter explores how the new police professionalism may affect the process and ethics of police research. Operation Turning Point, a randomised controlled trial testing diversion against prosecution, is used as a case study to explore this through a discussion of the impact on research motivation, consent, risk and harm assessment and the researcher role.

Key definitions

Applied police research: As described by Cockbain and Knutsson (2014), a collaborative, mixed methods approach to field research in policing.

New police professionalism: A concept coined by Stone and Travis (2011) and developed by Neyroud and Sherman (2013) to suggest that policing should, within democratic accountability become an evidence-based profession, underpinned by a systematic body of knowledge.

Police science: Weisburd and Neyroud (2011) and Neyroud and Weisburd (2014b) used this term to describe the body of systematic knowledge in policing.

Randomised controlled trial: An experimental test in which the participants are assigned to comparison groups by random assignment.

Introduction

Debates about a professional police and its relationship with research are almost as old as modern policing. Over 80 years ago, August Vollmer, police chief of

Berkeley, California and an academic, argued for a science base to the profession of policing (Vollmer, 1936). Vollmer's 'professional' vision encompassed a university-based education, a code of ethics to regulate individual practice and partnership with universities to develop scientific evidence to support practice (Telep, 2014).

Vollmer and his disciple O. W. Wilson (1950) saw research 'for' policing as something that should both contribute directly to the strategy of the organisation and which required significant internal leadership and involvement. They were both Police Chiefs[1] with one foot in the academic world, committed to a professional model of policing underpinned by a code of ethics. However, the professional model of policing that developed from their thinking was largely discredited by a wave of external research 'on' policing that followed in the 1960s and 1970s (Manning, 2005). Wilson's tactics, which have been summed up as the '3R's' – rapid response, random patrol and reactive investigation (Sherman, 2013) – were demonstrated by the very research that Vollmer had advocated to be ineffective (Skogan and Frydl, 2004) and their consequences discriminatory and problematic for police legitimacy (Sklansky, 2014). As a result, the first 'professional model' of policing became characterised as a 'technological conceit' intending to achieve crime control but paying insufficient attention to the unintended consequences for society (Manning, 2010: 137).

More recently, the wheel has come full circle. A 'new police professionalism' has emerged (Stone and Travis, 2011), with a renewed emphasis on 'science' as a driver of transformation (Weisburd and Neyroud, 2011). The 'new' professionalism has a clearer emphasis on legitimacy and democratic values and a different set of drivers. In the USA, it has become a response to a crisis in American policing, characterised by lethal force and stop and frisk in black communities, which led to the first Presidents's Task Force on 21st Century Policing (2015) since the 1960s. In the UK, Australia and Canada, there has been a 'perfect storm' of austerity, a crisis of legitimacy and new demands on the police (Neyroud, 2015) to which a science-based profession has become seen as a critical part of the reform agenda (Neyroud and Sherman, 2013).

Research has provided the basis for this response, as it has increasingly identified how the police can be effective at reducing crime and tackling problems of disorder (Skogan and Frydl, 2004 and Sherman, 2013). Whilst there have been competing methods used, with experimental or action research being the most prominent, the research has tended to be 'for' the police and developed in collaboration with the police. The growing availability of information systems and the increasing challenge to police to focus on reducing crime have also encouraged police to invest in research partnerships and embedded relationships with researchers (Klofas et al., 2010; Braga and Davis, 2014).

It is the implications of the 'new professionalism' – a science-based police professionalism driven from within the profession – which provides the central focus for this chapter. In particular, the chapter explores the ethical issues exposed when the 'new profession' takes ownership of the research agenda and 'new professionals' become directly involved in the process of research. After reviewing the key debates about police research and the ethical implications that arise, this chapter develops the issues further through the analysis of a case study, Operation Turning Point. The latter was a large randomised controlled trial (RCT) that the author managed as a researcher, having previously been a career police officer.

Researching the police

Bradley and Nixon (2009) described the process of police research as a 'dialogue of the deaf'. In their analysis, the police and the academic community have fundamental problems in understanding each other. They identified that the problems stemmed from contrasting views of the purpose, process and outcomes of research. A large part of the research on policing to that point had been from a critical tradition, which, as Cockbain and Knutsson (2014) argue, saw policing as both marginal to crime reduction and potentially racist and oppressive (Galliher, 1999). On the other hand, Police Chiefs and the 'new professionalism' institutions such as the National College of Policing and the Society of Evidence-based Policing, are committed, just as Wilson (1950) advocated, to seek research that tests practice and supports policy and strategy development – in short, 'what works?'

Hirschi (1993) accused the proponents of this type of research of being 'administrative criminologists' (p.349), who practice a 'practical criminology' (p.350), which is short on theory and uncritical of the role of government in addressing crime problems. Instead, Galliher and Galliher (1995) argued that research must be informed by human rights values and present a moral vision independent from government and institutional funders. Hirschi (1993) described crime as a 'moral problem that is beyond the reach of experimentation' (p.350). In effect, Hirschi suggests that research in criminal justice should be the preserve of independent (from government) scholars.

It is unsurprising, therefore, that the two main traditions of police research – 'critical' and 'police policy research' (Bradley and Nixon, 2009) or 'applied police research' (Cockbain and Knutsson, 2014) – have very different approaches to research and its outcomes (Manning, 2005). The former seeks to examine the organisation and its impacts critically as a means of holding the police to account, the latter to 'develop theories, frameworks and/or empirical evidence to inform and support policing policy and practice' (Cockbain and Knutsson, 2014:2). As a result of the very different starting points, the methods, style and philosophy of research have tended to be very different. Critical research prides itself on detachment and independence from the police. The focus of the research is to provide an expert voice to inform the thinking of the citizen and those charged with the governance of the police (Bradley and Nixon, 2009).

Police policy research, on the other hand, is committed to much closer engagement and partnership with the organisation, with a view to improving and developing policing policies and practices based on evidence. Its advocates have argued that the 'threat of less objectivity is outweighed by the gains in better understanding of contextual influences' (Engel and Whalen, 2010: 111). Moreover, as Greene (2014) demonstrated, applied police research in no way implies that the research is uncritical or unable to explore and report uncomfortable findings.

However, even within the 'police policy research' tradition, there is a vigorous epistemological debate about the meaning and validity of 'evidence' and the role of the profession in developing it. Sherman et al. (1997), Weisburd and Hinkle (2012), Mazerolle, Lum and Braga (2014) and Sherman (2013) have all provided strong advocacy in favour of 'testing' using experimental designs in order to answer questions of effectiveness. Bullock and Tilley (2009), Sparrow (2011) and Greene (2014) have countered that this approach to 'evidence-based policing' is 'unrealistic, reductive, prescriptive, scientifically flawed and detached from the realities of crime and policing (Cockbain and Knutsson, 2014:3).

At the heart of this debate are very different conceptions of the nature and the occupation of policing. For Neyroud and Sherman (2013) the police can properly aspire to develop as a profession, supported by a discrete body of scientific knowledge. Indeed, in contrast to Hirschi's stance, they suggested that police needed the support of tested evidence to underpin their legitimacy. The moral purpose of police research, in their argument, is to find evidence to maximise the benefits of policing and minimise the harms. Weisburd and Neyroud (2011) used the analogy of the medical profession to argue that the police, in furthering this enterprise should be engaged in clinical research to build the body of knowledge and should assume a degree of 'ownership' in the science of policing.

On the other hand, Kennedy (2014) has argued that the medical analogy is unhelpful. Drawing on Thacher (2001), he suggested that just as police tactics cannot be compared to a medical intervention, so policing should not be thought of as a profession. In the same way, operational policing could not be judged by the equivalent of medical trials because there were too many confounding issues. Policing, Kennedy argued, is a craft not a science, which needs to be developed by practice rather than learning from testing. In fact, there is a considerable amount of 'craft' in medical training and the science derived from medical trials can be just as controversial as police science. Goldacre (2015) has stated 'well documented problems exist in the funding and prioritisation of research, the conduct of trials, the withholding of results, the dissemination of evidence, and its implementation with patients' (p.350).

The debate about the scientific validity and realism of testing and, specifically, experiments in policing opens up an important debate about the utility and generalizability of any police research. The case against using experimental designs is that they are complicated to carry out, biased against significant findings (Kennedy, 2014) and appear to argue for 'universal treatments', whereas 'crime and policing are complex and context-sensitive social problems' that are not susceptible to this approach (Cockbain and Knutsson, 2014).

Clarke and Cornish (1972), in their seminal critique of experiments in institutional settings, identified that there were ethical dimensions not just in the issues of practitioner and subject consent, but in the choice of a design – RCT –

that they suggested could undermine the fairness and justice of the institutional regime itself through random assignment of treatment and yet produce non-significant results. Farrington and Joliffe (2002) used Clarke and Cornish's framework to demonstrate that an RCT within a prison was not justifiable because the likely effect size and impact were not proportionate.

It is unarguable that experiments require care and discipline, but the case that they are more difficult than other forms of research is not well made. All of the 'applied' designs described in Cockbain and Knutsson's (2014) edited collection require the same strong partnership, effective implementation and careful evaluation as an experiment. In response to the question of context and generalisability, the key issue is to ensure that any experiment is underpinned by a good understanding of the theory that is being tested, rather than just being a narrow test of a specific tactic (Weisburd and Hinkle, 2012). McGloin and Thomas (2013) and Braga et al. (2014) in trying to bridge the sides of the argument, set out a convincing case that policing research needs a mixed methods approach to cope with the complexities of the field.

The debate about the balance between academic and professional ownership and direction of police research is important, but as Vollmer recognised 'police's knowledge needs must come from continuous and close partnerships between police and universities' (Bradley and Nixon, 2009: 434). The nature of that partnership and the role of the researcher, whether as independent expert, field research partner or academic adviser to police staff carrying out their own research makes a significant difference to the research motivation, process and consequences of police research and the ethical issues raised. In particular, the more that police own, control and act as the principal researcher, the greater the need to close the gap between ethics for policing and the ethics of research to provide appropriate standards for police research and mechanisms for the police to be self critical and responsive to criticisms.

Ethics of police research and the new police professionalism

A professionally led science in policing raises many ethical challenges for police research, but four specific areas deserve close attention: research motivation; consent; risk and harm; the role and status of the researcher. If 'ethical policing' can be defined as 'police officers doing the right things for the right reasons' (Neyroud, 2008: 686), then the motivation for police research must be considered equally significant (Sherman, 2010). There is, as yet, no clear and developed parallel in Police Codes of Ethics to the golden rule of medical ethics – 'do no harm'. Policing frequently provides the need to balance between competing harms and benefits. Confronted with this dilemma in exploring covert policing, Marx (1988) suggested adopting a matrix decision-model of 'intended' and 'unintended' consequences. He used this approach to suggest how police and policy makers could chart an ethical route between police deception and the duty to protect the public. The 'right things for the right reasons' in Marx's model would, therefore, derive from a careful weighing of the potential intended and unintended consequences from both the research proposed and the intervention under scrutiny.

With the development and publication of a new Police *Code of Ethics* in the UK (College of Policing, 2014), such a process of weighting should, in future, be informed by the Code's framework. The Code is also relevant to the issues of consent and risk. However, there is an undoubted tension between a Code designed to support self-regulation within a professional context and the need for independent assessment of the motivation of the participants in research, many of whom will be police officers and, therefore required to consent to their participation and willingness to share their data with researchers (Punch, 1986 and Miles and Huberman, 1994). Similarly, when it comes to the assessment of the harm, risk and benefits of the research, the dangers of being driven by the needs of the organisation rather than objective consideration of the impacts of the research from a wider perspective are real and obvious (Punch, 1986 and Miles and Huberman, 1994). Finally, as more research is conducted or driven by the profession, there is the question of the status and independence of the researcher, particularly where the aim of the research is to translate evidence into practice and test its implementation in the operational environment (Wiggers et al., 2004).

These four issues need to be considered alongside each other to determine the status, reliability, quality and ethical compliance of the research. There is no starker illustration than when Police Chiefs themselves engage directly in the research process. Whether they are researcher as in Ariel and Farrar (2013) or sponsor, as in Operation CARA (Strang et al., 2014) or the Essex Body Worn Video trial (Owens et al., 2014), when the projects are directly linked to their strategy, police research can be seen, as Wilson (1950) proposed, as a largely internal management activity. As such, there is a danger that the process and outputs from the research could be driven more by the practical needs of the organisation than the requirements of independent scientific inquiry. In the past, this effect was mitigated by the impact of funding bodies such as the National Institute of Justice and Home Office, which brought both the advantages of a wider national perspective and the potential disadvantages of a narrow political frame (Hope, 2004).

The conflation of institutional and research motivation also raises questions about consent and how judgments about harm and risk from research will be approached. Participants could see high-level sponsorship by a Chief as cutting across the requirement for consent, where, as in the Body Worn Video RCTs in Rialto and Essex, the participants are serving officers in the Chief's own force (Ariel and Farrar, 2013; Owens et al., 2014). Furthermore, the judgments about the benefits, harms and risks to subjects and the wider public could become internally focused on achieving the police force's aims rather than paying regard to the wider public interest. Holgersson (2014) and Knutsson (2014), writing as a serving police officer and the Director of the Swedish National Police Board's Evaluation Unit, found all of these concerns to be active issues.

To add a further dimension, in Rialto (Ariel and Farrar, 2013) and Operation Turning Point, the principal researcher was a serving or recently serving Police

Chief. This brings advantages in that the researchers have a good understanding of the tacit knowledge of policing (Nutley et al., 2007). It also provides a greater opportunity for the researchers to perform a role of expert consultancy alongside evaluation. However, trust between senior officers and frontline staff can be fragile (Cockcroft, 2013) and academic research is far from universally valued in policing (Weisburd and Neyroud, 2011 and Cockbain and Knutsson, 2014), posing potential challenges of credibility and engagement for the professional police officer as researcher.

The reason why this issue is so important is that the extent of police professional involvement in major research projects is changing rapidly. Braga et al. (2014) undertook a systematic review of RCTs in policing up until 2012. Of the 63 police experiments in their search, they found none where the principal or co-researchers were serving or recently serving police officers. Yet by 2014 there were twenty or more examples, either complete or in progress and more in preparation, together with new studies being conducted by the College of Policing, as the professional body for policing (Neyroud, forthcoming). The case study, which follows, Operation Turning Point, was one of that group.

Case study: Operation Turning Point

Operation Turning Point was designed as a RCT to test whether low harm offenders, who might otherwise have been prosecuted (the control condition), could be effectively dealt with by a combined treatment of deferred prosecution and tailored conditions to encourage desistance (Sherman and Neyroud, 2012; Neyroud and Slothower, 2013). A second, connected experiment explored the impact on victims (Slothower, 2014a). Given that Turning Point required police to randomly assign offenders to prosecution or diversion, it provides a particularly good illustration of the moral boundaries of research in policing, as well as the ethics of research in practice. The case study has been analysed against the four areas identified above: research motivation, consent, risk and harm and researcher role and status.

Research governance and ethics

The Programme Board, chaired by an Assistant Chief Constable, provided the forum for debate and approval of the research and 'weighed the consequences'. In framing the discussion, it drew on a set of standards for the research agreement, data protection and research approvals that had been put in place by the National Policing Improvement Agency (NPIA). They were a mixture of field practicality and government bureaucracy.

As the main research design was a randomised controlled trial, the research team followed the standards designed by Sherman and Strang (2009) for a pre-research CRIMPORT Protocol (Neyroud, 2011b). Sherman and Strang drew their standards from the CONSORT (2010) standards for medical trials. The

CRIMPORT for Turning Point was first approved by the Programme Board and then the senior researcher, before publication on the website of the Cambridge Institute of Criminology.

On top of the Programme Board and the CRIMPORT, there were two further elements of the research that called for individual, institutional approval. Surveys of victims, which formed a key part of exploring the victim's experience, required approval from the University of Maryland's ethics committee, because the researcher who carried out the surveys was a Maryland student. Interviews with practitioners involved in the trial were carried out by a student from the University of Queensland (UQ) and approved by UQ's ethics committee. In each case, therefore, there was a dual sign off by both the Programme Board and the academic institution. It would be fair to say that the process, involving three different countries, three different institutions and the police force, was complex. The unifying factors were that all the main researchers were members of the American Society of Criminology and, ultimately, all decisions required sign off by the Programme Board.

Research motivation and randomisation

Given at least four key stakeholders – the independent funder, the force, the Police and Crime Commissioner and the research team – there were subtle differences of emphasis around research motivation. The funder wanted a programme that offered an opportunity to reduce the use of prison, the force and the PCC a means of preventing reoffending cost-effectively and the researchers to test a hypothesis (Sherman, 2011; Sherman and Neyroud, 2012) which appeared to have potential to achieve both.

Punch (1986) and Miles and Huberman (1994) have argued that the ethical basis for research motivation lies in the 'worthiness' of the issue and the question as to whether or not there is sufficient evidence within the body of research to suggest that we already know the answer to the questions being examined. 'Worthiness', as they defined it, was clearly to be guided by the wider societal impacts rather than the narrower perspective of an agency's strategic plan. A further approach to support 'worthiness' was taken by the research team: Neyroud and Slothower (2013) reviewed the evidence for out of court disposals (OOCD) and found that relative effectiveness of prosecution and diversion, particularly conditional diversion, had rarely been tested and not at all in the UK. Yet, such OOCDs accounted for more than 30 per cent of all disposals and the Ministry of Justice had embarked on further reforms (Neyroud and Slothower, 2015). This suggests that the issue was of more than internal importance. Indeed, the review of the research identified that there were significant potential adverse consequences from inconsistent and poorly designed practice (Neyroud and Slothower, 2013).

However, in agreeing to the research, managers in the force were primarily motivated by the fit between the research and their strategy and the extent to which the research could be used as a driver of an 'evidence-based approach'. The need to test victim experience was also driven by pressure from the police force and the Turning Point Programme Board to address the issue of victim satisfaction with both the Turning Point process and prosecution. Running through all of these was a theme of enhancing the professionalism of their officers and encouraging the use of their discretion, which was a cornerstone of the Chief Constable's vision. The latter, professional agenda drove a critical part of the research programme which focused on improving decision-making by police officers (Slothower, 2014b). The professional agenda did not deflect the main research motivation but it did influence the design and focus of the research. 'Worthiness' was, at least partly, defined by its relationship to the force's vision and values.

On the other hand, the most controversial aspect of the research design – random allocation of cases between prosecution and diversion – was most strongly influenced by the research team. The experiment was not wholly unique in using randomisation in this way. Dunford (1990) has described how a National Institute of Justice programme had approached the challenge of persuading police and prosecutors to such an approach in the 1980's. The overall justification in both the National Institute of Justice studies (Dunford et al., 1982) and Turning Point was that an RCT provided the best design to determine the effectiveness of the treatment (Farrington and Bennett, 1981; Sherman et al., 1997).

In Turning Point there was, however, a unique process for randomisation. Aligned with the emphasis on professional discretion and taking advantage of the internet based 'Cambridge Gateway' (Ariel et al., 2012), randomisation was entrusted to the Custody Sergeants supported by triage questions embedded in the Gateway. The research team created the first version, but, after piloting in Stage 1, a revised version incorporated input from Custody Sergeants. They were also given the ultimate sanction of exclusion from the experiment, subject to stating their reasons. Exclusions were tightly monitored throughout the trial. Research by a member of the programme team showed high levels of consistency (Hobday, 2014).

As such, day-to-day ownership of the experiment lay with the police, particularly Custody Officers and Offender Managers (who were responsible for setting conditions and managing the contracts). The design sought to ensure that the experiment was as close to normal operational practice as possible. There was no special team ring-fenced for the experiment. Instead, Custody Officers and Offender Managers were provided with tools – the Gateway and a decision tool for setting conditions – that were developed to allow the experiment to run as part of existing processes.

As Clarke and Cornish (1972) found in a penal setting, achieving a balance between professional discretion, internal validity and ethical random assignment is a significant challenge. Randomly allocating potentially prosecutable cases raises important ethical considerations for the criminal justice system. The first consideration has to be to ensure that there is no breach of the fairness principle. Offenders should not be worse off as a result of randomisation, nor should the treatment provide a disproportionately tough set of conditions compared with the trial nor should they be assigned to a treatment that causes them harm or worse consequences than the control treatment (Torgerson and Torgerson, 2008 and Edwards et al., 1998). In order to satisfy this condition, offenders were not put to the Gateway until and unless a clear decision to prosecute had been taken by the police custody officer. Hence, were it not for the random assignment to the treatment, they would be prosecuted and be at risk of a criminal conviction and punishment. By being offered the experimental condition, their prosecution was deferred. In turn, the treatment conditions were designed by drawing on the research evidence in such as way as to ensure that conditions offered were supported by the best evidence available and that treatments identified as causing increased levels of offending were avoided. Finally, the proportionality of the treatment conditions under Operation Turning Point was both central to the training provided to officers and independently audited by the Crown Prosecution Service, who examined a sample of 20 or more of the early cases.

Consent to participate: offenders

Once an offender had been randomised by the Gateway, the question of consent to participation was the next major ethical issue (Punch, 1986; Miles and Huberman, 1994). Custody Sergeants rejected the idea that they should tell offenders assigned to prosecution that they were part of a trial. They argued that all subjects should be treated as normal. On the other hand, those assigned to Turning Point clearly needed to be informed and provide consent. Custody Officers were reluctant to add another bureaucratic process. Given that the experiment relied on their compliance, the programme board decided that subjects assigned to Turning Point would not be asked for consent until after assignment and would only be asked to consent to detailed conditions after their interview with an offender manager. Consent was sought in two stages: agreement to consider the experiment and return voluntarily to the police station at an appointed time (but with the clear warning that failure to attend would trigger prosecution); fully informed consent, following a detailed, structured interview. As such, consent to the experiment was wrapped up with consent to the conditions and agreement to compliance with the Turning Point 'contract', which also meant that the subject was recognising the consequences of breach would be to trigger prosecution.

Given the potentially coercive nature of a police custody and offender management environment, access to a legal adviser provided an important safeguard to support informed consent and the programme team ensured that local duty solicitors were briefed about the experiment and that solicitor's concerns were carefully monitored. With over 700 cases in all four stages, there were no recorded solicitors' objections to the Turning Point treatment. Their interventions were confined to a small number of cases where the treatment was withdrawn or they considered the conditions too onerous.

The process of securing consent and the protections for the subject of the research were, therefore, part and parcel of the operational processes within custody and offender management. Mosera et al. (2004) found that even in the more coercive setting of a prison, offenders were able to make informed decisions to participate. In this experiment, the stability of 'normal' practice was also important to underpin the external validity of the experiment.

Risks, harm and benefits

Having settled the design, process and consent, there were a number of further risks and harms that needed to be considered. Farrington and Bennett (1981) highlighted the risk that diversion could widen the net by including cases that would otherwise have been cautioned. Landau and Nathan (1983) drew attention to the potential for disproportionate decisions. Equally, it was possible that the experiment could include potentially harmful and persistent offenders, in a way that might adversely impact on public protection and, ultimately, the legitimacy of the experiment in the eyes of the public.

The process to exclude those who might otherwise have been cautioned, relied on the fact that the Gateway was not triggered unless a decision to prosecute had been made. In an effort to exclude the harmful, the Gateway questions were designed to exclude high harm and persistent offenders by criteria that excluded offenders with multiple convictions, those likely to be sentenced to imprisonment and those whose offending fitted one or more of the exclusion criteria.

Offenders who have not admitted the offence are normally excluded from diversion. However, prior research on cautions and diversions, such as that by Landau and Nathan (1983), suggested that the reliance on admission to trigger diversion may have discriminatory impacts. Landau and Nathan found lower levels of admission amongst black suspects and, therefore, lower levels of cautioning. Although some of the difference could be accounted for by the nature of the offending behaviour, a significant element appeared to be linked to lower levels of trust in the police and criminal justice system.

A decision was taken very early on in the Programme Board to include all eligible offenders as long as the Custody Officer was satisfied that there was sufficient evidence to prosecute and a public interest to do so. This decision was driven more by the professional ethical requirement for fair and equitable practice, which was reinforced by a new Police Professional Ethical Code (College of Policing, 2014), as any research requirements.

The victim: consent and engagement

Including subjects who had not admitted offences was one of a number of challenges when ensuring that victim's were engaged and satisfied with their treatment. The Code of Practice for Victims of Crime (Ministry of Justice, 2013), which was introduced in 2006, provides a statutory framework for the obligations to victims in the criminal justice system. The Code places an obligation on the police and Crown Prosecution Service (CPS) to ensure that vulnerable victims or victims with special needs are identified and their needs taken into account and that victims are informed about significant events or changes in the investigation. The latter includes the decision to caution or divert an offender or to charge an offender to go before the court. However, the decision to divert remains with the police and CPS, having taken account of the victim's wishes. In the interviews with the officers participating in the experiment, protecting victims and ensuring that they received a good service ranked as a very important professional duty for the police.

Within the experimental design, the Programme Board recognised a clear difference between crimes with no personal victim, property crimes and crimes against the person. They concluded that there should be a sliding scale of obligation on the officers dealing with the crimes, with a greater obligation on the police to consult the victim in crimes against the person. From an early stage the police officers, frontline and managers, raised concerns about the impact of a decision to treat an offender through Turning Point on the victims. The research team responded by conducting an exploratory survey of personal victims from the first two stages, which identified problems with the way victims were being consulted and exposed limitations on the force's ambitions to use Turning Point to expand the use of restorative justice (Slothower, 2014a).

The concerns were potentially serious enough to have halted the experiment. Instead, the police force responded by adding a dedicated victims team to the programme, who worked with the research team to construct a model of victim engagement based on restorative justice (Slothower, 2014a). Consistent with the wider professional commitment to test new practice, the Programme Board supported the research team in expanding the experiment to include a RCT of victim treatment.

Role conflict and the status of the researcher

Turning Point was a complex experiment. Indeed, it is better described as two experiments nested within a programme which included several strands of practice development. As we have seen, the force was committed to an evidence-based approach, but there was also a wider context. One of the local commanders was a leader of the emerging Society for Evidence-based policing and the principal researcher was the co-author of 'controversial' (Engel and Henderson, 2014) papers advocating the transformation of the police through science (Weisburd and Neyroud, 2011, Neyroud and Weisburd, 2014a and 2014b) and of a review of policing that had led to the creation of the new professional body, the National College of Policing (Neyroud, 2011a). On both sides of the partnership, police and research team, there was a commitment to scientific testing of practice innovation and a shared vision of the police station as a learning and teaching environment (Weisburd and Neyroud, 2011 and Neyroud, 2011a).

That commitment extended to an exploration of the lessons of conducting and managing the experiment as part of a wider study of police experiments. This illustrated both the strengths and the limitations of a professionally owned science in policing. On the one hand, the principal researcher's background as a former Chief Officer provided the type of insights and knowledge that Nutley et al. (2007) suggest can be important. On the other, a relationship between frontline staff and researcher which is, at least partly defined by rank (even if former rank) and the persistence of courtesy titles such as 'sir' and 'boss', is not the norm in such relationships.

Summary

This chapter has explored the ethical challenges presented by a professionally owned and directed research in policing. The emergence of a new police professionalism with a strong commitment to testing practice and building partnerships with higher education remains a relatively recent phenomenon. For some, like Hirschi (1993), such an enterprise cannot succeed, because 'the state may be said to be responsible for crime "control" only in a technical and figurative sense, and the first obligation of the criminologist is to explain this fact to public officials' (p.249).

The considerable body of work in areas such as situational prevention and policing suggests that Hirschi overstated his case. However, his caution about the theoretical base and independence of institutionally or professionally led research serve as constant reminders that the process of building knowledge through research must respect wider standards of ethics, methods and publication to support the wider legitimacy of practice that Neyroud and Sherman (2013) have argued is achievable.

The ethical considerations in Turning Point were complex and research and operational issues were intimately interconnected. Miles and Huberman (1994) suggest that research tends to involve dilemmas and conflicts and that negotiated trade offs need to be made as the research progresses. In this trial, those choices were largely made within the context of the governance structure of the experiment. But they were also made within the wider context of the trial – sharply falling budgets and an urgent need for the police to find new and financially sustainable ways of reducing offending.

The lessons of Turning Point suggest that a new police professionalism, underpinned by science, is not unattainable. However, for the research to maintain credibility and high standards, strong partnerships with Universities and careful attention to the ethics, process and peer-reviewed publication of research are critical. Universities partnerships are critical not only because of the research skills, but also their research standards and ethics, external to police, provide an important degree of assurance of independence and critical focus. In the same way, it is also important that as the ethics of the new profession are developed, they include the ethics of research and the relationship between the professional as researcher and the wider research community.

Review questions

1. How might the ethical issues set out in the Turning Point case study be applied to a randomised trial to test a new less lethal weapon such as a conducted electrical device (such as TASER)?
2. Are there limitations to the idea of police ownership of 'police science'?
3. What are the benefits of police ownership of 'police science'?

Case examples

The chapter uses Operation Turning Point as one case example and references two studies of Body Worn Video (Ariel and Farrar, 2013 and Owens et al., 2014), which provide a very different experimental method.

Guide to further reading

Weisburd and Neyroud (2011) and Neyroud and Weisburd (2014b). The first proposed a new approach to police science, the second responded to the emerging debate that followed.

Greene, J. (2014). New Directions in Policing: Balancing Prediction and Meaning in Police Research. *Justice Quarterly*, 31(3): 193–228. Provides a critique of the limits of police science and police ownership of it.

Cockbain, E. and Knutsson (2014). A collection of essays about a non-experimental, applied police research approach.

Sherman (2013). Proposes a systematic discipline of police use of science based around a Triple T of Targeting, Testing and Tracking.

Note

1 Police Chief is used throughout to describe the police officials leading police agencies in executive roles as distinct from elected officials such as Sheriffs or Police and Crime Commissioners who have a responsibility for the political direction and governance of police.

References

Ariel, B. and Farrar, J. (2013). *The Effects of Body-worn Video on Police Citizen Encounters: an RCT*. Presentation to the 2013 Conference on Evidence-based Policing: http://www.crim.cam.ac.uk/events/conferences/ebp/2013.
Ariel, B., Vila, J. and Sherman, L. W. (2012). Random assignment without tears: how to stop worrying and love the Cambridge Randomiser. *Journal of Experimental Criminology*, 8: 193–208.
Bradley, D. and Nixon, C. (2009). Ending the 'dialogue of the deaf': evidence and policing policies and practices. An Australian case study. *Police Practice and Research: An International Journal*, 10(5–6): 423–435.
Braga, A. A. and Davis, E. F. (2014). Implementing science in police agencies: the embedded researcher model. *Policing: A Journal of Policy and Practice*, 8(4): 294–307.

Braga, A. A., Welsh, B. C., Papachristos, A. V., Schnell, C. and Grossman, L. (2014). The growth in randomized experiments in policing: the vital few and the salience of mentoring. *Journal of Experimental Criminology,* 10(1): 1–29.

Bullock, K. and Tilley, N. (2009). Evidence-based policing and crime reduction. *Policing: A Journal of Policy and Practice,* 3(4): 381–387.

Clarke, R. V. G. and Cornish, D. B. (1972). *The Controlled Trial in Institutional Research – Paradigm or Pitfall for Penal Evaluators?* London: HMSO.

Cockbain, E. and Knutsson, J. (Eds.) (2014). *Applied Police Research: Challenges and Opportunities.* Abingdon: Routledge.

Cockcroft, T. (2013). *Police Culture: Themes and Concepts.* Abingdon: Routledge.

College of Policing (2014). *Code of Ethics: a Code of Practice for the Principles and Standards of Professional Behaviour for the Policing Profession of England and Wales.* Downloaded from http:// www.college.police.uk/What-we-do/Ethics/Pages/Code-of-Ethics.aspx on 11.02.2015.

CONSORT (2010). *Consolidated Standards of Reporting Trials.* Downloaded from http:// www.consort-statement.org/consort-2010 on 11.02.2015.

Dunford, F. (1990). Random assignment: practical considerations from field experiments. *Evaluation and Program Planning,* 13: 125–132.

Dunford, F., Osgood, W. and Weichselbaum, H. F. (1982). National Evaluation of Diversion Projects: Final Report. Washington, DC: National Institute of Justice.

Edwards, S. J. L., Lilford, R. J., Jackson, J. C., Hewison, J. and Thornton, J. (1998). Ethical issues in the design and conduct of randomised controlled trials. *Health Technology Assessment,* 2(15): 1–146.

Engel, R. S. and Henderson, S. (2014). Beyond rhetoric: establishing police-academic partnerships that work. In Brown, J. (Ed.). *The Future of Policing.* Abingdon: Routledge.

Engel, R. S. and Whalen, J. L. (2010). Police academic partnerships: ending the dialogue of the deaf, the Cincinnati experience. *Police Practice and Research: An International Journal,* 11(2): 105–116.

Farrington, D. P. and Bennett, T. (1981). Police cautioning of juveniles in London. *British Journal of Criminology,* 21(2): 123–135.

Farrington, D. P. and Joliffe, D. (2002). *A Feasibility study into using a Randomised Controlled Trial to evaluate Treatment Pilots at HMP Whitemoor.* London: Home Office.

Galliher, J. F. (1999). Against administrative criminology. *Social Justice,* 26(2): 56–59.

Galliher, J. F. and Galliher, J. M. (1995). Professional ethics, personal moral commitment and the law. *The American Sociologist,* 26(1): 4–7.

Goldacre, B. (2015). How medicine is broken and how we can fix it. *BMJ* 2015: 350.

Greene, J. (2014). New directions in policing: balancing prediction and meaning in police research. *Justice Quarterly,* 31(3): 193–228.

Hirschi, T. (1993). Administrative criminology. *Contemporary Sociology,* 22: 348–50.

Hobday, J. (2014). Targeting Reasons for Rejecting Random Assignment in an RCT. M.St. Dissertation: Institute of Criminology, University of Cambridge.

Holgersson, S. (2014). An inside job: managing mismatched expectations and unwanted findings when conducting police research as a police officer. In Cockbain, E. and Knutsson, J. (Eds) (2014). *Applied Police Research: Challenges and Opportunities.* Abingdon: Routledge.

Hope, T. (2004). Pretend it works: evidence and governance in the evaluation of the Reducing Burglary Initiative. *Criminology and Criminal Justice,* 4(3): 287–308.

Kennedy, D. (2014). Working in the field: police research in theory and in practice. In Cockbain, E. and Knutsson, J. (Eds) (2014). *Applied Police Research: Challenges and Opportunities.* Abingdon: Routledge.

Klofas, J. M., Hipple, N. K. and McGarrell, E. F. (2010). *The New Criminal Justice: American Communities and the Changing World of Crime Control*. New York: Routledge.

Knutsson, J. (2014). Politics, promises and problems: the rise and fall of the Swedish police Evaluation Unit. In Cockbain, E. and Knutsson, J. (Eds.). *Applied Police Research: Challenges and Opportunities*. Abingdon: Routledge.

Landau, S. F. and Nathan, G. (1983). Selecting delinquents for cautioning in the London Metropolitan area. *British Journal of Criminology*, 23(2): 128–149.

McGloin, J. M. and Thomas, K. J. (2013). Experimental tests of criminological theory. In Welsh, B. C., Braga, A. A. and Bruinsma, G. J. N. (Eds.). *Experimental Criminology: Prospects for Advancing Science and Public Policy*. New York: Cambridge University Press.

Manning, P. (2005). The study of policing. *Police Quarterly*, 8(1): 23–43.

Manning, P. (2010). *Democratic Policing in a Changing World*. Boudler: Paradigm.

Marx, G. T. (1988). *Under Cover: Police Surveillance in America*. Berkeley: University of California Press.

Mazerolle, L., Lum, C. and Braga, A. A. (2014). Using experimental designs to study police interventions. In Reisig, M. D. and Kane, R. J. (Eds). *The Oxford Handbook of Police and Policing*. Oxford: OUP.

Miles, M. B. and Huberman, A. M. (1994). *Qualitative Data Analysis*. Thousand Oaks, CA: Sage.

Ministry of Justice (2013). Code of Practice for Victims of Crime. London: Ministry of Justice. Downloaded from https://www.gov.uk/government/uploads/system/uploads/attachment_data/file/254459/code-of-practice-victims-of-crime.pdf [accessed 14.12.14].

Mosera, D. J., Arndta, S., Kanza, J. E., Benjamina, M. L., Baylessa, J. D., Reesea, R. L., Paulsena, J. S. and Flauma, M. S. (2004). Coercion and informed consent in research involving prisoners. *Comprehensive Psychiatry*, 45(1, January–February): 1–9.

Neyroud, P. W. (2008). Policing and ethics. In Newburn, T. (Ed.). *The Handbook of Policing*. 2nd Edition. Cullompton: Willan.

Neyroud, P. W. (2011a). *Review of Police Leadership and Training*. London: Home Office. Downloaded from: https://www.gov.uk/government/uploads/system/uploads/attachment_data/file/118227/report.pdf [accessed 15.12.14].

Neyroud, P. W. (2011b). *Operation Turning Point: an experiment in 'Offender Desistance Policing'*. Jerry Lee Centre for Experimental Criminology, Institute of Criminology, University of Cambridge: Downloaded from http://www.crim.cam.ac.uk/research/experiments/rex-post/operation_turning_point.pdf [accessed 15.12.14].

Neyroud, P. W. (2015). Future perspectives in policing: a crisis or a perfect storm: the trouble with public policing? In Wankehede, P. and Weir, D. (Eds.). *Police Services: Leadership and Management Perspectives*. Heidelberg: Springer.

Neyroud, P. W. and Sherman, L. W. (2013). Dialogue and dialectic: police legitimacy and the new professionalism. In Tankebe, J. and Liebling, A. (Eds.) *Legitimacy and Criminal Justice*. Oxford: OUP.

Neyroud, P. W. and Slothower, M. P. (2013). *Operation Turning Point: a Second Interim Report on a Randomised Trial in Birmingham, UK*. Unpublished report: Institute of Criminology, University of Cambridge.

Neyroud, P. W. and Slothower, M. P. (2015). Wielding the Sword of Damocles: the challenges and opportunities in reforming out-of-court disposals in England and Wales. In Wasik, M. and Santatzoglou, S. (Eds.). *Who Knows Best? The Management of Change in the Criminal Justice System*. Basingstoke: Palgrave MacMillan.

Neyroud, P. W. and Weisburd, D. W. (2014a). Transforming the police through science: some new thoughts on the controversy and challenge of translation. *Translational Criminology*, Spring: 16–19.

Neyroud, P. W. and Weisburd, D. W. (2014b). Transforming the police through science: the challenge of ownership. *Policing, A Journal of Policy and Practice*, 8(4): 287–294.

Nutley, S. M., Walter, I. and Davies, H. T. O. (2007). *Using Evidence: How Research can Inform Public Services*. Bristol: Policy Press.

Owens, C., Mann, D. and McKenna, R. (2014). *The Essex Body Worn Video Trial: the impact of Body Worn Video on criminal justice outcomes of domestic abuse incidents*. National College of Policing. http://college.pressofficeadmin.com/repository/files/BWV_Report.pdf

President's Task Force on 21st Century Policing (2015). *Final Report of the President's Task Force on 21st Century Policing*. Washington, DC: Office of Community Oriented Policing Services.

Punch, M. (1986). *The Politics and Ethics of Fieldwork*. Beverley Hills, CA.: Sage.

Sherman, L. W. (2010). An introduction to experimental criminology. In Piquero, A. R. and Weisburd, D. (Eds.). *Handbook of Quantitative Criminology*. New York: Springer.

Sherman, L. W. (2011) Al Capone, the Sword of Damocles, and the Police–Corrections Budget Ratio. *Criminology & Public Policy*, 10: 195–206.

Sherman, L. W. (2013). The rise of evidence-based policing: targeting, testing and tracking. In Tonry, M. (Ed.). *Crime and Justice in America: 1975–2025*. Chicago: University of Chicago Press.

Sherman, L. W. and Neyroud, P. W. (2012). *Offender Desistance Policing and the Sword of Damocles*. London: Civitas.

Sherman, L. W. and Strang, H. (2009). *Criminological Protocol for Operating Randomised Controlled Trials*. Downloaded from www.crim.cam.ac.uk/research/experiments/crimport.doc on 11.02.2015.

Sherman, L. W., Gottfredson, D., MacKenzie, D., Eck, J., Reuter, P. and Bushway, S. (1997). *Preventing Crime: What Works, What Doesn't, What's Promising*. Washington, DC: Office of Justice Programs.

Sklansky, D. A. (2014). The promise and perils of police professionalism. In Brown, J. (Ed.) *The Future of Policing*. Abingdon: Routledge.

Skogan, W. and Frydl, L. (Eds.) (2004). *Fairness and Effectiveness in Policing: The Evidence*. Washington, DC: The National Academies Press.

Slothower, M. P. (2014a). Victim Satisfaction and Perceptions of Police and Criminal Justice Legitimacy: Mediating Impacts of Perceptions of Problem-Solving Motive Achievement and Matching. MA: University of Maryland.

Slothower, M. P. (2014b). Strengthening police professionalism with decision support: bounded discretion in out-of-court disposals. *Policing*, 8(4): 353–368.

Sparrow, M. K. (2011). *Governing Science: New Perspectives in Policing*. Washington, DC: Department of Justice, National Institute of Justice.

Stone, C. and Travis, J. (2011). *Towards a new Professionalism in Policing. New Perspectives in Policing*. Washington, DC: Department of Justice, National Institute of Justice.

Strang, H., Chilton, S., Cornelius, N. and Rowland, J. (2014). *Project CARA: Conditional Cautioning and Relational Abuse*. Presentation to the 7th International Conference on Evidence-based Policing. Downloaded on 13.04.2015 from http://www.crim.cam.ac.uk/events/conferences/ebp/2014/slides/112%20-%20TUES%20-%20Project%20CARA%20-%20Hampshire.pdf.

Telep, C. (2014). *Back to the future with ASC's new Division of Policing*. OUP Blog, November 15th 2014. Downloaded from http://blog.oup.com/2014/11/asc-new-division-policing/ [accessed 13/7/2015].

Thacher, D. (2001). Policing is not a treatment: alternatives to the medical model of police research. *Journal of Research in Crime and Delinquency*, 38(4): 387–415.

Torgerson, D. J. and Torgerson, C. J. (2008). *Designing Randomised Trials in Health, Education and Social Services.* Basingstoke: Palgrave Macmillan.

Weisburd, D. W. and Hinkle, J. C. (2012). The importance of randomised experiments in evaluating crime prevention. In Welsh, B. C. and Farrington, D. P. (Eds.). *The Oxford Handbook of Crime Prevention.* Oxford: Oxford University Press.

Weisburd, D. W. and Neyroud, P. W. (2011). *Police Science: Toward a New Paradigm.* Cambridge, MA: Harvard, Kennedy School of Government.

Wiggers, J., Jauncey, M., Purss, K., Considine, R., Daly, J., Kingsland, M., Purss, K., Burrows, S., Nicholas, C. and Waites, R.J. (2004). Strategies and outcomes in translating alcohol harm reduction research into practice: the Alcohol Linking Program. *Drug and Alcohol Review,* 23: 355–364.

Wilson, O. W. (1950). *Police Administration.* New York: McGraw-Hill.

Vollmer, A. (1936). *The Police and Modern Society: Plain Talk Based on Practical Experience.* Berkeley, CA: University of California Press.

6

THE ETHICS OF RESEARCH ON SOCIAL WORK IN CRIMINAL JUSTICE

David Smith

In this chapter I consider some of the main ethical issues in research in criminology and criminal justice, as they are expressed in the relevant literature and as I encountered them in my own work. In order to illustrate these issues in what I hope is a concrete and practical way, I draw extensively on my own research experience as well as the experience of others. This approach is also consistent with the view – developed at length and convincingly in relation to research by Macfarlane (2009) and following the broad arguments of MacIntyre (1985) – that ethics are best understood in terms of the virtues associated with situated social practices. Codes of ethical practice can of course provide important guidance and reminders (and some degree of legal security for universities), but because they are necessarily general and decontextualized they are of little help to researchers wondering in the very act of research what they should do next. As Macfarlane (2009: 3) puts it, 'Developing an understanding of what to do is always a more challenging prospect than issuing edicts about what it not right'.

Key points

1. Research on social work in criminal justice raises ethical issues that also arise in other social work research, as well as some that are distinctively criminological.
2. Government-funded research is not inherently objectionable in ethical terms. Still, researchers should approach it with caution.
3. Total conformity with the principles of non-maleficence and confidentiality is rarely if ever achievable.
4. A practical commitment to the virtues associated with academic research is preferable to anxious adherence to formal codes of ethics.

Key definitions

Evaluation: The assessment through research of the effectiveness of interventions in the field of criminal justice, generally concerned with processes of implementation as well as with outcomes.

Administrative criminology: Research conducted within or for government departments. The term is usually used to convey disapproval on the grounds that such research is excessively policy-oriented and insufficiently critical.

Privatisation: The involvement in criminal justice practice of commercial interests and hence the emergence of competition and concerns with profitability. A relatively recent but increasingly important process in British criminal justice.

Introduction: keeping confidences about crime

Criminological and criminal justice research is sometimes seen as liable to raise particularly difficult ethical issues, as it deals with subject-matter that is inherently sensitive (Fogel, 2007; Renzetti and Lee, 1993). The same is arguably true, however, of any research on social work – certainly of research that involves an attempt to understand the experience of service users, who are almost by definition vulnerable in ways that the general population may not be. Interviews, for example, are always going to have the potential to raise issues which research participants may find difficult and distressing. This clearly applies to interviews with people defined as offenders, and also to victims of crime, who may find it painful to recall their experience of victimisation, most obviously but not only in relation to violent victimisation (e.g. Clark and Walker, 2011). But the sensitive ethical issue that is more nearly specific to criminological research is the possibility that research participants may reveal past criminal acts that are not known to the police and thus not already on record, or, still more problematically, future acts which they are planning or contemplating. Can the principle of confidentiality apply in such situations?

There are criminological researchers who argue that research subjects must be given a complete and unbreakable guarantee of confidentiality, but in practice it seems more usual to offer limited confidentiality. Thus, researchers may make a commitment to anonymity and confidentiality except in relation to serious offences already committed or being meditated. Interviewees would then be told that they will not be asked about such offences, but if they disclose them the researcher will pass the information on to the police or another official agency. Otherwise researchers could find themselves in a position that is ethically impossible even if it might be legally defensible: imagine knowing about, but feeling unable to reveal, information about past offences of serious violence or planned offences of armed robbery or child abuse (in the case of future offences, the issue of public safety is particularly sharp). In my experience the kind of pragmatic approach that acknowledges that some topics are out of bounds has worked well enough: research participants understand the issue and frame their responses accordingly. But while it may be a pragmatic solution to the confidentiality problem it is not a logically tidy or watertight one. What counts as a serious offence, for example?

While it would not be sensible to claim that there is absolute consensus on this, the best evidence is that across developed western societies there is a high level of agreement, which is stable over time, on the ranking of offence seriousness (O'Connell and Whelan, 1996; and successive sweeps of the International Crime Victims Survey (ICVS)). So judgements on this are not just a matter of preference or the whim of the researcher, and there is every reason to think that people who offend are generally within the broad moral consensus. We can more or less assume a shared understanding of the issues between researcher and research participant. This does not dispose of all difficulties: interviewees may reveal serious past or proposed offending despite the interviewer's advice that they should not. But limited confidentiality remains in my view the most practical and morally defensible approach, and the one most in line with the virtues associated with ethical research.

Research for governments

Much criminal justice research in the UK and elsewhere has been funded directly by government departments or through public agencies such as the probation or prison services; indeed, the volume of such research would be much smaller without these sources of funding. There was therefore some stir in criminological circles with the publication by the respected Centre for Crime and Justice Studies (located at the time within King's College, University of London) of two essays that argued that criminologists should not conduct government-sponsored research, or at least should be very wary of doing so (Hope and Walters, 2008). Both wrote following unhappy experiences, with the Scottish Executive in Walters' case, with the Home Office in Hope's. Of the two, Walters took the more thoroughly rejectionist position, arguing for a boycott by academics of Home Office and Scottish Executive research (the equivalents in 2015 would be the Ministry of Justice and the Scottish Government). His complaint is partly that academics who accept research funds from these bodies are likely to be badly treated or ignored, but more fundamentally that the agenda of governments is (and has probably always been) inherently oppressive: 'I am strongly opposed to academics (notably to senior academics) engaging in contract research or consultancy advice with the Home Office or the Scottish Executive that simply grants legitimacy to the ongoing criminalisation and marginalisation of some of the poorest and most marginalised members of society'. The alternative to resistance to 'existing trends' in the relationship between governments and academia 'is a form of intellectual collusion that is akin to corruption' (Hope and Walters, 2008: 23). Hope did not go as far. He suggested (p. 29) that things had been better when he worked as a researcher at the Home Office – from 1974–91 – but that his experience in the early 2000s was that the Home Office did not practise peer review of research as it claimed to and that its 'manipulation of the publication process' (p. 32) (so as to highlight the most favourable interpretation of the results of a burglary prevention initiative) denied the researchers 'the opportunity to account properly for ourselves'. Like Walters, he complained of a lack of integrity not only in government officials but in academic colleagues.

Hope is convincing enough that there is a risk in government-funded research that inconvenient research findings will be delayed, obscured or suppressed altogether. But it could be argued that to a degree this risk applies to all research: assessors for peer-reviewed journals may be unsympathetic or (in the minds of frustrated authors) wilfully obtuse; and as a former editor of a fairly reputable journal (the *British Journal of Social Work*) I can testify that some authors are liable to believe that publication of their work is being hindered by editorial incompetence or malevolence. Walters also complained of delays in publication on the part of the Scottish Executive of the evaluative research on which he worked, and of over-management by the Home Office of the flow of publications; while his particular targets were the 'New Labour' government in 2006–07 and the then Home Secretary John Reid, he did not seem to share Hope's view that things used to be better. His criticism of academics for doing research that gives 'legitimacy' to oppressive government policies seems to be meant to apply generally, rather than only to some kinds of research on some topics. He complains of criminology that is 'embedded', by which he means something very like what 'administrative' criminology came to mean.

This term comes from the 'left realist' criminology that developed in the 1980s: in Jock Young's (1986) essay on 'The failure of criminology' it referred to a loss of interest in the social causes of crime, which Young associated with the Research and Planning Unit of the Home Office. As Hough (2014: 216) notes, it 'acquired other connotations, most of them unflattering: unimaginative, atheoretical, politically suborned and corrupted by the pressures of grantsmanship'. Hough was a colleague of Tim Hope's at the Home Office, moving to academia in 1994, where he has continued to work on government-funded research. He is therefore understandably interested in defending himself and other possibly 'embedded' criminologists from these criticisms – and in my view does so successfully. But he accepts that the relationship between research conducted in or for the Home Office and policy-makers has changed since the 1970s, when 'links with policy divisions…were distant' and '[t]here was no direct political involvement (as I recall) in the publication process' (Hough, 2014: 217). During the 1980s 'the unit progressively lost a great deal of its autonomy', until '[by] the start of the 1990s, ministerial approval was required for all items in the annual research programme, and all publications were subject to ministerial scrutiny'[1]. In 2014, he writes:

> There is now much tighter political control on the commissioning and publishing of policy research, leaving much less autonomy and 'voice' to the researchers involved. Especially since the late 1990s, working on government research reports has typically involved a prolonged tussle over questions of

tone and language between researcher and commissioner – the latter keeping
a close eye over their shoulder for signs of a ministerial frown.

(Hough, 2014: 217–8)

In the latter part of this chapter I give two accounts of my own experience of doing
government-funded research in Scotland, as Walters did. For now, here are briefer
reflections on my experience of working on two pieces of Home Office-funded
research, one in the late 1980s, the other in the early 2000s. The first, on which I
worked with my then colleague Harry Blagg, was on social crime prevention projects
for young people. Our main contacts in the Home Office were Tim Hope and Mike
Hough, who were invariably supportive and collegial. After we had submitted our
report, however, we learned that a Home Office minister had taken a belated and not
entirely welcome interest in the research and was not happy with it: we had, apparently,
failed to answer the questions we were supposed to answer. We complained to the
effect that the goalposts had been moved at a late stage of our work, an argument that
was accepted at least in part by a senior member of the Home Office research staff; but
it was clear that the Home Office would not publish the report. Some material from
it appeared in Blagg and Smith (1989), so it was not suppressed. All the same, the
experience was not free of conflict resulting from political pressure.

The second project, led by Ali Wardak at the University of Glamorgan and
published as Calverley et al. (2004), was on Black and Asian men's experiences of
probation and criminal justice. Two particular issues of interest were whether there
was support from the interviewees for the provision of separate probation programmes
for ethnic minority offenders (there was not), and whether there was evidence of
discrimination in criminal justice decision-making (there was, in ways that arguably
worked to the detriment of minority ethnic offenders) (Calverley et al., 2004; Raynor
and Lewis, 2011). The topic was clearly politically sensitive, but as I recall the sources
of tension at the publication stage mainly concerned the number of authors of the
report (nine was said to be too many) and a discussion of the problems some probation
areas seemed to have in identifying which offenders on their caseloads were Black or
Asian (this eventually appeared as an appendix to the report).

Neither experience, then, was entirely problem-free – but as suggested above,
freedom from problems is not a sensible expectation of any research or publication
process. Both experiences are broadly in line with what one would expect from the
accounts of Hope and Hough. But they are not, in my view, in line with the apparent
argument of Walters that research on topics that interest the government by definition
grants legitimacy to the criminalisation and marginalisation of poor and vulnerable
people. The 'social' crime prevention which was the focus of the first project was
seen by Harry Blagg and myself, and by Hope and Hough, as a politically progressive
and optimistic alternative to purely 'situational', exclusionary approaches (see also
Hope and Shaw, 1988). The possibility of discriminatory disadvantage on the basis of
ethnicity was an important focus of the second project. In both cases, then, the
research had more potential to contribute to egalitarian and inclusive policy and
practice than to legitimate oppression. In conducting the research my colleagues and

I were perhaps 'embedded', though temporarily – but it does not follow, because the research inevitably had policy implications, that we were inevitably corrupted.

Now for some more extended autobiographical reflection and, I hope, reflexive self-criticism. Like many academics in the field, I have undertaken evaluative research on projects and programmes that had some experimental or innovative aspect which led someone – the agency responsible for the project or the government department that funded it – to be interested in its evaluation. In the published work that resulted from some of these evaluations, the project is discussed without any attempt at disguise. There is nothing exceptional about my work in this regard, as readers familiar with the literature on programme evaluation will know[2]. But, looking back, I wonder if I should have taken more care about identifying some of those involved, project and agency staff as well as those on the receiving end of the project's work – offenders and, sometimes, victims.

Example 1

This is the evaluation colleagues and I undertook of a pioneering victim-offender mediation scheme (Smith et al. 1988). This was funded by the local probation service, whose managers were proud of the project and keen that it should be publicised. The title of the main publication that emerged from this gave its location as 'South Yorkshire'; and the text was more specific about where it operated, from two named probation offices. It was also made clear that the project was small in scale, being essentially run by two probation officers and their senior, who was named as the author of two of the sources cited. The only pseudonyms used in the article were for a mining village and an estate in Rotherham, but anyone who knew the area – and certainly anyone who knew of the project's work – would have had little difficulty in working out their true identities. It is doubtful that any further efforts at disguise would have been effective ('an innovative mediation project run by the probation service in a mining area – at the time becoming an ex-mining area – in the north of England' would have been clumsy, and several references that independently identified South Yorkshire would have had to be removed). Even so, on re-reading the paper I felt uneasy about the amount of detail in the accounts given of some of the cases the project worked with, especially those in the pseudonymous mining village. More troublingly, I was reminded of a worry I felt at the time – that because the project was so small it would have been easy for an informed reader to identify individual workers. The paper discussed the different outcomes of offers of mediation between the two probation offices, but only very cautiously hinted at what for me was a crucial factor in making for success or failure – 'differences in the styles of two officers involved' (Smith et al. 1988: 380). What this cryptic formulation meant was hinted at by the reference that followed to Truax and Carkhuff (1967), but the idea that the qualities of the individual worker were a crucial differentiating factor was not spelled out. We hoped that by avoiding saying this explicitly we would avoid hurting the feelings of one of the workers, or at least reduce the hurt. We may not even have managed this, but we certainly reduced the scope and depth of the analysis by our evasion. I am still unsure if we got right the balance between telling the truth as we saw it and avoiding possible hurt to one of the people involved (in this case, someone whose helpfulness and openness had made the research possible).

Example 2

Another evaluation from around the same time, also on a project that sought to bring victims and offenders together, was reported in Smith and Blagg (1989). The Cumbrian project was one of four funded by the Home Office on a trial basis; all were discussed in the overall evaluation by Marshall and Merry (1990). The Home Office also commissioned the evaluation, so as researchers we were treated with slightly more reserve than had been the case in South Yorkshire, and our account of the project had to be approved by Home Office staff before publication; it was also read by a senior manager in Cumbria probation service before being submitted to the Home Office. (He drew our attention to a detail about the location of one of the offences we discussed which could have led to the identification of the victim, and we removed it.) At the time, victim-offender 'reparation' – what came to be called restorative justice – was still a novelty in Britain, and was attracting the attention of researchers. While recognising the difficulties identified by others in using reparation in the service of diversion (Davis et al. 1988), we tried to defend the practitioners in Cumbria against what we called the 'lofty didactic tone' and 'grandly dismissive' language of Davis and his colleagues, who we felt underestimated the sensitivity and capacity for self-criticism of reparation workers (Smith and Blagg, 1989: 273–4). So we were concerned to treat the workers with respect and to avoid the condescension sometimes displayed by researchers towards social workers in the criminal justice system, as when they explain that while the workers may think they are being helpful they are really only part of the social control system (and that it takes a properly sceptical researcher to point this out): that is, to avoid the unhelpful, patronising kind of research criticised long ago by Stanley Cohen (1975). I think we were right about this, but on re-reading the paper I found at least one passage that could well have been unhelpful in a different way. The main stated aim of the project was diversion from prosecution: the police brought cases to a multi-agency panel which considered the feasibility of reparation as an alternative to prosecution. As in the South Yorkshire evaluation, the area in which the project worked was stated openly (as was also true of the four areas discussed by Marshall and Merry (1990)), and enough detail was given about the four divisions of the county to make it possible for anyone with basic geographical knowledge to identify individual towns, and for someone with some inside knowledge of the project to identify individual workers. Thus, we said (p. 261):

> The probation staff tended on the whole to a sceptical view of the motives of the police, alleging that cases were often brought to the panels for discussion for the sake of 'window-dressing', and that time was wasted in

symbolic argument over cases which were obvious candidates for cautions. In South division in particular, the reparation worker felt that the police had 'been keeping the cautioning rate artificially high by formalizing what used to be dealt with informally on the street', especially in petty criminal damage cases…where the police felt under local pressure to be seen to be doing something.

No-one complained about this passage, either before or after publication, but the views attributed to the probation staff amount to quite a sharp criticism of the motives and practices of the police. By the time the paper was published the project had come to the end of its two years of funding, but even so we had given a glimpse of probation staff attitudes that the local police might understandably take exception to; certainly the passage was unlikely to promote the good inter-agency relations on which the success of the project – and of any subsequent projects aiming to divert juveniles from prosecution – depended.

Example 3

In 1995, I began a five-year evaluation of the Freagarrach Project, which was set up to work with the most persistent juvenile offenders in what was then Central Region in Scotland (Lobley at el., 2001; Lobley and Smith, 2007). The Scottish Office, as it then was, had invested substantial resources and hopes in the project, and the officials involved believed strongly in the importance of having it evaluated. The evaluation was to have both quantitative and qualitative dimensions, concerned respectively with its effects on known reoffending and the experiences the young people, their families, the project workers and staff in other agencies had of the project. As with the mediation projects discussed above, the project and its location were (inevitably in this case) explicitly identified.

For the civil servants associated with the project, an important element of the quantitative evaluation was that it should allow for the medium-term outcomes from Freagarrach to be compared with those for young offenders receiving some other form of intervention. Early on, the model proposed was for a control group matched with the Freagarrach group on as many variables as possible, not only on offending history. The ideal was the approach of Sheldon and Eleanor Glueck (1950), who matched 500 known delinquents with 500 young people with similar characteristics who were not known to have offended. But the Gluecks' research entailed a level of intrusion into the lives of the young people in both groups (but most pertinently for ethical considerations in the control group) that could not possibly be allowed given the concern with the protection of research subjects that has developed since the 1940s. In their re-working of the Gluecks' findings, Sampson and Laub (1993) noted (p. 24) 'the unique substantive properties of the Gluecks' data', and remarked (p. 29) that the 'level of detail and the range of information sources in the Glueck study will likely never be repeated, given contemporary research standards on the protection of human subjects'. The

Freagarrach research, while more generously funded than most such evaluations, could not have come near the Gluecks' range and depth of data even if there had been no ethical problems associated with rights to privacy, confidentiality and freedom from disruption, but the ethical (rather than practical) impossibility of getting an exactly matched control group was the most important reason why the aspiration to repeat the Gluecks' approach never got off the ground. Some of the ethical issues that arose from the long-term nature of the research, which allowed for a five-year follow-up of some of the young people, and from the identification of a comparison group, much more roughly matched than had been originally envisaged, will be described below.

A different set of worries about how to present the findings of research in an ethically responsible and respectful way arose when, as a result of having been given the contract to research Freagarrach, I was asked to undertake the evaluation of another Scottish project aimed at reducing persistent juvenile offending. This was the CueTen project in Fife, run by Apex Scotland, a charity committed to the provision of training and employment opportunities for offenders, and informed by the belief that productive participation in the labour market should be protective against continued offending. Scottish Office officials had been sufficiently impressed by the presentation by Apex Scotland to find further funding for CueTen (all the funding originally earmarked having been committed to Freagarrach). CueTen was funded for three years (compared with five for Freagarrach) and the evaluation period was correspondingly shorter. Our report was published in 1999 (Lobley and Smith, 1999) and subsequently adapted along with the Freagarrach evaluation for publication in Lobley and Smith (2007). The appearance of the two evaluations in the same book made comparisons between the projects inevitable, though no doubt some readers had been comparing them since the publication of the Freagarrach report in 2001.

Very briefly, neither project produced dramatically impressive results in terms of known reoffending, though Freagarrach could make the more convincing claims to have had a positive effect (and there was no doubt that on the whole the young people it worked were more persistent and serious offenders). Both in the 2001 report and in the 2007 book, we presented Freagarrach as a successful project overall: its methods of working with the young people were in line with what research suggested ought to be effective in reducing the reoffending risk, and – crucially and unusually for a specialist project – it had been from its outset well integrated with mainstream services in social work, education, and the police. This integration, designed into the planning of the project, was never quite as complete as had been envisaged, and it frayed at the edges as local government reorganisation replaced a single authority – Central Region – with three smaller authorities. We duly reported this, along with an analysis that was as complete and rigorous as we could make it of the before-and-after offending histories of the young people who attended the project. While (I hope) we did not obscure or minimise the problems and limitations that we found, readers of our work would have been in no doubt that we approved of Freagarrach's design and ways of working, and liked and respected the staff involved.

Our account of CueTen was considerably less positive. Contrary to what practitioners whose work is subject to evaluation may sometimes (and sometimes with reason) think, evaluators who are not *a priori* ideologically hostile to social work and related welfare activities would much rather report success than failure, and our dutiful reporting of the difficulties CueTen encountered left us uncomfortable throughout the evaluation. We tried to maintain a distinction between criticism of the model on which CueTen operated and criticism of the staff who had to try to make the model work. In very brief summary, we concluded that the way of working on which the CueTen model was based was not practical as an approach with persistent juvenile offenders, many of whom had barely attended school for years: it was too school-like (or further education-like), too didactic and not participative enough. It did not help that in sharp contrast to Freagarrach CueTen was not well connected with the systems of relevant local agencies and therefore struggled to gain acceptance – and, at the level of immediate practice, to maintain an adequate flow of referrals of young people in the intended target group. The report made all of this clear, while also trying to convey that the project staff worked hard and conscientiously in circumstances that were consistently difficult. My impression was that the staff who worked directly with the young people accepted our account as fair and accurate: they knew better than anyone how fraught everyday life in CueTen often was. The then Director of Apex Scotland, Jeane Freeman, later a prominent figure in Scottish public and political life, did not accept it, and stated this publicly, saying that we had not sufficiently recognised how the project had developed and been adapted over time. The willingness of the staff to try new ways of working and their readiness to learn from experience were actually prominent themes of the report, but its overall message was inevitably a negative one that was bound to produce some sense of hurt and disappointment.

In this sense it is impossible to claim that the research could not have caused distress to anyone who participated in it, raising the question of whether evaluative research that produces negative findings can ever fully satisfy the principle of non-maleficence or doing no harm, on which everyone concerned with research ethics ostensibly agrees (Macfarlane, 2009). In discussions of ethics in criminal justice research, the subjects seen as potentially vulnerable to harm are usually offenders (Fogel, 2007; Healy, 2009). The *Statement of Ethics* of the British Society of Criminology (2015), however, expresses the point in a way that allows for a wider application of the principle. Researchers should recognise:

> that they have a responsibility to minimise personal harm to research participants by ensuring that the potential physical, psychological, discomfort or stress to individuals participating in research is minimised by participation in the research [and]…[s]trive to protect the rights of those they study, their interests, sensitivities and privacy.
>
> *(British Society of Criminology, 2015: 5)*

The Code continues in a way that makes clear that the authors mainly had in mind the rights and interests of vulnerable research subjects, in this case people defined as offenders or otherwise deviant – those who are rightly the main focus of thinking about ethics in this field. If, however, the principle is to apply to every research participant (and it would be hard to find agreement on who it should not apply to), then it is bound to be broken to some degree by evaluative research that gives a truthful account of negative findings. We can say, plausibly enough, that some people are better able than others to withstand a threat to their sensitivities, but we should still recognise that the non-maleficence principle in its absolute form is impossible to achieve in this context.

Since part of the evaluation of both projects involved the collection and analysis of data on the young people's known offending during their time at CueTen or Freagarrach, and a comparison with groups of offenders as similar (in terms of offending) as we could find, we had access to the offending histories of over 200 young people from Fife and the central belt of Scotland. The records on the young people at CueTen and in the comparison groups were relatively unproblematic in ethical terms, since they included only offences that led to some official action – though they still required careful handling and storage, since they were not anonymous. They thus differed from the kind of data typically available to criminologists studying large data sets (such as that produced by the Police National Computer or the Home Office Offenders Index) to identify patterns of offending, which are anonymous or are made so before they reach the researcher. It should also be said that while the young people who attended the projects knew that we were interested in their criminal records, the young people in the comparison groups did not, so even if we were to claim – stretching a point – that the CueTen and Freagarrach groups gave us their informed consent this was certainly not the case for the comparison groups. The Freagarrach data were also problematic in that they came from an information system (TRACE) that was unique to Central Scotland Police and contained far more than a record of officially processed offending (i.e. offences that resulted in a sentence, some form of reprimand, or a formal decision from the Children's Hearings System). The Freagarrach staff had access to this system throughout the period of our evaluation, an unusual example of willingness on the part of the police to share sensitive data which led to some raised eyebrows and concerns about confidentiality in other police areas. As researchers we also had full access to TRACE data (in paper form), so that by the end of our work I had filing cabinets full of records that gave the names, ages and addresses of the young people who attended Freagarrach as well as details not only of adjudicated offences but of charges, which in many cases went no further and of which the young people may well have been innocent. I hope I handled and stored this material with appropriate care, but when I was moving to another office a couple of years after completing the research, and had to treat it as confidential waste, I was sharply reminded of just how sensitive it was.

I will conclude this section with two more examples from my own experience: one that again relates to evaluation research but raises a different issue (one that may well become more pressing for research on probation-type programmes and interventions); and one from more 'purely' criminological research, in that it was not primarily policy-focused, which returns the discussion to a fundamental question for criminological researchers at the start of the chapter.

Example 4

Again with my colleague David Lobley, who worked on both the Freagarrach and CueTen evaluations (Lobley and Smith, 1999), I evaluated (1998–2000) the pilot of the use of electronic monitoring (tagging) of offenders in Scotland[3]. In a summary of the evaluation for a mainly academic readership, I wrote (cautiously):

> The issue of costs proved to be a vexed one for the evaluation…because commercial confidentiality was invoked at a late stage of the evaluation process as a reason why a full account of the costs of the orders could not be given, and why no comparison should be made between the costs of the two contractors.
>
> *(Smith, 2001: 209)*

I went on to name the two companies which provided the tagging service and suggested that if the argument of commercial confidentiality were to be generally applied to research on community sentences delivered by commercial organisations it would be impossible for their costs to be available for public scrutiny. I also reported our estimates of the costs of orders involving tagging and argued that some fairly optimistic assumptions had to be made before it could be claimed that the tagging orders had produced any cost saving for the system. What I did not write, but do now, was that (for the first and still only time in my research experience) we were put under direct pressure to present our findings in a way that would present the tagging orders in a positive light. One form this persuasion took was a radical re-writing, without consultation, of parts of our report. Perhaps rather grandly, I said that if it were published in this revised form I would insist that my name be removed, and – though probably not as a direct result of this – a more senior civil servant decided that the report should be published as we wrote it. Another interesting intervention was a complaint by one of the pre-publication readers of the report that our estimate of the cost of a 6-month tagging order as £4860 gave a misleading impression of accuracy and that it would be better to 'round' it – but down to £4500, not up to £5000 as normal arithmetical rules would require. In the event, the unrounded figure survived in the published report.

Of course, it is embarrassing to report this, since it looks like an effort to present myself in a good light; but I am not claiming any special virtue, only the degree of integrity that ought to be and is generally assumed to be exercised by social researchers (Macfarlane, 2009). The more important issue is that with the growing role of the private sector in criminal justice, in custodial institutions and – in England and Wales since mid-2014 – in the community (Ministry of Justice, 2013a; 2013b), there is a risk that the kind of pressure I experienced in a small way in 2000 will become a normal feature of criminal justice research, in the name of protecting commercial interests. Independent researchers will resist such pressure, but publications resulting from their work are likely to be more muted in their criticism than they would have been without it, and some important findings on costs and benefits may never see daylight. And/or, independent researchers will become unwilling to do evaluative work in such circumstances. These are not inevitable results of privatisation, but they are certainly risks attendant on it.

Example 5

This comes from research on the perpetrators of racially motivated violence in Greater Manchester. The main findings have been given in various publications (e.g. Ray et al., 2003a; 2003b; Ray et al., 2004; Ray and Smith, 2004) and I will not repeat them here. The core element of the research was a series of interviews conducted by Liz Wastell, the research officer on the project. Most were tape-recorded, which meant that I had another body of sensitive material (fortunately anonymous) in my office that had to be carefully looked after and eventually disposed of. But the points I want to raise here concern the nature of the relationship between the researcher and the interview subjects. While they mostly had not been convicted at any stage of their lives of the most serious offences, their criminal records were certainly more serious than those of the CueTen or Freagarrach groups; and while their racist sentiments were not usually of an extreme ideological kind they were often worrying enough to make it difficult to feel much sympathetic rapport with the interviewees. In a general way, I am as susceptible as most people to the appeal of an ethic of love and care, as advocated by Denzin and Giardina (2007), but even if a way of operationalising this could be found in some research projects it is far from clear what it would mean for research with people who have committed acts of racially motivated violence. As Hammersley and Traianou (2014: section 3.8) suggest, one problem with Denzin and Giardina's 'alternative ethics' is whether the approach is meant to apply to *any* group of people (in which case, what would it mean to express care for and solidarity with racists?), or only to 'those groups with whom they [researchers] share a sense of ethical or political solidarity' – which would seriously restrict the scope of research undertaken on Denzin and Giardina's principles.

As we reported (Ray et al., 2003a), the subjects of this research had much in common with other offenders in contact with the probation service – more in common, in fact, than we had expected at the start of the research. With the possibility in mind that we would encounter serious violent offenders, we agreed at the outset that interviewees would be told that if they disclosed that they had committed serious offences that had not led to any official action, or that they intended to commit such an offence, we could not keep this information to ourselves. We – or the researcher, Liz Wastell – thus offered them 'limited confidentiality', meaning, as Healy (2009: 173) puts it, 'that confidentiality is honoured except in situations where actual or intended harm to self or others is disclosed'. As Healy noted, both the British Society of Criminology (2015) Statement of Ethics and the American Sociological Association (1999) Code of Ethics suggest that considerations of confidentiality can be over-ridden by legal obligations, and that (as in the present example), participants should be 'fully and clearly informed about the limitations that apply to confidentiality before they take part in the research' (Healy, 2009: 174).

But, as argued above, there is surely a moral as well as a legal obligation here. It is difficult to see why criminal justice researchers should be exempt from the moral requirements that apply to everyone else – and which the researchers would surely regard themselves as being subject to in their everyday, non-professional lives. Palys and Lowman (2001) argue for strict confidentiality on three grounds: non-maleficence – research subjects should not be exposed to penalties as a result of what they tell the researcher; honesty – the scope of the research will be restricted if some topics are declared out of bounds; and safety – researchers may be vulnerable to reprisals if their disclosure of an offence leads to the arrest of the offender. Of these three arguments, the second seems the strongest: if we offer only limited confidentiality we have to accept that there are some questions (which might produce interesting answers) that we cannot ask. As to the first argument, while strict confidentiality may help to ensure that the research does no harm to its subjects, I argued above that it may entail a risk of harm to others; and if someone is arrested for an offence disclosed to a researcher, the latter's safety may well be compromised even if strict confidentiality has been guaranteed, since the person arrested – or their associates – may not believe the guarantee.

Summary

After a brief statement of position in favour of a virtue-based approach to thinking about research ethics, the chapter considered the issue of confidentiality as a particular problem in criminological research. It also considered arguments about the ethics of policy-oriented research in a field where recent policy in Britain has tended to become harsher and more punitive. Questions of confidentiality were then considered in terms of the possible negative impact of published research on practitioners or on efforts by public agencies to work in productive co-operation with other parts of the criminal justice system. An example was given of the worries that can arise when researchers have perhaps too much data on individuals who cannot honestly be said to have given their informed consent. Another example illustrated the pressures to which researchers may be subject when commercial interests are involved, as they increasingly are in criminal justice. Finally, the chapter considered some ethical issues arising from research with people of whom one disapproves, and returned to the question of complete or partial confidentiality as it arose in an actual research project.

Until recently, research on social work in criminal justice was generally understood to include research on probation. One of the most distinguished and influential researchers in this field over the past 30 years or so is Peter Raynor, who in a recent article (Raynor, 2014) uses the image of the Ship of Fools to describe developments in probation policy in England and Wales in the twenty-first century. He argues that in the current climate the kind of research on effective practice that the government used to be interested in has become almost impossible. His 'solution has been to move much of my research (though not myself) offshore': specifically, to the island of Jersey where, perhaps counter-intuitively, 'probation is a public service for the benefit of the community', free from political interference and committed to using research evidence to improve its practice (Raynor, 2014: 304). We can't all move our research to Jersey – though Scotland might be a possible alternative – but we can all continue to argue that research on social work in criminal justice is worthwhile and worth doing with integrity.

Review questions

1. What are the arguments against offering only limited confidentiality in criminological research?
2. How can evaluation researchers find a balance between the accurate reporting of negative results and the avoidance of distress to practitioners?
3. Does doing research for government departments compromise academic integrity?

Guide to further reading

Hammersley, M. and Traianou, A. (2012) *Ethics in Qualitative Research*. London: Sage. Is comprehensive and authoritative.

Macfarlane, B. (2008) *Researching with Integrity*. London: Routledge. Is particularly relevant to the arguments in this chapter because of its case for 'virtue ethics' in academic research.

The British Society of Criminology Statement of Ethics (2015) (http://www.britsoccrim. org/new/docs/BSCEthics2015.pdf) is the most relevant of the various codes on offer.

You could also try, in addition to some of the work listed above:

Buckland, G. and Wincup, E. (2004) Researching Crime and Criminal Justice in J. Muncie and D. Wilson (eds.), *Student Handbook of Criminal Justice and Criminology*. Abingdon: Cavendish, which is helpfully student-friendly.

Davies, P., Francis, P. and Jupp, V. (2011) *Doing Criminological Research* (2nd edition). London: Sage, which has a useful chapter on 'ethics and politics'.

Notes

1   Note that in Hough's account political interference began well before the first 'New' Labour government was elected in 1997.

2 The same applies to much research on prisons, including classic (and critical) work such as that of Mathiesen (1965), King and Elliott (1977) and Sparks et al. (1996). Some academics – including the examiners of a recent Lancaster PhD thesis – believe that in research on prisons the prisons should appear pseudonymously. It is not clear that this would deceive the informed reader.

3 Electronic monitoring might count as an example of the oppressive trend in criminal justice policy complained of by Reece Walters, and I did not hope as strongly as I did for Freagarrach and CueTen that we would be able to report positive results. In the event, electronic monitoring was extended in Scotland although our report (Lobley and Smith, 2000) hardly judged the pilots to have been resoundingly successful.

References

American Sociological Association (1999). 'Code of Ethics and Policies and Procedures of the ASA Committee on Professional Ethics', at http://www.asanet.org/sites/default/files/savvy/images/asa/docs/pdf/CodeofEthics.pdf.

Blagg, H. and Smith, D. (1989). *Crime, Penal Policy and Social Work*, Harlow: Longman.

British Society of Criminology (2015). 'British Society of Criminology Statement of Ethics 2015', at http://www.britsoccrim.org/documents/BSCEthics2015.pdf.

Calverley, A., Cole, B., Kaur, G., Lewis, S., Raynor, P., Sadeghi, S., Smith, D., Vanstone, M. and Wardak, A. (2004). *Black and Asian Offenders on Probation* (Home Office Research Study 277), London: Home Office.

Clark, J.J. and Walker, R. (2011). 'Research Ethics in Victimization Studies: Widening the Lens', *Violence Against Women*, 17, 12, pp. 1489–1508.

Cohen, S. (1975). 'It's All Right for You to Talk: Political and Sociological Manifestos for Social Work Action', in Bailey, R. and Brake, M. (eds.), *Radical Social Work*, London: Edward Arnold.

Davis, G., Boucherat, J. and Watson, D. (1988) 'Reparation in the Service of Diversion: The Subordination of a Good Idea', *Howard Journal of Criminal Justice*, 27, 2, pp. 127–34.

Denzin, N.K. and Giardina, M.D. (eds.) (2007). *Ethical Futures in Qualitative Research: Decolonizing the Politics of Knowledge*, Walnut Creek, CA: Left Coast Press.

Fogel, C. (2007). 'Ethical Issues in Field–based Criminological Research in Canada', *International Journal of Criminal Justice Sciences*, 2, 2, pp. 109–18.

Glueck, S. and Glueck, E. (1950). *Unravelling Juvenile Delinquency*, New York: The Commonwealth Fund.

Hammersley, M. and Traianou, A. (2014). 'An Alternative Ethics? Justice and Care as Guiding Principles for Qualitative Research', *Sociological Research Online*, 19, 3, p. 24.

Healy, D. (2009). 'Ethics and Criminological Research: Charting a Way Forward', *Irish Probation Journal*, 6, pp. 171–81.

Hope, T. and Shaw, M. (eds.) (1988). *Communities and Crime Reduction*, London: HMSO.

Hope, T. and Walters, R. (2008). *Critical Thinking about the Uses of Research*, London, Centre for Crime and Justice Studies.

Hough, M. (2014). 'Confessions of a Recovering "Administrative Criminologist": Jock Young, Quantitative Research and Policy Research', *Crime Media Culture*, 10, 3, pp. 215–26.

King, R.D. and Elliot, K.W. (1977.) *Albany: Birth of a Prison, End of an Era*, London: Routledge and Kegan Paul.

Lobley, D. and Smith, D. (1999). *Working with Persistent Juvenile Offenders: An Evaluation of the Apex CueTen Project*, Edinburgh: The Scottish Office.

Lobley, D. and Smith, D. (2000). *Evaluation of Electronically Monitored Restriction of Liberty Orders*. Edinburgh: Scottish Executive.

Lobley, D. and Smith, D. (2007). *Persistent Young Offenders: An Evaluation of Two Projects*, Aldershot: Ashgate.

Lobley, D., Smith, D. and Stern, C. (2001). *Freagarrach: An Evaluation of a Project for Persistent Juvenile Offenders*, Edinburgh: Scottish Executive.

Macfarlane, B. (2009). *Researching with Integrity: the Ethics of Academic Enquiry*, New York and London: Routledge.

MacIntyre, A. (1985). *After Virtue: A Study in Moral Theory*, London: Duckworth.

Marshall, T.F. and Merry, S. (1990). *Crime and Accountability*, London: HMSO.

Mathiesen, T. (1965). *The Defences of the Weak: A Sociological Study of a Norwegian Correctional Institution*, London: Tavistock.

Ministry of Justice (2013a). *Transforming Rehabilitation: A Revolution in the Way We Manage Offenders* (Consultation Paper CP1/2013), London: Ministry of Justice.

Ministry of Justice (2013b). *Transforming Rehabilitation: A Strategy for Reform* (Cm 8619), London: TSO.

O'Connell, M. and Whelan, A. (1996). 'Taking Wrongs Seriously: Public Perceptions of Crime Seriousness', *British Journal of Criminology*, 36, 2, pp. 299–318.

Palys, T. and Lowman, J. (2001). 'Social Research with Eyes Wide Shut: The Limited Confidentiality Dilemma', *Canadian Journal of Criminology*, 43, 2, pp. 255–67.

Ray, L. and Smith, D. (2004) 'Racist Offending, Policing and Community Conflict', *Sociology*, 38, 4, pp. 681–99.

Ray, L., Smith, D. and Wastell, L. (2003a). 'Racist Violence from a Probation Service Perspective: Now you See it, Now you Don't', in Lee, R.M. and Stanko, E.A. (eds.) *Researching Violence: Essays on Methodology and Measurement*, London and New York: Routledge.

Ray, L., Smith, D. and Wastell, L. (2003b). 'Understanding Racist Violence', in Stanko, E.A. (ed.) *The Meanings of Violence*, London and New York: Routledge.

Ray, L., Smith, D. and Wastell, L. (2004). 'Shame, Rage and Racist Violence', *British Journal of Criminology*, 44, 3, pp. 350–68.

Raynor, P. (2014). 'Consent to Probation in England and Wales: How it was Abolished, and Why it Matters', *European Journal of Probation*, 6, 3, pp. 296–307.

Raynor, P. and Lewis, S. (2011). 'Risk–need Assessment, Sentencing and Minority Ethnic Offenders in Britain', *British Journal of Social Work*, 41, 7, pp. 1357–71.

Renzetti, C.M. and Lee, R.M. (eds.) (1993). *Researching Sensitive Topics*, Newbury Park, CA, London and New Delhi: Sage.

Sampson, R.J. and Laub, J.H. (1993). *Crime in the Making: Pathways and Turning Points through Life*, Cambridge, Mass and London: Harvard University Press.

Smith, D. (2001). 'Electronic Monitoring of Offenders: The Scottish Experience', *Criminal Justice*, 1, 2, pp. 201–14.

Smith, D. and Blagg, H. (1989). 'The Cumbrian reparation scheme', *British Journal of Social Work*, 19, 3, pp. 255–75.

Smith, D., Derricourt, N. and Blagg, H. (1988). 'Mediation in South Yorkshire', *British Journal of Criminology*, 28, 3, pp. 378–95.

Sparks, R., Bottoms, A.E and Hay, W. (1996). *Prisons and the Problem of Order*, Oxford: Clarendon Press.

Truax, C.B. and Carkhuff, R.R. (1967). *Towards Effective Counseling and Psychotherapy*, Chicago: Aldine.

Young, J. (1986). 'The Failure of Criminology: The Need for a Radical Realism', in Matthews, R. and Young, J. (eds.) *Confronting Crime*, London: Sage.

PART II

Foregrounding sensitive issues
Politics, ethics and dilemmas

Introduction to Part II

The second part of this book considers 'sensitive issues'. Although the chapters variously describe the sensitivity of the matters they address, it is helpful to start with a broad definition of what is under consideration in the part; Lee (1993) is a much-cited source in this area; he suggests that 'sensitive topics present problems because research into them involves potential costs to those involved in the research, including, on occasion, the researcher' (Lee, 1993: 4). The chapters in this section considers – sex offenders, child victims of sexual assault, war crimes and environmental issues. Malcolm Cowburn highlights the need for respecting the dignity of sex offender research participants in construing, designing, implementing and reporting research. He explores issues relating to managing confidentiality whilst ensuring that no harm comes from the research. Additionally he considers ethical issues related to the dissemination of research findings. Simon Hackett notes that research on the impact of sexual abuse on children has in the past been confined to retrospective studies with adult survivors. He argues strongly that well-managed research can be conducted with children who have been affected by sexual abuse if ethically and developmentally sensitive methodologies are adopted. As part of this, consideration of the identities (gender, ethnicity and so on) and power of researchers is of fundamental importance. Issues of informed consent, confidentiality, the safety and protection of research participants, and managing distress and disclosures are explored. Kirsten Campbell identifies three key sets of ethical challenges in researching war crimes. The first is epistemological and concerns how the researcher defines and theorises the nature of war crimes. The second set of ethical challenges relate to the context of conflict, which inevitably situates the researcher in a violent and politicized research field. The third challenge which is intrinsic to research quality and integrity and concerns the choice of methodology and methods. In considering 'green criminology' Avi Brisman and Nigel South note the extensive range of issues under consideration, and the diversity of methods used ranging from analysis of epidemiological and large data sets to localised anthropological and visual analysis. The sensitive nature of green criminological research lies in the delicate negotiations for gaining (and sustaining) research access to data sources that are often protected by gatekeepers, and possibly central to political and/or cultural conflicts, and power imbalances. Ethical and political issues may arise where research is critical of state and corporate systems and makes calls for more rigorous regulatory and legal interventions.

Reference

Lee, R. M. (1993). *Doing research on Sensitive Topics*. London: Sage.

7

RESEARCHING SEX CRIMES AND SEX OFFENDERS

Some ethical and epistemological considerations

Malcolm Cowburn

This chapter reflects issues involved in conducting research, with sex offenders, which is respectful of the dignity of research participants. It addresses epistemological tensions underpinning utilitarian motivations for research. It focuses on respectful interactions that recognise and support the dignity of offenders throughout the research process. One key area considered is the management of confidentiality. Dissemination raises issues related to: the involvement of research participants, the nature of forensic treatment, external influences of publication and the (written) representation of acts of sex harm.

Key points

1. Epistemological assumptions shape the nature and focus of research on sex offenders.
2. Forensic research focuses on the convicted population of offenders.
3. Epistemological standpoints affect how researchers behave in the collection of qualitative data (e.g. how distress is managed).
4. Confidentiality is a problematic concept that needs clear delineation. Researchers have a duty to report harmful unreported acts or intentions expressed by research participants.
5. Researching sex crimes and sex offenders has the potential to create distress for researchers and research teams.
6. Dissemination of research findings may be problematic, particularly in contract research, where funders may have a policy-driven agenda, or anticipate using research findings to secure further funding.
7. Disseminating graphic accounts of sex crimes may cause further distress to victims without further developing knowledge of sex crimes.

Key definitions

Epistemic: Relating to particular ways that knowledge constructed.
Epistemology: The study of how knowledge is achieved. An epistemological inquiry scrutinises assumptions behind research questions, and their associated methodologies.

Introduction

> In the forensic and correctional arena there is the added complication of a strong ethical overlay, that is, offenders have frequently inflicted serious harm on members of the community and are being punished as well as researched or treated. In light of what is at stake for both offenders and the wider community, it is incumbent upon researchers and practitioners to examine their ethical and epistemic assumptions about offenders and their problems carefully.
>
> *(Ward and Willis 2013: 109)*

The dominant academic discipline researching sex offenders and their crimes is undoubtedly forensic psychology; it focuses on convicted populations and is motivated by utilitarian objectives to identify and improve how 'society' responds to sex offenders. Implicit in this approach is a polarised population: the small group of offenders and the wider society of non-offending people:

> In the scientific study of anomalous behavior, the indispensible role of classification is well established. Understanding the taxonomic structure of a deviant population is the keystone of theory building and the cornerstone of intervention. It provides a pivotal understanding for research on a population and is an essential prerequisite for determining the optimum response of society to deviance.
>
> *(Knight and Prentky 1990: 23)*

Ignoring, for the moment, the tautological tendency of 'scientific study' providing a 'pivotal understanding for research'; in the above quotation the components of psychological study of sexual violence are indicated; they are:

1. a clearly defined 'deviant' population;
2. a key research aim – to understand 'the taxonomic structure' of the problematic population; and
3. a clear methodological approach – 'the scientific study'.

However, there are problems with this if the 'optimum response of society' is to be enhanced:

1. Most sex offenders are unconvicted and are not, therefore, part of a clearly identified ('deviant') population (see for example Percy and Mayhew 1997, who estimate that there are 15 times more unreported sex offenders than reported ones, the bulk of sex offenders have not been brought to public notice and their offences remain unacknowledged in the private domain).
2. Studies of the prevalence of people experiencing sexually harmful behaviours (see Pereda et al. 2009) and self-report studies of men's 'proclivity' to rape and acceptance of 'rape myths' (Malamuth 1981, Bohner et al. 2010) suggest that sex crimes may not be 'anomalous' behaviours.
3. Feminist research and theory is either ignored or marginalised (for example Purvis and Ward (2006) comment that feminist perspectives and research in relation to sex crime have little or no 'clinical utility').

Both the focus of study and what is ignored constitute an epistemological issue, but are also political and an ethical matters. The concerns are how a research question is formulated, what literature informs the research question and what sort of research attracts funding. It could be argued, for example, that whilst psychological research projects develop knowledge in relation to people convicted of sex offences, this knowledge does not address the social problem of sex crimes or community safety.

The epistemological tensions in construing research on/with sex offenders point to the different challenges from the main ethical standpoints: utilitarianism is concerned with the well-being of the majority – 'the greater good of the greatest number'; whereas Kantian ethics is less concerned with outcomes and more focused upon the processes (means) whereby outcomes are achieved. A utilitarian perspective would require rigorous consideration of the wider benefits of research. It may question the predominant focus on convicted offenders to the exclusion of wider social issues. A Kantian perspective requires that research be conducted respectfully and without causing harm. This chapter reflects issues involved in conducting research, with sex offenders, which is respectful of the dignity of research participants. It addresses epistemological tensions underpinning utilitarian motivations for research. It focuses on respectful interactions throughout the research process that recognise and support the dignity of participants. Finally it considers matters concerned with dissemination of findings.

Developing research projects: ethical implications of knowledge

Two issues are focussed on in this section: First, the epistemological issues of 'framing' or defining a research topic and how this relates to Utilitarian motivations to understand sexual violence; Second, the imperative to develop 'new knowledge' in the context of ensuring that research 'does no harm'; central to this is how confidentiality is defined and managed.

Epistemology, epistemic values and forms of knowledge

Theories developed to understand or explain sexual offending are not merely heuristic devices; they also imply ways of reducing sex offending. Psychological theorising concentrates on the individual offender and seeks to identify (more) effective therapeutic approaches to reduce the risks posed by individual offenders. The ultimate objective of psychological theory is to improve the clinical response to sex offenders. Evidence for an improved clinical response is complex, but much attention is focused on re-conviction rates. Sociological (including social anthropological) theories consider sex offending as a social phenomenon. Sociological theory locates sex offending as a social problem that may require a social/public policy response.

Apart from disciplinary preferences, 'epistemic values' (Fricker 2007; Robertson 2013) are of fundamental importance in construing research on sex offenders and sex crimes. Highlighting epistemic values draws attention to the socially constructed nature of knowledge. Societies and communities variously influence and shape what is deemed to be relevant to the development of knowledge at any particular time, in any particular area, and how the constellation of relevant factors are subsequently interpreted to produce a body of knowledge. The body of knowledge ('discourse' – Foucault 1984), is not only socially and culturally located, it is also historically fixed. Robertson (2013: 302) has more recently given a fuller summary of what is involved:

> philosophers of social science often grant that the social location of the researchers and their corresponding experiences may be relevant to the question that they choose, the way they frame the problems to be studied, and the theories they employ.

By giving detailed attention to cultural, social and chronological aspects of 'knowledge' and the operation of power Feminist, Post-Colonial and Queer theorists have indicated that much natural and social scientific knowledge, whilst adopting methodologies predicated on 'objectivity', emanates from a socially dominant group (white, middle-class, able-bodied, heterosexual men) and as such represents the viewpoint of this group (see for example Harding 2006; Fricker 2007; Said 1978; and Rich 1980). When the power to define who is, and who is not, a sex offender is considered, and what characteristics of the sex offender are relevant in policy, sentencing and treatment terms, in the 'Western'[1] world the academic discipline that is most influential is forensic psychology. As Robertson (2013: 302) observes:

> The knowledge generated largely by dominant groups may be biased in the sense of giving an incomplete picture of the domain of study, one biased towards the interests and experiences of the dominant group.

The interests and experiences of forensic psychologists are located within a convicted population. However, the pervasive presence of sex crimes has been repeatedly highlighted by feminist commentators, who recognize that sex crimes are rarely reported and those that are reported rarely result in a conviction. Kelly et al. (2005), for example, note that findings from the 2001 British Crime Survey indicated that by the age of 16, seven per cent of women had suffered at least one serious sexual assault; five per cent had been raped. They also found that of 3,527 crime reports of rape only 8 per cent resulted in a conviction. Similar patterns of attrition are noted in relation to all sex crime reports across Europe and beyond (Jehle 2012).

Feminist theory not only widens consideration of sex offences, it also challenges over-dependence on what is legally defined as a sex crime. Kelly (1988) presented qualitative data from sixty women who had experienced some type of sexual violation; from this material she developed a continuum of sexual violence that ranged from unwanted non-physical approaches (including sexualised verbal abuse) through to rape. Kelly's continuum continues to be a very influential framework for recognising and understanding the place of coercive sex within a wider range of personal relationships. Gavey (2005) uses it in her study of sexual coercion within Western cultures. Similarly, the work of Sanday (2003) is of central importance in theorising sexual offending in a social context. In her work spanning three decades she has drawn attention to the characteristics of 'rape free' and 'rape prone' societies and communities. Feminist research and theory point to both the social context and the gendered nature of sex crimes.

Thus in construing/designing a research project, it is important to recognize wider fields of knowledge, and the implications they have for the aims and objectives of particular research projects (Cowburn 2005a).

The epistemic framing of research on sexual violence is centrally linked to the Utilitarian motivations that underpin such research. Whilst 'clinically' focussed research with convicted populations of sex offenders is important in developing more effective penal responses and therapeutic programmes, it should not be conflated with wider utilitarian aspirations in relation to sexual violence and community safety. Research concerned with finding ways to develop safer communities is misinformed if it focuses solely on convicted populations of sex offenders, whose harmful actions may well be unrepresentative of the wider (unconvicted) population of people who sexually harm others, but are not dealt with by the criminal justice system.

Developing 'new' knowledge without harming others: the challenge of confidentiality

Research into sexual offending generally seeks to enhance community safety by developing knowledge about people convicted of harming others. A key part of this knowledge focuses on harmful behaviours, and what is not known about them (for example the extent of offending behaviour or intentions to commit further offences) may be of greatest interest to those developing strategies to improve the safety of the general public. In order to obtain such information, researchers generally guarantee research respondents some degree of confidentiality and anonymity (Cowburn 2005b). Traditionally, criminological research held sacrosanct the confidential nature of the relationship between the researcher and the researched (see for example Baldwin, 2000; Cowburn 2005b), and breaching such a trust was considered unethical. However, when researching sex offenders, the issue of undisclosed harmful behaviour is problematic. To know of unreported harms and to take no action may leave victim(s) at risk of further abuse. To know of a research participant's intentions to harm someone (or her/himself), and not to take action because of a confidentiality agreement, raises many issues. Potentially, the researcher can be seen as knowingly colluding with behaviours that are harmful to other people, and thus failing to protect members of the public.

The privileged nature of confidentiality in criminological research has been questioned by a number of researchers; for example research undertaken in prisons (King 2000), and some research undertaken with sex offenders (Cowburn 2005b) now recognizes there are constraints on the extent of confidentiality a researcher can offer.

The British Society of Criminology (BSC 2015: para 12) notes, in relation to breaking confidentiality that 'researchers should not breach the 'duty of confidentiality' and not pass on identifiable data to third parties without participants' consent'.

However, the issue of disclosure with the consent of the participant is problematic and may lead to situations of impasse or potential danger for the researcher; the Society adds this further guidance:

> Offers of confidentiality may sometimes be overridden by law: researchers should therefore consider the circumstances in which they might be required to divulge information to legal or other authorities, and make such circumstances clear to participants when seeking their informed consent.
>
> *(BSC 2015: para 12)*

The British Psychological Society (BPS) (2014: 22) states that 'the duty of confidentiality is not absolute in law and may in exceptional circumstances be overridden by more compelling duties such as the duty to protect individuals from harm'.

The exceptional circumstances are defined further (BPS 2009: 11):

> 3. (vi) Restrict breaches of confidentiality to those exceptional circumstances under which there appears sufficient evidence to raise serious concern about:
>   (a) the safety of clients;
>   (b) the safety of other persons who may be endangered by the client's behaviour; or
>   (c) the health, welfare or safety of children or vulnerable adults.

It could be argued that this approach to confidentiality prevents a full exploration of issues that may develop understanding. Some methodological choices offer a way of learning more, whilst not acquiring detailed knowledge that would require further action on the part of the researcher. Whilst qualitative methods invariably involve interviews, and thus personal contact with an identifiable person, large-scale surveys have the advantage of being anonymous. Abel et al.'s (1987) self-report study of 561 'non-incarcerated paraphiliacs' discovered much about sex offender behaviour that was previously unknown (Fisher 1994). The success of the study, in part, depended on the elaborate procedures that were in place to protect both confidentiality and anonymity. Additionally respondents were encouraged to reveal only general features of unreported offending; research documentation was elaborately coded and elaborate steps were taken to prevent criminal justice agencies accessing the data.

However, qualitative research with sex offenders has the potential to discover more nuanced detail about sex offenders' offending behaviour, how they make sense of it, and how it fits into their lives. Managing the potential for the disclosure of harmful intentions of unreported offences is of key importance. For example, King (2000) and Abel et al. (1987) suggest that researchers can explicitly discourage research participants, when talking about unreported offences or intentions to offend, from identifying specific details that would identify potential victims. Similarly researchers can remind research participants of the boundaries of confidentiality each time they interview them (Cowburn 2005b). Whilst these suggestions do not fully overcome the ethical dilemma outlined above, they do allow the researcher to show respect for the research participant, and also potentially to develop new areas of knowledge.

Doing research with convicted sex offenders: ethical issues throughout the research process

Whilst ethical considerations in developing a research project emphasise utilitarian and associated epistemological issues, managing the parameters of confidentiality highlights both the problems in developing 'new' knowledge and conducting research in a manner that is respectful to research participants. This section is concerned with ethical practice in the *conduct* of research, and as such is influenced by consideration of both Kantian and character-relationship ethics.

Two concepts are of central importance here: 'respect' and 'dignity'. Butler and Drake (2007) identify two distinct usages of the term; respect as consideration and respect as esteem. It is primarily the first usage that is of relevance to the conduct of research. Respect as consideration can be seen as the most basic form of respect, and is recognition that in a civil society we should treat one another in an honest, polite, courteous and considerate manner. Respect defined in this way need not be earned; it is an implicit entitlement in good/right human relationships. It recognises and responds to the basic 'dignity' of all human beings. 'Dignity' is a complex concept with a long and convoluted history (see Riley 2010 for a full exposition).

Dignity is central to Kantian ethics, but notions of dignity transcend Kantian ethics, and influence, amongst other things, the human rights discourse that developed after the Second World War (Riley 2010). For the purposes of this chapter, the following definition of dignity is adopted:

> Dignity denotes the equal and high value of all human beings … and functions as an anchor point for any subsequent ethical reasoning within research contexts.
>
> *(Ward and Willis 2013: 98)*

However, in accord with Kantian and character-relationship ethics, dignity is not conceived as an *outcome* of a process, it is achieved and sustained *through* a process; in this case, the process of research – in particular project design, data collection, data analysis and the dissemination of 'findings'.

Project design

Whilst the conceptual origins of a project may lie in researchers' engagement with research literature and, to some extent the empirical field, it is in the detailed designing of a project that involves a range of stakeholders/potential participants, that the ethical tenor of the endeavour is set. Ward and Willis (2013: 107) note that the active involvement of 'stakeholders … clearly reflects commitment to moral equality, fairness and impartiality'. Dependant on where the research is planned to occur, stakeholders may be sex offenders, victim-survivors of sex crimes, community leaders, women's groups, health service staff, police officers, social workers, probation officers and prison staff (of various grades). Dependant on the scale of the project, it may be necessary to convene a stakeholders advisory group which could inform the development of the design and the ongoing conduct of the project; generally advisory groups meet in the early stages of a project and then periodically until the project is complete. This enables stakeholder involvement in design *and* implementation of the project.

Key issues to be resolved in the design stage of a project are:

- from whom data is collected;
- how is collected; and
- how it is analysed.

Associated with these issues is the preparation of research instruments – these may be standardised questionnaires, interview schedules, focus group schedules, participant information sheets, consent forms and associated letters of introduction. Project documentation is usually developed in consultation with advisory groups.

Prior to commencing the research it is subject to ethical scrutiny – either from a University Ethics Committee or (increasingly in the UK) research ethics committee convened by the Health Research Authority (HRA) (http://www.nres.nhs.uk), which is responsible for monitoring research involving prisoners. It is interesting to note that HRA convened committees, in particular, are interested to know whether patients/service-users/carers have been involved in the development and delivery of research projects (the standardised application form specifically asks questions in relation to this), and in whose interests the research is developed (i.e. what are the risks and benefits to people participating in the research).

Linked to the issue of risks and benefits to research participants is the thorny matter of informed consent. Three issues are of particular importance:

1. Is there sufficient evidence that potential research participants have received sufficient information about the project to make an *informed* choice about their participation?
2. How do projects deal with people who lack the capacity (either through their young age or their mental incapacity) to consent?
3. Is it clear that participants are not coerced into participation?

Whilst all of the above questions are of importance to sex offender research, attention is focused on the final question. Ward and Willis (2013: 107) note:

> Issues related to informed consent and competency are to the forefront when prisoners are involved in research projects, and there is a heavy burden of proof on researchers to establish in forensic and correctional settings offenders were under no pressure to consent, and were, indeed psychologically competent to do so.

The participant information sheet is the key document where the boundaries of the research are outlined to potential participants, for example:

*   How confidentiality and disclosures of past, unreported harm or future intentions to harm self or others are managed is fundamental.
*   The benefits and harms of participation require careful expression – particularly, where the research is undertaken with prisoners or people on community licences, that participation in research is unrelated to and, does not affect any criminal justice process, e.g. parole.
*   Research in this area carries the potential to distress research participants, particularly qualitative in-depth interviews. Potential participants need to know this and how the project will help them if they become distressed.
*   All research participants need to know that they can end their involvement at any time without any detriment to themselves.

Ward and Willis (2013: 109) caution against presenting information and taking consent in a way that is based on 'Western' assumptions – particularly that consent is an individual's decision. Many African, Asian and Aboriginal communities emphasise the involvement of families and extended networks in the decision making of community member (see also Owusu-Bempah and Howitt 2000). Thus taking informed consent may require more time for some potential participants.

Data collection

Research with sex offenders has made use of the extensive repertoire of social research methods that are widely available – e.g. ethnographic, interview-based, focus groups and experimental research designs. Each of these approaches contains ethical considerations in relation to respecting participants and treating them fairly (i.e. showing respect for their dignity). Ward and Willis (2013: 105) highlight problems with the allocation of sex offenders to 'treatment' and 'non-treatment' groups in research adopting experimental designs:

> The problem with restricting research and treatment in these ways is that offenders can be denied legitimate access to treatment, access that they are ethically entitled to receive according to human rights declarations, and, more fundamentally their moral equality.

In qualitative research a range of issues arise in conducting research including:

- the location of the research interview/focus group;
- recording of the data;
- managing potential disclosures;
- managing distress; and
- caring for the research team.

Qualitative research with sex offenders involves many 'sensitive' issues (Lee 1993; Cowburn 2005(b)); the place where data collection occurs needs to be private and anonymous, but it also needs to ensure that researchers are not left in isolated and vulnerable situations. Most commonly research takes place in Criminal Justice agency settings (e.g. prison or probation offices) where privacy, anonymity and researcher safety can be assured; it is inadvisable for research to take place in the homes of offenders.

The participant information sheet should tell participants how the data collection is recorded, and that they can refuse to be electronically recorded. Generally, this is unproblematic, except in focus groups where if one group member does not wish to be recorded, the proceedings of the group will be manually recorded.

Issues relating to managing disclosures have been addressed above, but there is one setting where it is not possible to guarantee any level of confidentiality; this is the focus group. The researcher cannot guarantee that other group members will not discuss what was said in the group; it is therefore advisable to warn group members to be aware there is no guarantee of confidentiality outside of the group.

Researching sensitive issues carries the likelihood that research participants may become distressed as they speak about their personal histories, including the harmful acts that they have experienced or perpetrated; how the researcher responds to this distress is both an ethical, an epistemological and a methodological matter. The key issue concerns the nature of the scientific endeavour. Researchers who favour a methodology that gives a central position to objectivity, with the researcher being little involved with the research participant, except to facilitate the extraction of information, may choose only minimal engagement with a distressed research participant. This largely consists of ensuring the participant is able to access support outside of the research interview. Researchers who view the interview process as a dialogical event may consider they have a duty of care for the research participant in a more immediate way, for example by using interpersonal or therapeutic skills in engaging with the other person's immediate distress (Cowburn 2010).

Research teams may be as small as a lone researcher, but they may also include research assistants, transcribers and supervisors (Lalor et al. 2006). Emotionally engaged research may produce more in-depth and detailed data, but the cost of such engagement on the researcher(s) may be high. This is likely to be the case in research with sex offenders. Listening to accounts of sexual violence is emotionally demanding on the researcher (Cowburn 2007), the people transcribing the interviews (Cowburn 2002; Lalor et al. 2006), and people offering support to the research team, although these impacts may vary according to the identities (for example, gender, ethnicity, and age), and experience of the workers concerned. In the interests of doing no harm it is essential that appropriate supports for everyone be identified (Cowburn 2013) at the outset of the research project.

Data analysis and the presentation and dissemination of 'findings'

Denscombe (2007) amongst many others identifies five stages of data analysis for both quantitative and qualitative research:

- data preparation;
- initial exploration of the data;
- analysis of the data;
- representation and display of the data; and
- validation of the data.

In the space available in this chapter, it is not possible to explore in any in-depth issues relating to each of these stages. However, a key issue that relates to all of them is *transparency*; at each of these stages it should be clear how researchers have proceeded, and their methodology and their analysis should be open to interrogation and challenge. So issues of accuracy and the limitations of the study are acknowledged and the method of interpretation of the data is outlined.

Research practice that is respectful of research participants and seeks to accord them equal moral value needs to show how participant involvement has contributed not only to data collection, but also to the analysis and presentation of data. The issues considered in this section of the chapter are:

- the involvement of research participants in post-data collection activities;
- the practical implications of forensic research;
- external influences on the publication of results;
- the problem of representation.

Involvement of research participants in post-data collection activities

Ward and Willis (2013: 104) suggest that:

> because research participants consent to become involved in a project they have a claim on the data yielded and therefore should be entitled to co-ownership of the data.

Generally, co-ownership would involve ensuring the accuracy of interview/focus group transcripts and approving of how data is subsequently used in publications. However, this process is not easy to achieve. Dependant on where the research takes place, there may be difficulties for research participants in participating fully in these processes. In my own doctoral research (Cowburn 2002), which involved life history interviews with sex offenders in prison, all of the men I interviewed refused my offer of sharing the interview transcript with them. They were fearful that if such a revealing document were to go astray their safety would be seriously jeopardised. Given the length of the transcripts, they did not want to sit in a private room with me and read them. However, wherever possible sharing transcripts and developing joint interpretations of the data is desirable, and treats research participants as 'equal moral agents' (Ward and Willis 2013). For example, Sullivan et al. (2007) provides an example of work jointly published by prisoners and researcher.

The other key area of research participant involvement is in access to research reports and other publications. Ward and Willis (2013) suggest sharing reports and publications recognises the equal moral status of research participants, and is particularly important in forensic and correctional settings, where power imbalances between researcher and research participants are most marked. Whilst this is a laudable aspiration, and should be discussed with research participants, it may be other dangers in these settings that pose more serious threats to both participants' safety and dignity. Accordingly, if participants decide against having access to written material relating to the research, this should be respected. Moreover, in institution-based research there may be many stakeholders, some with more power than others, and it is essential to secure the agreement of all parties before research reports are shared. For example, Cowburn et al. 2010 is a report of research undertaken in a maximum-security prison; it was shared with prisoners, following the agreement of prison managers.

However, whilst research participants' (non-) involvement in the preparation and presentation of data may have negative consequences for them, there are other issues in forensic research to consider.

Practical implications of forensic research

Ward and Willis (2013: 106) highlight the importance of reporting, and that forensic research is located in current clinical theory:

> research on sex offenders that fails to distinguish between risk levels and variables that are known to effect outcomes such as age, sexual deviancy, emotional regulation and so on is misleading and ethically unacceptable.

Moreover, forensic research should clearly describe sample characteristics and size, and methodology employed. Similarly it should spell out limitations of the study, and the extent to which generalisations may be made from it. Failure to provide this level of detail is not only academically sloppy; it may have serious consequences for sex offenders being assessed in the Criminal Justice System. Ward and Willis (2013: 103) thus advocate:

> careful communication of risk assessment research data, especially acknowledgement of the limitations of interpreting risk assessment findings with respect to individual offenders.

Furthermore, they suggest failure to exercise such care is a violation of offenders' dignity (Ward and Willis 2013: 103).

An associated area highlighted, again, by Ward and Willis (2013: 104) is the failure to publish negative study findings. They suggest:

> This is both an epistemic (knowledge related) and an ethical violation – epistemic, because failure to disclose may result in poorly grounded inferences about treatment efficacy, and an ethical violation because it denies individuals the best chance to improve their personal well-being and, furthermore to create a safer society.

External influences on the publication of results

However, failure to publish negative results is not always the researcher's responsibility. Senior (2013: 359) points to the distinction between 'pure' and 'applied or contract' research:

> The former is typically commissioned via research council funding and taking place within an academic context ostensibly in pursuance of knowledge for its own sake, and the latter may be commissioned via local and national government, individual organisations, and other charitable sources with a problem-oriented approach designed to impact in a more immediate way upon policy and practice.

The distinction is not quite clear-cut. The Economic and Social Research Council (2015) gives central consideration to issues of impact in assessing research proposals and subsequent reports. However, the immediacy and problem-oriented nature of contract research clearly influence both how the research is undertaken and what is written in any report or subsequent publication. Senior (2013) highlights how contract research is often focused on evaluating a criminal justice intervention. This may be delivered by a voluntary sector project dependant upon a positive evaluation for continued funding. The pressure on the contract researcher to produce positive results is strongest during the preparation of the final report. Commenting on the experience of contract researchers, Senior (2013: 365) identifies:

> The pressure to produce a piece of work that was descriptive of the project but did not essentially challenge the aims was acute. Researchers often fed back on the pressure to provide a report that showed unconditional support for the programme under evaluation.

Moreover, Senior (2013) also indicates how funders amend the contents of reports and at times, delay or prevent their publication. Clearly respecting the dignity of research participants is not always given prime consideration in the presentation of research reports.

The problem of representation

Qualitative research can co-create graphic descriptions of unpleasant and offensive thoughts and behaviours; such descriptions both provide information and cause distress. However, it is important to ask whether the detailed presentation of sexual offences enhance general understanding or revictimise victims, and (re)offend or (re)harm other groups. The answer to this question is probably 'both'. However, in relation to understanding sex offences, is it appropriate to present the 'voice' of the offender, without additional comment, describing his offences? It could be argued that to do so gives insight into sex offenders, but, equally, it could be argued that merely to present the offender's account is to deny or ignore the experience of victims. Moreover, to present graphic detail of offences without adequate explanation and justification may be experienced as offensive or distressing.

Summary

Research with sex offenders can have impact on conceptual, policy and practice levels. This chapter has considered ethical and epistemological issues involved in researching sex offenders. To understand and develop knowledge about sex offenders requires researchers to locate themselves in relation to the various disciplinary perspectives concerning sexual violence. Epistemology and ethics are inextricably interwoven, not only when research is being designed, but also when practical boundaries of conduct are being defined.

Review questions

1. What are the strengths and the shortcomings of research that seeks to improve clinical practice with the convicted population?
2. How does research with sex offenders keep in mind their 'equal moral value', whilst also ensuring that it does not collude with intentions to harm others?

Case study 1: managing distress

Michael[2] is 31 years old. He is serving a 7-year sentence for the rape of his ex-partner. He was 29 at the time of the offence. He has no previous convictions for any type of offence. His offence was brutal and very violent. However, he appears to be a thoughtful man, trying to make sense of his life and what he had done to his ex-partner.

His childhood was unremittingly neglectful and abusive. He was taken into care of the local authority when he was 3 years of age and spent the remainder of his childhood there. He had little contact with his birth family.

The interview sessions with Michael are gruelling in many ways (including his account of his offences), but one persistent feature is his emotional pain, which appears to have strong links with his negative experiences of childhood.

You are aware of a range of resources that could help Michael in his struggle to understand the influence of his childhood on the distress that he has felt and continues to feel as an adult. Should you share this information with him? Reflect on the methodological implications of your epistemological standpoint (e.g. the significance of scientific practice) and how these influence your response.

Case study 2: epistemology, ethics and (non-) dissemination

The researcher is evaluating a sex offender treatment programme. The evaluation uses both quantitative and qualitative methods – the quantitative measures comprise a range of psychometric tests administered before, during and at the end of the programme. The qualitative measure is an open-ended interview at the home of each person that had completed the programme.

The researcher visits 'Bill'[2] at home one evening where he and his female partner live together. The results of his psychometric tests are positive and indicate a change in his attitudes. Bill is asked to talk about his experience of the programme, and whether it had changed him in any way. He speaks positively about the programme and states that it had changed him. Prior to being on the programme he was an 'MCP' (male chauvinist pig) and now he is no longer a MCP. However, as he speaks about these changes he instructs his partner to make tea, then to iron his clothes for their evening out and finally then he instructs her to obtain some money for their evening's entertainment.

In the interim report to the funder the researcher reflects upon the discrepancy between the psychometric scores, the personal changes identified by Bill, and his actual behaviour. The research contract is immediately cancelled without any explanation.

What could the researcher have done differently? What compromises could be made? Would they be ethical acceptable?

Guide to further reading

Cowburn, M. (2010). Principles, virtues and care: ethical dilemmas in research with male sex offenders. *Psychology Crime & Law, 16*(1–2), 65–74.

Cowburn, M. (2005). Confidentiality and public protection: ethical dilemmas in qualitative research with adult male sex offenders. *Journal of Sexual Aggression, 11*(1), 49–63.

Ward, T., and Willis, G. (2013). Ethical Issues in Sex Offender Research. In K. Harrison and B. Rainey (Eds.), *The Wiley-Blackwell Handbook of Legal and Ethical Aspects of Sex Offender Treatment and Management* (pp. 97–112). Chichester, UK: John Wiley & Sons.

Notes

1   This term is problematic, but I use it to refer to Western Europe, North America and Australasia.
2   This is a pseudonym.

References

Abel, G. G., Becker, J. V., Mittelman, M. S., Cunningham-Rathner, J., Rouleau, J. L., and Murphy, W. D. (1987). Self-reported sex crimes of non-incarcerated paraphiliacs. *Journal of Interpersonal Violence, 2*(1), 3–25.

Baldwin, J. (2000). Research on the criminal courts. In R. D. King and E. Wincup (Eds.), *Doing research on crime and justice*. Oxford: Oxford University Press.

Bohner, G., Pina, A., Viki, G. T., and Siebler, F. (2010). Using social norms to reduce men's rape proclivity: perceived rape myth acceptance of out-groups may be more influential than that of in-groups. *Psychology, Crime and Law, 16*(8), 671–693.

BPS (British Psychological Society). (2014). *Code of Human Research Ethics*. Leicester: The British Psychological Society.

BPS (British Psychological Society). (2009). *Code of Ethics and Conduct: Guidance published by the Ethics Committee of the British Psychological Society*. Leicester: The British Psychological Society.

BSC (British Society of Criminology). (2015). *Statement of Ethics*. www.britsoccrim.org.

Butler, M., and Drake, D. H. (2007). Reconsidering respect: its role in her Majesty's prison service. *Howard Journal of Criminal Justice, 46*(2), 115–127.

Cowburn, M. (2002). *Men and Violence: life hi/stories of male sex offenders*. Unpublished PhD, University of Sheffield, Sheffield, UK.

Cowburn, M. (2005a). Hegemony and discourse: reconstruing the male sex offender and sexual coercion by men. *Sexualities, Evolution and Gender, 7*(3), 215–231.

Cowburn, M. (2005b). Confidentiality and public protection: ethical dilemmas in qualitative research with adult male sex offenders. *Journal of Sexual Aggression, 11*(1), 49–63.

Cowburn, M. (2007). Men researching men in prison: the challenges for profeminist research. *Howard Journal of Criminal Justice, 46*(3), 276–288.

Cowburn, M. (2010). Principles, virtues and care: ethical dilemmas in research with male sex offenders. *Psychology Crime & Law*, *16*(1–2), 65–74.

Cowburn, M. (2013). Men researching violent men: epistemologies, ethics and emotions in qualitative research. In B. Pini and B. Pease (Eds.), *Men, masculinities and methodologies* (pp. 183–196). Basingstoke: Palgrave Macmillan.

Cowburn, M., Lavis, V., with Bird, H. (2010). Appreciative Inquiry into the Diversity Strategy of HMP Wakefield: Full Report. http://researchcatalogue.esrc.ac.uk/grants/RES-000-22-3441/read (Accessed 30 August 2016).

Denscombe, M. (2007). *The good research guide for small-scale social research projects.* Maidenhead, UK: Open University Press.

Economic and Social Research Council (2015). 'What is impact?' http://www.esrc.ac.uk/funding-and-guidance/impact-toolkit/what-how-and-why/what-is-research-impact.aspx (Accessed 19 March 2015).

Fisher, D. (1994). Adult sex offenders: who are they? Why and how do they do it? In T. Morrison, M. Erooga, and R. Beckett (Eds.), *Sexual offending against children: assessment and treatment of male abusers* (pp. 1–24). London: Routledge.

Foucault, M. (1984). *The history of sexuality: an introduction* (R. Hurley, Trans. 1984 ed. (Vol. (i)). London: Peregrine.

Fricker, M. (2007). *Epistemic injustice: power and the ethics of knowing.* Oxford: Oxford University Press.

Gavey, N. (2005). *Just sex: the cultural scaffolding of rape.* London: Routledge.

Harding, S. (2006). *Science and social inequality: feminist and postcolonial issues.* Urbana and Chicago: University of Illinois Press.

Jehle, J.-M. (2012). Attrition and conviction rates of sexual offences in Europe: definitions and criminal justice responses. *European Journal of Criminal Policy & Research*, *18*, 145–161.

Kelly, L. (1988). *Surviving sexual violence.* Oxford: Polity Press.

Kelly, L., Lovett, J., and Regan, L. (2005). *A gap or a chasm? Attrition in reported rape cases.* London: Home Office Research, Development and Statistics Directorate.

King, R. D. (2000). Doing research in prisons. In R. D. King and E. Wincup (Eds.), *Doing research on crime and justice* (pp. 285–312). Oxford: Oxford University Press.

Knight, R. A., and Prentky, R. A. (1990). Classifying Sexual Offenders: The development and corroboration of taxonomic models. In W. L. Marshall, D. R. Laws, and H. E. Barbaree (Eds.), *Handbook of sexual assault* (pp. 23–54). New York: Plenum.

Lalor, J. G., Begley, C. M., and Devane, D. (2006). Exploring painful experiences: impact of emotional narratives on members of a qualitative research team. *Journal of Advanced Nursing*, *56*(6), 607–616.

Malamuth, N. M. (1981). Rape proclivity among males. *Journal of Social Issues*, *37*, 138–157.

Owusu-Bempah, K., and Howitt, D. (2000). *Psychology beyond Western perspectives.* Leicester: British Psychological Society.

Percy, A., and Mayhew, P. (1997). Estimating sexual victimisation in a national crime survey: a new approach. *Studies on Crime and Crime Prevention*, *6*(2), 355–362.

Pereda, N., Guilera, G., Forns, M., and Gómez-Benito, J. (2009). The prevalence of child sexual abuse in community and student samples: a meta-analysis. *Clinical Psychology Review*, *29*(4), 328–338.

Purvis, M., and Ward, T. (2006). The role of culture in understanding child sexual offending: Examining feminist perspectives. *Aggression and Violent Behavior*, *11*, 298–312.

Rich, A. (1980). Compulsory heterosexuality and lesbian existence. *Signs*, *5*(4), 631–660.

Riley, S. (2010). Human dignity: comparative and conceptual debates. *International Journal of Law in Context*, *6*(2), 117–138.

Robertson, E. (2013). The epistemic value of diversity. *Journal of Philosophy of Education*, *47*(2), 299–310.

Said, E. (1978). *Orientalism*. New York: Pantheon Books.

Sanday, P. R. (2003). Rape-free versus rape-prone: how culture makes a difference. In C. B. Travis (Ed.), *Evolution, gender, and rape* (pp. 337–362). Cambridge, MA: The MIT Press.

Senior, P. (2013). Value for money? The politics of contract research. In M. Cowburn, M. Duggan, A. Robinson, and P. Senior (Eds.), *Values in criminology and community justice* (pp. 359–379).

Sullivan, E., Gyamfi, E., Joyce, J., and Pamphile, F. (2007). Straight from the horse's mouth. *Prison Service Journal*, *173*, 9–14.

Ward, T., and Willis, G. (2013). Ethical issues in sex offender research. In K. Harrison and B. Rainey (Eds.), *The Wiley-Blackwell handbook of legal and ethical aspects of sex offender treatment and management* (pp. 97–112). Chichester: John Wiley & Sons.

8

RESEARCHING CHILD SEXUAL ASSAULT

Towards a child sensitive methodology

Simon Hackett

Researching the 'experiences' of people who have been sexually abused as children or who have themselves committed sexually abusive acts raises a range of methodological and ethical dilemmas. In the past, researchers have often relied on retrospective research designs, with the majority of studies of child sexual abuse undertaken with adults who are asked to recall their childhood experiences of abuse. However, there are compelling reasons to involve children in research in order to hear their voices and experiences directly. At the same time, the complex dynamics inherent in child sexual abuse and sexual exploitation pose specific practical and ethical challenges to researchers wishing to undertake research in this area. Key issues that are addressed in this chapter are: the benefits of involving children who have been affected by sexual abuse in research, choosing ethically and developmentally sensitive methodologies, the gender and power of researchers, confidentiality and informed consent, safety and protection of research participants, and managing distress and disclosures.

Key points

1. User perspectives in the sexual abuse field, particularly the perspectives of children and young people affected by sexual abuse, are under-developed.
2. Research into sexual abuse has the potential to give voice to the experiences of children and young people who have been victimized.
3. Researchers in the field of child sexual abuse need to be particularly mindful of the dynamics of children's abuse experiences in planning and designing research studies.
4. Obtaining consent is a core researcher skill and an ongoing process in research with children who have experienced sexual abuse.

5. Research designs that share power and actively involve children and young people as partners in child abuse research are warranted.
6. The choice of research methods should be informed by attention to the child's age, developmental status, abilities and preferred modes of communication. Researchers need to be prepared to demonstrate creativity and responsiveness to children's needs.
7. Gender and culture are key considerations in this research and require researchers to address issues of power and how it affects methods of data collection and data analysis.
8. Children who are prior victims are not necessarily more vulnerable to emotional distress in answering sensitive research questions about violence than non-victims.
9. Safeguarding considerations and risk issues are inevitable elements of research focusing on children's experiences of sexual abuse. Researchers need clear written information sharing protocols to assist in decisions about disclosures.
10. Researchers need to ensure that children are offered appropriate support at all stages of the research process.

Key definitions

Abuse: Defined by the Working Together (2013) document as 'a form of maltreatment of a child. Somebody may abuse or neglect a child by inflicting harm, or by failing to act to prevent harm'.

Sexual abuse: Defined by the Working Together (2013) document as 'forcing or enticing a child or young person to take part in sexual activities, not necessarily involving a high level of violence, whether or not the child is aware of what is happening'.

Sexual exploitation: Defined by NSPCC as a type of sexual abuse in which children are sexually exploited for money, power or status (https://www.nspcc. org.uk/preventing-abuse/child-abuse-and-neglect/child-sexual-exploitation/).

Introduction

The sexual abuse and exploitation of children is a highly sensitive phenomenon that occupies a particular position in current society. It represents an experience that affects a significant minority of children and young people. In their study of a nationally representative sample of children living in the UK, Radford and colleagues (2010) found that 0.5 per cent of under 11s, 4.8 per cent of 11–17s and 11.3 per cent of 18–24s reported contact sexual abuse as defined by the criminal law at some point in their childhoods. Radford and colleagues (2010) found that most perpetrators of sexual abuse were known to their victims and 65.9 per cent of the contact sexual abuse reported was perpetrated by young people under the age of 18. Despite this, open and balanced debate about the true extent and nature of child sexual abuse and its causes and consequences remains rare. Recent media reporting of historical cases of celebrity 'paedophiles' such as that relating to the Savile case and Operation Yewtree, whilst raising the spectre of widespread sexual abuse in society, have also tended to promote a distorted discourse of sexual abuse that happened at a now distant period in our history, 'out there' in institutions, perpetrated by renowned and, at least in retrospect, easily identifiable, odd, adult men. The true and ongoing risks to children from those known to them are arguably being hidden in the face of these more lurid reports of high profile scandals.

It is against this particularly controversial societal backdrop that research into child sexual abuse takes place. Whilst there have been a huge number of studies internationally into sexual abuse over the last three decades, the evidence base into child sexual abuse remains inadequate in several important dimensions. Specifically, in a recent review of the evidence into child sexual abuse in the family, Horvath and colleagues (2014) conclude that there is a considerable amount of literature addressing victims' experiences from practitioners' perspectives, but there is less drawing directly upon victimized children's views and experiences.

In this chapter, I explore some of the ethical and methodological challenges that working with children and young people on studies of child sexual abuse entails and I seek to propose ways in which they can be overcome. Attention is given to the benefits of involving children who have been affected by sexual abuse in research, choosing ethically and developmentally sensitive methodologies, confidentiality and informed consent, safety and protection of research participants, and managing distress and disclosures. Although the chapter does not focus specifically on gender and culture, these are key considerations and are referred to when considering issues of researcher power.

Why involve children and young people in research into sexual abuse?

Service users in health, welfare and criminal justice systems have a right to be consulted about their experiences, especially when these experiences are critical, sensitive and harmful, such as experiences of sexual abuse. At the same time, researchers have an ethical responsibility to protect the rights of participants in and through research. If participation in research leads to a significantly greater probability of harm than non-participation, then it challenges the boundaries of this responsibility. Thus, the principle of beneficence, in other words maximizing the benefits of doing research whilst minimizing risks to research subjects, is often cited as a core element of research ethics (Ybarra et al., 2009). Harming anyone who has experienced sexual abuse through involving them in research is not justifiable, but equally not consulting them may also contribute to the ongoing silencing of victims. This means that the design of any study into sexual abuse that actively involves human participants, irrespective of their age, requires careful ethical consideration on the part of researchers. Such designs include, most obviously, surveys or interview based studies of people known to have been affected by sexual abuse as victims or perpetrators (such as the Case Example at the end of this chapter), as well as more general population based surveys where it can be assumed that a proportion of those responding will have experienced abuse (such as Radford and colleagues' (2010) prevalence study referred to above).

It is now widely acknowledged internationally that service user perspectives should be a central feature not only of service planning and evaluation in health, social care and criminal justice systems (Warren, 2007) but also in social research in these areas (e.g. Lowes and Hulatt, 2005). However, in contrast to the general momentum that has been generated on this issue, user perspectives in the sexual abuse field, particularly the perspectives of children and young people affected by sexual abuse, remain woefully under-developed. For example, Hackett and Masson's (2006) study of the views and experiences of young people one year or more following the end of therapeutic interventions as a result of their problematic sexualised behaviours represents one of only a few attempts to establish children's views in the sexual aggression field. In this study, service users often considered unreliable and hard-to-reach were keen to share their views in order to help the professional system improve for other users who would follow them.

Considerable work on research methodology over the last two decades has charted a conceptual shift from research *on* children, to research *for* and *with* children (Lewis, 2004). Involving children and young people in research about their experiences of sexual abuse and exploitation has been viewed as important in that it can provide different and more accurate estimates of the prevalence of abuse (Cashmore, 2006), as well as distinct insights that are crucial in developing services for children and families affected (Masson, 2004). Additionally, sexual abuse is a crime that often takes place in secrecy and through which the perpetrator seeks to silence the child who is victimized. One of the powerful dimensions of research into sexual abuse is, therefore, its potential to give voice to the experiences of children and young people who have been victimized. Involving children and young people affected by sexual abuse in research studies should not, of course, be seen as either therapy or a substitute for post-abuse professional support, but it may nonetheless have important emancipatory and therapeutic benefits in the aftermath of abuse.

Save the Children (2004: 10–14) suggest that the benefits of involving children in research about violence can be delineated into: benefits for the child; benefits for the research; and, benefits for society. In Table 8.1, I draw on the work of Save the Children to summarize and develop these benefits as they pertain to involving children and young people in research on child sexual abuse and exploitation.

TABLE 8.1 The benefits of involving children in research about sexual abuse and exploitation (adapted and developed from Save the Children, 2004).

Benefits	Themes	Elements
To children	Assertion of their right to participate	Children have the right to decide if they wish to get involved, to what degree and how.
		Active participation by children can help to challenge the silence about sexual abuse and the stigmatization of those children who have experienced it.
	Participation can help to protect children	Children are most vulnerable to sexual abuse in situations where they have little opportunity to voice their views. A participative approach can help build skills to resist exploitation.
		Participation in research teaches children how to access information which can be crucially important in survival following sexual abuse.
		Increased self-confidence is protective.
	Children's participation can help to heal the past	The process of involvement, if supportive and understanding, can help children to explore past experiences and regain confidence for the future.
		Participation can be a tool out of victimisation, passivity and silence.
To research	Children's participation can bring new insights	Participation of children in research can produce better quality data, as it helps focus the research, and clarify the analysis and the interpretation of data.
		Unique perspectives and insights on abuse are provided by children.
		The nature of child sexual abuse is shifting given new technologies. Retrospective studies of adult survivors' experiences of child sexual abuse may not reflect the current realities for children.
		Adult researchers may have less insight into the daily lives of children than they think they have.
	Children's participation can focus the research	Obtaining data from children themselves increases the possibility of presenting a picture of child abuse that is freer of adult interpretations.
		As a population group, children are disproportionately affected by sexual abuse and exploitation. Therefore the natural way to obtain information about abuse is to work with them as informants or co-researchers.

TABLE 8.1 continued

Benefits	Themes	Elements
To society	Enhances children's position as active citizens	Working in partnership with children challenges the status quo in terms of what children can realistically contribute and challenges existing notions of children's capacities and vulnerabilities.
		Research with children on violence and abuse can contribute to positive intergenerational communication, which may increase the chance that children are listened to and their opinions taken into account.

Connecting the dynamics of child sexual abuse with the challenges of engaging children and young people in research

If the benefits of involving children and young people in research are so extensive, then why have researchers traditionally shied away from approaches to research into child sexual abuse that actively involve children and young people, either those who have been victimized or those who have victimized others? Two primary justifications are often given for not engaging children: first that they are somehow unreliable given their immature status; and second that they are vulnerable to exploitation by researchers (Kirk, 2007). However, as Kirk (2007) maintains there is now a growing body of literature that demonstrates that children can be competent participants in research as long as researchers make their participation possible and recognise the ways in which children communicate. Likewise, there are very many ways of meaningfully involving children and young people that utilize their capacity for agency in non-exploitative ways.

However, research into child sexual abuse may be particularly challenging in both of these regards. First, adults rarely speak openly to other adults, let alone to children, about sex and abuse. How should researchers communicate with children on such matters and what would the impact of this be? Second, children who have been affected by sexual abuse have already by definition been exploited as part of their abuse experience and there are legitimate concerns about research processes replicating this exploitation. For example, asking a child to meet in a private space with a researcher to talk with an unknown adult on personal issues, offering that such exchanges are confidential and not to be shared with anyone outside the room, using distinct techniques to win the child's trust and establish rapport, and videoing or audio recording such interactions, are part of the standard repertoire of qualitative social research approaches. However, they are also mirrored closely by the processes of grooming, coercion and emotional force that sexual abusers often use in the commission of their abusive acts. This means that researchers in the field of child sexual abuse need to be particularly mindful of the dynamics of children's abuse experiences in planning and designing research in order for their involvement to be an ethical, positive and corrective interpersonal experience, rather than one which however inadvertently replicates their earlier abuse experience. In the sections below, I explore the practical consequences of this in respect of a number of key ethical dimensions.

Consent

Consent in any research with children is a contested issue, especially the difference between assent and consent and children's legal and cognitive abilities to make decisions about their own participation. Consent issues in research with children who have experienced sexual abuse are particularly sensitive. In overt ways, child sexual abuse is an assault on consent. Children who have been sexually abused have experienced their boundaries being transcended by an abuser who, in the commission of the abuse, rides roughshod over the child's ability to consent to key aspects of their body, behaviour and sexuality. Children cannot, of course, consent to being abused, yet often an abuser will use deliberate strategies to coerce children into the abuse and to make them believe that they are willing and 'consenting' participants.

The legacy of distorted consent in abuse can leave some, though by no means all, children who have been sexually abused with a variety of consequences which include: suspicion of the motives of others; inhibited trust of adults; a feeling that saying no is not meaningful; pressure to go along with things to meet others' needs even if this is contrary to their own needs; and, a lack of belief that they are valid individuals with a real say in what happens to them. Researchers need to be particularly mindful of these possibilities when devising ways in which to negotiate consent with children affected by abuse. Researchers should:

- offer clear information, in developmentally appropriate and understandable formats about the study that specify precisely what participation would entail;
- clearly state that participation is voluntary, that non-participation is a legitimate choice and that withdrawal is possible at any point;
- emphasise that non-participation or withdrawal from the study would not affect any professional services being received by the child or family;
- be explicit about how any information gathered will be used, who will have access to it and how it will be presented; and
- allow adequate time for the child to ask questions and receive answers prior to agreeing consent.

Obtaining consent is both a core researcher skill and represents an ongoing process in research with children who have experienced sexual abuse, and should not be viewed merely as something to be signed off at the beginning of a study. In the Case Example offered below, for example, consent had to be negotiated and renegotiated before, during and after interviews with young people affected by gang sexual violence.

One particularly difficult question is whether children and young people affected by sexual abuse should be able to give consent to participate individually or whether parents or carers are also required to give their consent alongside that of the child. In the Case Example, the researchers delineated sub groups of young people at different ages with different consequences for parental consent. Many research ethics committees expect to see parental *consent*, in addition to child *assent* to research participation. In this context, assent is:

> different to consent in that it is not a legally endorsed process, assent refers to children's affirmation to participate. Assent recognizes that while children might be unable to give legally valid consent for themselves, it is important to involve them as much as possible in the decision about whether they would like to participate, or not, in the research.
>
> *(Lambert and Glacken, 2011: 787)*

Yet, this distinction is often not straightforward to maintain in cases of child sexual abuse. It would, for example, be highly unethical for a child who wishes to talk about abuse experiences to be constrained by a parent who has perpetrated that abuse or who does not believe the child's account.

In their very helpful paper reviewing approaches to issues of consent in research with children across studies, Lambert and Glacken (2011) note ambiguity in the way in which researchers address issues of parental consent and considerable variation in the way in which the legal position is interpreted across research organisations and contexts. They note, for example, that the Royal College of Paediatrics and Child Health advises researchers to seek parental consent for all children under the age of 18 years, whilst the UK Health National Research Ethics Service (NRES) states that it is 'possible to apply' the principle of Gillick competence to research studies not governed by the Medicines for Human Use (Clinical Trials) Regulations and that 'children who are felt to be competent to understand the research proposal and thus make decisions can give consent on their own behalf' (cited Lambert and Glacken, 2011: 785). Although the principle of Gillick competence does not specify a minimum age at which children should be regarded as competent, NRES further states that it would be unwise to use this principle for children younger than ten years of age. The Department of Health (2001), by contrast, recommends that it is good practice even where children are deemed legally competent to involve their family in any decision-making process. One suggestion put forward by the National Children's Bureau (1993), and cited by Lambert and Glacken (2011), is that children should give ultimate consent to participation, whereas parents should give consent for the researcher to invite their child to participate in the study.

Confidentiality

It is usual for researchers to negotiate issues of confidentiality alongside those relating to consent. Anonymous survey designs are the only way of guaranteeing absolute confidentiality to child participants. The standard practice in much interview based research is to give children a commitment in advance of the interview that what they say as part of taking part is confidential and will not be shared with anyone else, unless there are issues of risk identified, in which case this information might need to be shared with someone outside of the research team in order to protect the child or other persons at risk. Usually, this then leads to a further clarification of the anonymity of data, and an explanation on the part of the researchers that any information offered by the child could be used by the researchers in reports or publications, but giving a commitment that this information would not be used in a way that identifies the individual child.

This standard position may be problematic in research based research with children and young people who have been affected by abuse, including both those who have perpetrated abusive behaviours and those who have been victimized. As highlighted above, much child sexual abuse is facilitated by secrecy and attempts on the part of the abuser to control and silence those victimized by coercing them into a position whereby the abusive behaviour is regarded as 'our secret'. Researchers may have to actively work against this with children in order to delink any connection for the child between confidentiality (which in research terms is meant as a guarantee of safety) and secrecy (which in abuse terms is a threat and means of silencing the child). In addition, the orthodox research position described above places the power and control of the information squarely with the researcher, who the child is asked to trust to manage this information. My own approach to this issue in interview situations has been to explain carefully the limits of confidentiality with children and give guarantees about how I will protect their privacy and identity in the use of the data, but at the same time emphasizing that participants own their own information along the lines of:

> You can tell anyone you like everything that I say to you today. None of what I say to you is a secret if you choose it not to be. But I will keep what you say safe and private and make sure that I use the information you give me in the following ways...

This kind of language and approach models openness, participant control and utilises the decision-making abilities of the child. In the Case Example below, the researchers went one step further. Here, worried that young people may have felt, in retrospect, that they had disclosed too much to researchers about their experiences, they offered young people a cooling off period of one month after the interview during which time it was possible for them to ask for any aspect of what they had said to be discounted by the researchers. The specific approaches required in relation to confidentiality will, of course, vary according to the research design, aims and focus of different studies. However, this is an area that needs careful planning and consideration.

Researcher power issues

Mostly, even those researchers who have sought to include children affected by sexual abuse in research have tended to do so with children as passive recipients or research subjects. Few studies have directly involved such children more directly as active partners in the research process. This mirrors the passivity of children in abuse situations. If researchers wish to model an approach to research with children affected by abuse that counters the dynamics of that abuse, it is important to use research designs that involve children and young people as actively as possible. This may include, for example, recruitment of children and young people as expert informants to research planning processes, advisors on the appropriateness of data collection measures, consultants on data analysis, members of research advisory groups and co-authors of research reports. Models of community based participatory research (CBPR) are particularly well suited to researching with children and young people affected by sexual abuse as these approaches are designed explicitly to minimize the power imbalance in the research process. Jacquez, Vaughn and Wagner (2013) highlight how CBPR is diverse in terms of the particular methods used, but the common factor is 'the shift from the typical power dynamic inherent in the adult/child relationship to include youth as active participants in one or more phases of the research process' (p. 177).

One important dimension of research power which is important for researchers to address is that of gender. Sexual abuse is a highly gendered phenomenon. Particular care needs to be taken with the gender of researchers, especially if interview based methods are used. Researchers need to ensure that children and young people are presented with and can exercise free choice about which gender of researcher to engage with. This is not about the skills or safety of the individual researcher, but it is about the legacy and impact of the sexual abuse upon the child.

A second and critical power dimension relates to culture. In a paper on speaking out about sexual abuse in British South Asian communities, Cowburn, Gill and Harrison (2015) outline how cultural dynamics may influence the ways in which sexual abuse is discussed within and between communities. They emphasize the importance of culturally sensitive approaches to the issue of sexual violence and abuse in order to better support victims and to empower communities to respond to sexual abuse. Likewise, Gilligan and Akhtar (2006) highlight how cultural beliefs and values may impact on the effects of abuse and they urge professionals to avoid practice based in generalized assumptions about ethnicities, cultures or religions.

Abuse sensitive methods

It is beyond the scope of this chapter to outline specific methodological approaches that are developmentally sensitive and appropriate for children affected by sexual abuse, but readers are referred to the textbook of Grieg, Taylor and MacKay (2007), which is listed in the key resources section below and contains many practical suggestions for appropriate methods to use with children. Needless to say, researchers should be guided by the particular age, developmental status, abilities and preferred communication modes of the children to be engaged in research and should be prepared to demonstrate creativity and responsiveness to children's needs. As two brief examples, Masson et al. (2013) used social media as a vehicle for data collection on sensitive topics to do with sexual offending with young adults (see Masson et al., 2013 for a fuller description). Here, the use of social media offered a means for some individuals who did not want to have a face-to-face interview to share their experiences at their own pace, using a means of communication that they controlled and with which they were familiar. Second, in the Case Example below, the researchers developed an approach to interviewing that allowed young people to talk in the third person about their experiences of gang-related sexual violence.

It is also important for researchers to consider how some orthodox methods may be inappropriate for specific populations of children and young people. For example, the widespread practice of video or audio recording interviews may be highly problematic for children who have been recorded by sex offenders as part of their sexual abuse experience. Focus groups may be inappropriate for young people abused in peer group contexts. Similarly, online survey methods may need caution for children who have been sexually exploited online.

Emotional distress

Researchers or gatekeepers, such as professionals who may grant access to young people or members of ethical review bodies, are frequently worried about the potential for children and young people who have experienced sexual abuse to be distressed by taking part in research. In my experience, this is the most frequently cited reason why permissions to undertake research with children on this subject is withheld. The concerns relate to the potential that children could find the nature of questions about violence or abuse distressing as a consequence of their experiences or that in some way the questions could trigger memories of the abuse that would set back or interrupt the child's recovery from the abuse. Is this legitimate or just research paternalism and infantalization of young people?

Ybarra and colleagues (2009) investigated self-reported stress to questions about violence in a US national online survey of over 1,500 young people aged 10–15 years old. In almost all cases, young people who reported being victims were no more likely to report being upset by the survey questions than non-victimized youth. At the same time, across both victim and non-victimised groups, age did appear to be a factor in emotional distress. Specifically, 10 year olds were three times more likely to be upset by questions on violence than 15 year olds. It could be that developmental variation is more significant than abuse experience as a factor in influencing participant distress. In another important study, Priebe, Bäckström and Ainsaar (2010) investigated factors determining discomfort amongst adolescents in answering survey questions about sexuality and sexual abuse in

Estonia and Sweden. They found that the majority of adolescent participants did not feel discomfort when completing the survey and participants who reported experiences of penetrative sexual abuse did not differ from non-abused participants in their emotional response to the survey.

Ybarra et al. (2009) conclude that although it is important to be sensitive to the potential vulnerability of victims in research, their findings do not support concerns that prior victims are more vulnerable to emotional distress in answering sensitive questions about violence than non-victims. This is also reflected in my own experience of research in this field. I have repeatedly seen the resilience of children who have lived with abuse and have integrated it into their personal experience, often with considerable strength. In my view, it is important for researchers not to under-estimate the capacities of children who have survived abuse. As long as the researchers are skilled in asking questions about abuse in non-blaming and clear ways, it need not be a stressful or distressing experience for children to answer them.

Handling disclosures and protecting participants

In research with children of their experiences of sexual abuse, it is inevitable that safeguarding and risk issues are going to be present. Researchers should have knowledge of procedures in the local areas or organizations in which the research is being conducted and have clear written information sharing protocols. These need to be agreed with participants and gatekeepers prior to any data collection, not left to the point when a child says something which may be concerning. When agreeing protocols with children, I have found it important to be explicit with, and give concrete examples of, what would need to be shared and what would not.

When a child makes a disclosure of abuse in the course of research, the researcher may have little or no prior knowledge of the child's experiences and therefore whether the information being shared is already known or not. Where there is current or previous professional involvement in the life of the child, it is likely that the data generated will include both experiences that are known and information that may not have been communicated previously. In an interview situation, it is possible for researchers to discuss this with the child, but in other designs, such as survey research, this may be impossible. In making decisions about whether any information offered by a child in the course of research needs to be shared, in other words breaking the general principle of confidentiality, researchers should not be driven by the question of whether that information is previously known or not. Rather the focus should be on whether any information (either historical or current) is indicative of ongoing risk to either the child concerned or anyone else. If so, this would be reason to inform the child that the researcher needs to discuss this with another person. In general, the literature suggests that researchers should do this with the permission of, and in conjunction with the child, though as Wiles and colleagues (2008) highlight, there is little explicit reference in the literature as to what to do if this permission is not forthcoming. Managing situations where it is necessary to break confidentiality requires a high level of skill on the part of researchers and in practice such situations represent real ethical dilemmas. It is important for researchers not to give false assurances to the child about the possible outcomes of information sharing. Researchers also need good supervision and support themselves in order to be able to seek advice about these dilemmas.

Similar dilemmas exist about statements that self-incriminate a young person over the age of criminal responsibility. Wiles et al. (2008) found that while researchers felt duty bound to break confidentiality where participants were at risk of harm, this did not extend to a perceived duty to disclose information relating to involvement in crime or other illegal activity. This has also been my approach in studies I have conducted with young people whose sexual behaviour has harmed others, where I have not shared evidence of illegal activity unless it is indicative of risk to the participant or any other person. This is a rather controversial interpretation of an ambiguous legal situation. For a fuller discussion of this issue and the inherent tensions it brings, the reader is advised to consult the excellent paper of Wiles and colleagues (2008).

Post involvement support

The overriding principle here is that the safety and protection of children and others who are vulnerable or who may be at risk should be the paramount concern not only during the data collection process but also afterwards. Researchers should put mechanisms in place to ensure that appropriate independent support is available for the child after their involvement in research. For example, in an interview based study of children who had been sexually abused, we not only asked at the end of interviews whether children would like to access support, but we agreed with them that we would make contact two days after the interview in order to check the impact of taking part and help identify any ongoing support needed. In planning post research contact, it is important for researchers to consider ongoing safety issues for children and ascertain, for example, whether is it safe to contact them and how best to do this. Researchers should also be very specific about how and when contact will be made and keep to this in order for children not to be left in situations of uncertainty.

Summary

This chapter has highlighted how it is both beneficial and practical to involve children and young people affected by sexual abuse directly in studies on the subject of sexual abuse and violence. Researchers need to take considerable care in ensuring that the research process does not inadvertently mirror aspects of the child's earlier abuse experience.

Review questions

1. What specific benefits are there in involving children and young people in research on sexual abuse, exploitation and violence: for them; for the research; and more widely? How can researchers realize these benefits?
2. What should researchers do to partner most effectively with children and young people in research on sexual abuse?
3. How far does research with children who have been affected by sexual abuse challenge received knowledge and orthodox practices around consent, confidentiality and the sharing of information? What would your approach to these issues be?

Case example

'It's Wrong, but you get used to it': a qualitative study of gang associated sexual violence towards, and exploitation of, young people in England.

The study was undertaken in 2013 by a team at the University of Bedfordshire led by Professors Jenny Pearce and John Pitts. Key reference: Beckett, H. et al. (2013).

Aim

The research was commissioned by the Office of the Children's Commissioner for England as part of its Inquiry into Child Sexual Exploitation in Gangs and Groups. The overall aim of the research was to consider the scale and nature of gang-associated sexual violence and exploitation in six areas of England.

Methods

Individual interviews were held with 150 young people who had experienced gang related violence and these were complemented by 11 focus groups with 76 professionals and 8 single-sex focus groups with 38 young people. The sensitive nature of the research and the potential vulnerability of research participants required great care on the part of the researchers to minimise issues of risk and harm to young people. A detailed ethical protocol was developed was used to structure the research.

All participants were accessed through agencies that could advise of any potential risks associated with young people's involvement in the research and ensure that appropriate follow-up support was in place. The researchers acknowledge that this requirement introduced a degree of bias into their sample and excluded other potential participants who were not involved in professional agencies, however they felt that the risks of engaging those outside of services were too high given the resources and timescales set for their study.

As the primary focus of the interviews was on young people's experiences of gang-related sexual violence and exploitation, both as victims and perpetrators, interviews were highly sensitive in nature. In order to make the interviews as comfortable as possible for young people, they were conducted so that young people could talk about issues in the third person, unless they actively chose to do otherwise. Interviews used a conversational format, using an interview schedule as a framework for discussion. The language and terminology used with young people was critical. As some young people did not recognise the violence and exploitation inherent in their personal circumstances, the researchers were careful to explore these issues within the wider context of 'relationships, sex and gangs: the good and the bad' in both the interviews and focus groups with young people rather than use prescriptive and value laden terms such as 'gangs' and 'violence' or 'abuse'.

Informed consent with young people was a critical issue in the study. For participants under the age of 16 years, parent/ carer consent was obtained in addition to that of the young person, unless this was deemed contrary to the best interests of the child. For those aged under 13, opt-in parental consent was obtained; for those aged 13–15, opt-out consent was obtained unless the policy of the facilitating agency required otherwise. The researchers, however, saw that informed consent was not just something to be agreed at the outset of the research but was a dynamic process to be negotiated and renegotiated throughout the research.

The researchers also sought to give young people control over the interview process and their contributions. Young people could terminate the interview at any point and did not need to answer any of the questions being asked. The researchers recognised that some young people may have inadvertently shared more than they planned to, so they checked with each young person at the end of their interview whether they had shared anything that they would rather not be used in the research. Any material designated as such by the young person was not included in the research. Young people were also able to withdraw their contribution within one month of their interview and were given explicit advice as to how to do this, both verbally and in writing.

Findings

The researchers found significant levels and many types of sexual victimisation within the gang-environment, with young women being particularly at risk. Young women were much more likely to recognise the exploitative and violent nature of sexual interactions being described than young men. Many young women were blamed by both young men and other young women for their experiences of sexual victimisation within gang contexts. Many young people viewed rape and sexual assault as 'normal' sexual behaviour with little recognition of the meaning of a sexual offence. Few thought that young people would report or talk about their experiences of sexual violence, and fewer still thought that they would talk to professionals as opposed to peers.

Methodological conclusion

The researchers were able to engage young people considered particularly hard-to-reach to talk about their experiences of widespread and extreme gang associated sexual violence. Their use of carefully constructed interview methods gave voice to a hitherto neglected area in the sexual violence field in the UK.

Guide to further reading

Grieg, A., Taylor, J. and MacKay, T. (2007). Doing Research *with* Children. London, Sage. This is an excellent textbook on research with children, including very helpful practical materials, approaches and exercises.

Lambert, V. and Glacken, M. (2011). Engaging with children in research: Theoretical and practical implications of negotiating informed consent/assent. *Nursing Ethics*, 18(6) 781–801. This is an excellent, focused paper on consent issues in research with children. It is a review paper which includes both conceptual and practical suggestions.

Priebe, G., Bäckström, M. and Ainsaar, M. (2010). Vulnerable adolescent participants' experience in surveys on sexuality and sexual abuse: Ethical aspects. *Child Abuse & Neglect*, 34, 438–447. One of the few empirical investigations of the impact of asking questions relating to sexual abuse to adolescents who have been sexually victimised.

Save the Children (2004). *So You Want to Involve Children in Research? A toolkit supporting children's meaningful and ethical participation in research relating to violence against children.* Stockholm, Save the Children. This is an excellent practical guide offering tips and advice for researchers who wish to involve children and young people in research on the subject of violence. It has two main parts, the first being a discussion of key ethical issues in engaging children in research, the second focusing on 'how to do it'.

Wiles, R., Crow, G., Heath, S. and Charles, V. (2008). The Management of Confidentiality and Anonymity in Social Research. *International Journal of Social Research Methodology*, 11, 5, 417–428. An excellent paper on issues of confidentiality and anonymity of relevance to research on sensitive topics, including abuse, with children.

References

Beckett, H with Brodie, I., Factor, F., Melrose, M., Pearce, J., Pitts, J., Shuker, L. and Warrington, C. (2013). *'It's wrong…but you get used to it': A qualitative study of gang-associated sexual violence towards, and exploitation of, young people in England.* University of Bedfordshire/Office of the Children's Commissioner's for England.

Cashmore, J. (2006). Ethical issues concerning consent in obtaining children's reports on their experience of violence. *Child Abuse & Neglect*, 30, 969–977.

Cowburn, M., Gill, A. and Harrison, K. (2015). Speaking about sexual abuse in British South Asian communities: offenders, victims and the challenges of shame and reintegration. *Journal of Sexual Aggression*, 21(1): 4–15.

Department for Education (2013). *Working together to safeguard children: a guide to inter-agency working to safeguard and promote the welfare of children.* London: Department for Education.

Department of Health (2001). *Consent–what you have a right to expect: a guide for children and young people.* London: Department of Health.

Gilligan, P. and Akhtar, S. (2006). Cultural barriers to the disclosure of child sexual abuse in Asian communities: listening to what women say. *British Journal of Social Work*, 36: 1361–1377.

Grieg, A., Taylor, J. and MacKay, T. (2007). *Doing research with children*. London: Sage.

Hackett, S. and Masson, H. (2006). Young people who have sexually abused: what do they (and their parents) want from professionals? *Children and Society*, 20: 183–195.

Horvath, M.A.H., Davidson, J.C., Grove-Hills, J., Gekoski, A. and Choak, C. (2014). *'It's a lonely journey': A rapid evidence assessment on intrafamilial child sexual abuse*. London: Office of the Children's Commissioner.

Jacquez, F., Vaughn, L. and Wagner, E. (2013). Youth as partners, participants or passive recipients: a review of children and adolescents in community-based participatory research (CBPR). *American Journal of Community Psychology*, 51: 176–189.

Kirk, S. (2007). Methodological and ethical issues in conducting qualitative research with children and young people: A literature review. *International Journal of Nursing Studies*, 44: 1250–1260.

Lambert, V. and Glacken, M. (2011). Engaging with children in research: theoretical and practical implications of negotiating informed consent/assent. *Nursing Ethics*, 18(6): 781–801.

Lewis, V. (2004). Doing research with children and young people: an introduction. In Fraser, S., Lewis, V., Ding, S., Kellett, M. and Robinson, C. (eds.) *Doing research with children and young people*. London: Sage.

Lowes, L. and Hulatt, I. (eds.) (2005). *Involving service users in health and social care research*. London: Routledge.

Masson, H., Balfe, M., Hackett, S. and Phillips, J. (2013). Lost without a trace? Social networking and social research with a hard-to-reach population. *British Journal of Social Work*, 43(1): 24-40.

Masson, J. (2004). The legal context. In Fraser, S., Lewis, V., Ding, S., Kellett, M. and Robinson, C. (eds.) *Doing research with children and young people*. London: Sage.

National Children's Bureau (1993). *Guidelines for research*. London: National Children's Bureau.

Priebe, G., Bäckström, M. and Ainsaar, M. (2010). Vulnerable adolescent participants' experience in surveys on sexuality and sexual abuse: Ethical aspects. *Child Abuse & Neglect* 34, 438–447.

Radford, L., Corral, S., Bradley, C., Fisher, H., Bassett, C., Howat, N. and Collishaw, S. (2010). *Child abuse and neglect in the UK today*. London: NSPCC.

Save the Children (2004). *So you want to involve children in research? A toolkit supporting children's meaningful and ethical participation in research relating to violence against children*. Stockholm: Save the Children.

Warren, J. (2007). *Service user and carer participation in social work*. Exeter: Learning Matters.

Wiles, R., Crow, G., Heath, S. and Charles, V. (2008). The management of confidentiality and anonymity in social research. *International Journal of Social Research Methodology*, 11(5): 417–428.

Ybarra, M., Langhinrichsen-Rohling, J., Friend, F. and Diener-West, M. (2009). Impact of asking sensitive questions about violence to children and adolescents. *Journal of Adolescent Health*, 45(2009): 499–507.

9

ETHICAL CHALLENGES

Researching war crimes

Kirsten Campbell

This chapter explores the complex ethical challenges of researching war crimes, using my research on sexual violence in the conflict in the former Yugoslavia as a case study. The chapter explores three key sets of ethical challenges in this area. The first concerns how the researcher defines war crimes, as this includes or excludes forms of conduct, and accordingly, categories of victims and perpetrators. The second set of ethical challenges arises from the context of conflict, which situates the researcher in an acutely violent and politicized research field. The third set of challenges relate to the choice of methodology and methods, which is integral to research quality and integrity in this difficult field. The chapter examines each of these ethical challenges through the practice of researching war crimes in the field. It connects practical ethics issues, such as confidentiality, to the broader ethical questions of the values and principles of research, such as social justice commitments, that this area inevitably raises.

Key definitions

Epistemic accountability: Evaluation of epistemic standards in terms of the transformative values of social justice.

Situated ethics: The critical position built through relationships of epistemic responsibility to others and to transformative social change.

Theoretical accountability: The explicit and reflexive engagement with values in a process of concept building.

Introduction

The study of war crimes is a growing area of research. The field has emerged in the context of the so-called 'new wars' and the new international criminal justice system of the 1990s. However, there is little consensus within this new and multi-disciplinary field on how to engage with the specific ethical challenges of researching war crimes. This chapter explores key ethical challenges and strategies for ethical accountability when undertaking war crimes research. It identifies three key sets of ethical challenges. The first challenge concerns how the researcher defines and theorizes the nature of war crimes, since this includes or excludes forms of conduct, and accordingly, defines categories of victims and perpetrators. The second set of ethical challenges arises from the context of conflict, which inevitably situates the researcher in a violent and politicized research field. The third challenge relates to the choice of methodology and methods, which is intrinsic to research quality and integrity in this difficult field.

This chapter explores these issues through the practice of researching war crimes, drawing on my research on prosecutions of conflict-related sexual violence in the former Yugoslavia. Most recently, this research involves a four year research project, 'The Gender of Justice' ('GoJ'), funded by the European Research Council. The project develops a new research framework for studying gender justice. It studies the 'gender' of international justice for sexual violence in armed conflict through a mixed-method case study of international prosecutions of conflict-related sexual violence before the International Criminal Tribunal for the former Yugoslavia ('ICTY'), and national prosecutions before the War Crimes Chamber of the Court of Bosnia and Herzegovina ('BWCC'). This study involves a multi-disciplinary team working across multiple field sites. The study exemplifies the ethical challenges of war crimes research, and the GoJ team has engaged in ongoing dialogue on these challenges. This dialogue has been integral part of the development of the approaches outlined in this chapter

From regulatory compliance to ethical accountability

The 'conventional story told about the emergence of research ethics' links modern principles to post-war prosecution of medical war crimes committed by German doctors in World War Two (Hay and Israel 2006). The judgement in this war crimes trial laid down the so-called 'Nuremburg Code', a set of ethical principles for conducting research on human subjects (Mehring 2014: 164). These ethical principles eventually moved from medical research to the social and political sciences.

These principles continue to inform the ethical frameworks of professional disciplinary associations and research councils, which will guide ethical practice in studying war crimes. Multiple disciplinary, country, and specialist subject specific guidelines may also be relevant. One strategy is to use research council guidelines as 'baseline professional ethics requirements' (Sriram 2009: 58). For example, the GoJ Project drew on the European Research Council ethics framework, together with the guidelines of the British Sociological Association, Social and Legal Studies Association (UK), and Economic and Social Research Council (UK) for subject specific issues.

These principles and guidelines are important for developing accepted ethical standards, and for complying with existing regulatory regimes. However, such compliance does not necessary guarantee ethical research in practice, particularly in the 'difficult situations' of conflict and post-conflict settings (Sriram 2009: 58). For example, a sexual violence survivor may wish to be named rather than appearing as an anonymous informant in publications because they wish to combat the 'stigmatization' of rape victims. Such informants are often well aware of the potential harm of disclosure, but 'want to draw attention to a situation that they perceive as unjust'. To refuse this disclosure 'may be at odds not only with the demands of our interlocutors, but also our goals as scholars, advocates, and advisers on policy' (Sriram 2009: 58). These important goals reflect the values that researchers have, and play a crucial role in how they undertake that work.

Acknowledging the crucial role of these values in the generation of knowledge shifts the model of ethical practice from regulatory compliance to ethical accountability. Given the complexities of ethical practice in war crimes research, applying mechanistic or technical solutions to these challenges will not necessarily provide ethical research. Rather, my approach acknowledges the interconnection between ethical norms governing the proper conduct of research, and epistemic norms governing the generation of knowledge. There is an imbrication of ethical and epistemological practices in war crimes research, and ethical accountability requires a relationship of responsibility of researchers to wider social and political values in their generation of knowledge. This approach shows how war crimes research inevitably connects practical ethics issues, such as confidentiality, to broader ethical questions of the values and principles of research, such as commitments to social justice. Accordingly, this chapter frames its discussion of specific ethical issues, such as informed consent, in the context of broader ethical strategies. Researchers can then use these strategies reflexively to develop appropriate practice for their research. To develop this approach, this chapter draws on feminist work on ethical research generally, with specific reference to ethical issues concerning conflict and sexual violence. This work offers sustained engagement with ethical issues in this challenging area, and reflects on the fundamental question of ethical accountability. Do epistemic practices reproduce inequalities and injustices, or promote social transformation and change?

Ethical challenge one: what are we researching? The challenge of theoretical accountability

The first ethical challenge that researchers face concerns how to select and define the object of investigation. Sandra Harding (1986: 22) points out that 'deciding what phenomena in the world need explanation, and defining what is problematic about them' always involves cultural and social values. The ethical challenge is to develop a reflexive understanding of how these values construct 'war crimes' as an object of research. This challenge is two-fold. The first aspect is the concept of criminality underlying models of war crimes. The second is how the research field shapes 'war crimes' as an object of inquiry.

Concepts of criminality

If criminology concerns a 'specific genre of discourse and inquiry about crime' (Garland 2002: 7), then what is the 'crime' that war crimes research focuses upon? This is a fundamental ethical question for the study of war crimes. It is fundamental because the concept of criminality determines which acts we will categorize as criminal, and which persons we will count as victims or perpetrators of these crimes.

Researchers in this area often assume that there is an obvious answer to this question. In the first approach, war crimes are seen as 'gross human rights violations', which breach human rights law or norms (Mullins and Rothe 2008). However, this 'human rights' approach does not provide an adequate conceptual basis for identifying war crimes. For example, to define conflict-related sexual violence as a human rights violation focuses upon the breach of the civil rights of the individual right-holder, and the state as guarantor (or violator) of those rights. However, breaches of human rights norms are not necessarily criminal offences or attract criminal sanctions. Moreover, this approach neglects the collective nature of this criminality, and of the legal protection and punishment of victims and perpetrators as members of groups (Campbell 2011). The second approach characterizes war crimes as violations of the legal or moral norms governing conflict (Treadwell 2012). However, this 'crimes in war' approach also fails to provide an adequate conceptual foundation. For example, to define conflict-related sexual violence as a war crime focuses upon violations of international humanitarian law, the law of armed conflict. However, not all breaches of these legal rules are criminalized, and it is only where the requisite elements of war crimes under customary international law, genocide, or crimes against humanity that such acts can be prosecuted as crimes under international law. To use the laws and norms of humanitarian law to define conflict-related sexual violence as war crime reproduces this 'compartmentalized and incomplete normative framework' (Bassiouni 1996: 560).

It is not possible to resolve this ethical challenge by focusing upon positive law or moral norms to define the object of study. If we define 'war crimes' according to positive law, then which legal regime should be used? For example, in the case of conflict-related sexual violence, the substantive definition of rape as a war crime differs between different international and national legal regimes. Alternatively, if we use moral norms to define war crimes, then exactly which values are we employing? For example, the 'right to sexual autonomy' that underlies international sexual offences is a specific cultural representation of sexual violence (see Campbell 2011). The ethical challenge is not to ensure that these concepts of criminality are value-free. Rather, it is to account for the values that shape concepts of war crimes, and to engage with the ethical consequences of how those values shape the focus of enquiry.

The ethics of visibility

The second aspect of the challenge of theoretical accountability concerns invisible and visible values in the research field. These values are also part of the 'specific genre of discourse and inquiry' of this field (Garland 2002). While this heterogeneous and multi-disciplinary field is still in the process of constitution, it is possible to identify key debates and approaches that shape our understanding of war crimes as an object of investigation. They form the contextual values of the field by providing a set of assumptions and judgments about what is known or not known about war and criminality. These assumptions may be taken for granted and widely held ideas about conflict, which are unexamined and hence 'invisible'. For example, Laura Sjoberg (2014: 3) points out that 'much of the scholarly work on war and conflict does not talk about women – much less gender – at all', but instead assumes male armies, masculine institutions, and men's peace. These invisible assumptions about gender and war shape our understanding of the object of inquiry. The ethical challenge is to make these assumptions visible, so that it becomes possible to critically examine the social and cultural values of the field.

The counterpoint to 'invisible' research assumptions is highly visible research problems. For example, conflict-related sexual violence has now become a highly visible problem (Buss 2014; Aoláin 2014). This is in contrast to the earlier invisibility of this issue when the current research field began to emerge in the 1990s. The emergence of new research problems may reflect shifts in broader social values, such as the rise of feminist activism in the 1990s (Campbell 2002). However, it may also be due to other values. These include 'the role of institutional culture(s), activist strategies and choice of "frames", policy entrepreneurs, and the operation of deep-seated gendered, racialized, and colonial ideologies' (Buss 2014). For example, the increasing focus upon of male victims of conflict-related sexual violence coincides with the increasing rejection of previous feminist work (Vojdik 2014: 938). The visibility of this new debate coincides with new funding, increased academic respectability, and policy attention to conflict-related sexual violence. The ethical challenge is how to critically intervene in the research field without reproducing these politics of knowledge.

Ethical strategy one: theoretical accountability

The first strategy is that of theoretical accountability. This involves constructing an ethically accountable concept of war crimes. This process of 'concept building' explicitly and reflexively engages with the values that shape the focus of enquiry. There are three elements in this process, which can be seen in the building of a new concept of the crime of conflict-related sexual violence in the GoJ project.

The first element builds upon the concept of criminalization, which focuses upon the social practices that make or constitute 'criminality'. This approach moves away from the legal and normative concerns that are often taken for granted in war crimes research. Instead, criminalization is a dynamic field of 'interlocking practices in which the moments of "defining" and "responding to" crime can rarely be completely distinguished and in which legal and social (extra-legal) constructions of crime constantly interact' (Lacey 2002: 197). It focuses upon the constitution of war crimes as such in legal rules and trial practices. Substantive law defines which conduct is criminal and which is not (such as the criminal act); who is a victim of that harm (such as consent); and who perpetrates it (such as intent). However, this process of criminalization also involves practices that adjudicate the alleged crime. These include the charging of offences, which determines what offences are brought before the court, witness evidence, which determines the harms that the court hears, and evidential proof, which determines the basis upon which the court makes its determination of criminality.

The second element focuses upon international criminal justice, and away from human rights or humanitarian law. It is now possible to identify a body of substantive and procedural law that can properly be called 'international criminal law'. This provides a means of identifying the category of criminalized conduct, as well as the relevant national and international criminal proceedings determining criminality. For example, sexual violence consists of a category of international crimes defined by customary international law. Such acts can be prosecuted as war crimes, genocide, or crimes against humanity if the requisite elements are met under customary international law. These so-called 'core crimes' can be prosecuted under national and international legal regimes, as this customary law binds all states. Following contemporary usage of 'armed conflict' rather than 'war' in this body of law, we will call these international offences 'conflict-related crimes'. This approach emphasises the connection between conflict and the commission of these crimes. It also offers a cohesive conceptual approach, and thereby avoids the problem of different legal or 'moral' norms across national legal systems. These two elements build a concept of the criminalization of conflict-related crimes, which provides a means of capturing how certain conduct in conflict becomes prohibited, and how certain persons become victims or perpetrators.

The third element explicitly inscribes transformative values in this process of concept building. This inscription aims to resist invisible assumptions about gender and war. This is because this model of conflict-related sexual violence as a crime can make visible how the process of criminalization creates 'gendered' acts and subjects in the legal rules and trial practices that construct the crimes of war. However, it also resists the current politics of knowledge by building on feminist work to highlight 'the limitations in what has been made visible' about conflict-related sexual violence (Buss 2014: 15). This approach does not focus upon war crimes against women or men as such, but instead considers how international criminal justice constructs *gender relations*. With this theoretical framing, it becomes possible to consider the making of gendered patterns of criminalization, and to ask whether those patterns reinforce or challenge existing gendered patterns of domination and power.

Ethical challenge two: the research field in the context of conflict and the challenge of situated research

The second ethical challenge arises from the context of conflict, which situates both researcher and researched in an often violent and politicized research field. This context of conflict may range from wars between states to protracted violence between irregular armed groups. The conflict may include physical, material, and symbolic violence. In such contexts, the demarcations between zones of war and peace are often unclear, with a society remaining in conflict, if not at war (Gagnon and Brown 2014).

The ethical challenge of this research arises because it is 'undertaken in difficult or dangerous settings, within societies that are often deeply divided, and with participants who may have witnessed or experienced violence' (O'Reilly 2015). In this context of conflict, observing the ethical principle of 'do no harm' becomes significantly more challenging and complex. In particular, it raises two key sets of ethical challenges for the researcher: data in conflict and situating knowledge.

Data in conflict

The conflict context can create an ethical challenge to the production of knowledge itself. This is the problem of 'data in conflict'. In conflict, truth claims often become both highly contested and evidentially underdetermined. Crimes of conflict still remain a significantly under-researched area (Aoláin 2014). Where data is available, it often suffers from inconsistent and unsystematic collection and analysis, or from under-developed methodological frameworks and methods (Cohen et al. 2013; Foreign and Commonwealth Office 2014). Where claims are made, they frequently become highly politicized and contested (Hansen 2000). For example, the estimated numbers of female victims of conflict-related sexual violence in the war in Yugoslavia ranges from 12,000 to 50,000 (Niarchos 1995). Exact numbers of female victims were difficult to establish for two reasons. First, these investigations faced not only the general challenges encountered when researching sexual violence, but the additional difficulty of doing so in the midst of an armed conflict (Bassiouni 1994). Second, as claims and counter-claims of sexual violence became part of the Yugoslavian conflict, these estimates themselves became the subject of 'wars of interpretation' (Kesić 2002: 317). Similar difficulties arose in investigating incidents of sexual violence against men. There are no comparable estimates for male sexual assault (Oosterhoff et al. 2004).

Due to the problem of data in conflict, the researcher confronts the issue of objectivity, and its negative counterparts, bias and partiality. In regulatory ethical frameworks, objectivity is often understood to require that researchers occupy the position of neutral observers of the world. This is often seen as particularly important in contexts of conflict, because 'in a divided society, the researcher must be someone who will strive for impartiality and be unbiased in his or her analysis' (Adetoun 2005: 48). The assumption is that without objectivity, researchers will necessarily become situated within the conflict itself, and so mired in its polarities. This approach requires that researchers must exclude value and valuation from their research, because to be objective is to be value-free.

The challenge of data in conflict, however, reveals the complexity of a value-free position in conflict and post-conflict societies. For example, a 'neutral' position that contends that all nationalities suffered equally during a war may ultimately give support to ethno-nationalist arguments about the nature of the conflict by failing to acknowledge differentiated patterns of perpetration and victimization (Boose 2002: 71–72; Mischkowski and Mlinarevic 2009). Similarly, if the researcher insists that some truth claims are warranted (while others are not), they have already positioned themselves in the field of competing truths. For example, while exact numbers cannot be known, it is now well established that there are significant differences in the gendered and ethnicized patterns and scale of male and female victims in the war in the former Yugoslavia (Campbell 2007). The ethical challenge does not concern how to exclude value and valuation so as to become impartial and unbiased, but rather to critically consider how these judgments shape our knowledge and situate us in the context of the conflicts that we are seeking to study.

This challenge includes reflexively examining the values that inform the decision to undertake research. These are the ethical problems of knowing too much, and knowing too little. The problem of 'knowing too much' arises when a particular conflict or international crime has been 'over-researched', with a resulting burden upon research participants and related distrust of researchers (Pittaway et al. 2010: 236). For example, there are significant gaps in the understanding of conflict-related sexual violence in the former Yugoslavia. It might seem that the most ethical approach is to interview survivors about their experiences. However, this focus can also operate as a 'narrative burden imposed on women victims of sexual violence' (Buss 2014: 17), with little apparent benefit to them or to their community (Helms 2013: 19). Conversely, the problem of 'knowing too little' arises when a researcher has 'under-researched' the conflict that they are seeking to investigate. This can have similar consequences to the over-researched conflict, with subjects growing increasingly wary of researchers with little knowledge of the particular field site, or experience of fieldwork.

Situating knowledges: the researcher and the researched in the context of conflict

Research on conflict-related crimes is a classical example of 'sensitive research' (O'Reilly 2015). Sensitive research requires particular care regarding ethical issues because of potential risks and costs to research participants, communities, or researchers (Renzetti and Lee 1993). In his classic study of research on sensitive topics, Raymond Lee (1993: 4) identifies these threats as including intrusion into the participant's private life or personal experiences, sanction where research is stigmatizing or incriminating; and political threat where research investigates the vested interests of powerful persons or political institutions, or relations of coercion or domination. The context of conflict clearly raises all the possibility of all three 'threats', and raises two key issues for undertaking ethical research. These are 'vulnerable subjects' and 'ethical disclosure'.

The first issue concerns 'vulnerable subjects' of research. The idea of 'vulnerability' in sensitive research is generally understood to refer to susceptibility to harm, whether because of the personal or social position of the research participant (Liamputtong 2007). In the conflict context, the vulnerable subject may be individual informants or vulnerable groups. For example, wartime sexual assault survivors in the former Yugoslavia have often experienced long-term detrimental impacts upon their physical or psychological health, and still live in precarious financial and social circumstances some twenty years after the war (Mischkowski and Mlinarevic 2009). It is common for both scholars and ethical reviewers to assume that these women form a 'vulnerable group', whether because of personal distress or social stigma. However, Downes et al. (2014: 2.8) point out that 'this means that victim-survivors are assumed to be unable to comprehend the potential risks and consequences that may unfold as a result of participating in research and the process of informed consent may not be possible for them'. This belief in the diminished autonomy of such groups often leads to the presumption that they require special safeguards to protect their rights (Liamputtong 2007: 2–3). Such safeguards are necessary in situations in which obtaining valid consent may be difficult due to incapacity (such as the age of a child or psychiatric illness) or circumstances (such as emergency settings). However, such situations should be distinguished from presumptive classification of the diminished capacity of a particular group because of their personal or social vulnerabilities. For example, the marginalized social position of many sexual violence survivors in the former Yugoslavia has not diminished their capacity or willingness to participate in research (Mischkowski and Mlinarevic 2009: 12). The 'vulnerable subject' requires the researcher to be responsible to that subject by identifying specific risks of harm due to personal disadvantage or social disempowerment. The ethical question remains for the researcher at every point: how do I minimise personal harm to participants? However, the researcher alone cannot answer this question. Rather than focusing upon diminished capacity, the researcher should engage in research practices that give agency to those participants in the research process.

An integral element and example of the ethical challenge of the 'vulnerable subject' involves the agency of informed consent. This concerns the information that respondents and researchers require to make a responsible decision about whether or not to participate in research. To have 'informed consent' entails that the prospective participant is informed of the nature of the project, and understands the potential risks and benefits that may follow from that participation. In terms of regulatory ethical compliance, this may include a project information sheet and consent forms. However, 'informed consent' is a process involving more than a form for participants to read and sign (WHO 2007). It may involve explaining the relevant information to participants. Alternatively, it may involve obtaining verbal consent from participants, where using written records is inappropriate or creates further risk of harm (Wood 2006: 379). If consent is understood as a process, then it may need to be sought an ongoing basis throughout the research, so that participants can make these decisions in the context of the development of the research, and of their own changing circumstances (MacKenzie et al. 2007: 307).

The second key ethical issue involves 'ethical disclosure'. This concerns the normative reasons for disclosure or non-disclosure of information obtained in the course of research. This problem arises because information may not only report and explain facts, but it may also ground claims to legal and/or social justice. In the context of conflict, ethical disclosure is a particularly important and complex issue because of the potential personal and social consequences of making (or not making) information public. This information may include sensitive personal or institutional information, legally protected information, or information provided in circumstances of confidentiality. Disclosure may involve the publication of information in any media, as well as revealing information to third parties.

For informants, disclosure raises issues of security, confidentiality, and identification. For researchers, it may also raise issues of legal or social impact of disclosure or non-disclosure, as well as legal requirements concerning restrictions upon disclosure or obligations to disclose. These requirements may involve different obligations arising in different jurisdictions (such as obligations under a national criminal code not to disclose the identity of protected witnesses) or regional regimes (such as European Union personal data protection regulations). For example, the GoJ project faced the challenge of complex ethical and legal obligations at both European and national levels concerning recording, storing, managing, and publication of sensitive personal and institutional data concerning conflict-related sexual violence prosecutions.

In terms of ethical accountability, these obligations cannot be determined legalistically or narrowly. Rather, obligations concerning disclosure may extend beyond direct interlocutors, and also involve 'research assistants and other collaborators as well as interviewees, to individuals such as their relatives and colleagues with whom one may have no direct contact' (Sriram 2009: 56). Equally, these obligations may not be to the persons, but to a society. Disclosure of information regarding perpetration of war crimes, or the effectiveness of the prosecution of these crimes, may be regarded as an integral part of public interest obligations. These can be articulated as legal obligations to report suspected criminal activities. However, these public interest obligations may also include broader ethical obligations to social values such as open justice and the rule of law. To engage with this challenge requires understanding disclosure as an ethical practice, in which all decisions about disclosure or non-disclosure must be considered in terms of their personal and social consequences in the conflict setting. In this context, the principle of 'do no harm' becomes fundamental to developing ethical practices of disclosure.

Ethical strategy two: situated ethics

The second strategy is that of 'situated ethics'. This involves building a new approach to situated research, with its ethical challenges of data in conflict and ethical disclosure. Following Donna Haraway (1991: 191), the concept of 'situation' refers to 'location, partial embodiment and partial perspective'. This standpoint of the researcher reflects their objective position in a social structure. However, rather than seeing this partiality as an ethical and epistemic problem, Haraway argues 'for situated and embodied knowledge claims and against various forms of unlocatable, and so irresponsible, knowledge claims'. To be objective is to acknowledge how our social position shapes the partiality and limits of our research. Rather than objectivity being seen as value-free research, this approach instead conceives objectivity as the acknowledgement of the situatedness of knowers and knowledge in an unequal social space. This enables researchers to generate less partial perspectives of the society they are seeking to study.

Following this model, the study of conflict-related crimes is a situated knowledge, in which both the researcher and researched are situated in conflictual social relations. However, this context of conflict also requires researchers to develop ethical accountability in their situated knowledges. Ethical accountability is the responsibility to 'know well' (Code 1987: 10). To 'know well' involves responsibility to others and to wider transformative values that seek to change social orders of conflict. For example, this strategy recognizes that research on conflict-related crimes should aim to resist, rather than reproduce, categories of social differentiation and domination. This is because conflict itself constitutes these categories through violence. Ethical accountability is a form of situated knowledge. It is situated because ethical research practices are located and embodied in social relations of conflict.

The strategy of situated ethics involves developing a critical position through knowing well, that is, through developing relationships of epistemic responsibility to others and to transformative social change. Accordingly, 'situated ethics' acknowledges the positions of researcher and participants in a differentiated social space that has been structured by and through conflict. It involves building relationships of accountability through, 'webs of connection called solidarity in politics and shared conversations in epistemology' (Haraway 1991: 191). A useful description of these relationships of accountability in practice can be found in Elissa Helms' (2013) discussion of her fieldwork in Bosnia and Herzegovina. Knowing well is necessarily relational, since it is the outcome of practices of communities of knowers, rather than the ethical act of a single scholar.

Using the strategy of situated ethics, then, is a means of addressing the challenge of research in the context of conflict. The GoJ project uses the strategy of situated ethics by integrating ethical accountability into research design and practice. Since the project was 'high risk' in ethical terms because of its subject matter, the research design sought to address this through the use of 'low risk' research strategies. For example, to deal with the issue of vulnerable subjects, the research does not use sexual violence survivors as key respondents. Rather, the project engages with key groups working with these survivors. To engage with the issue of ethical disclosure, the project uses a consultative strategy that circulates research to informant lawyers and local expert practitioners for review prior to dissemination. This aims to ensure that all potential ethical issues are addressed before the research moves into the public domain. The project involves continuing collaboration and consultation with key informants, practitioners, and advocacy groups. Because ethical accountability is a situated knowledge, it must be continually re-examined in relation to the changing contexts of conflict. In this approach, ethical accountability is an ongoing process.

The ethical challenge of researching: value in methods and methodologies

The third ethical challenge relates to the choices of methodology and methods, which are integral to research quality and integrity in this difficult field. This is the other element of 'knowing well', which involves reflecting upon the values that inform our epistemic practices. To 'know well' is to be responsible for our epistemic practices, so that we reflect on our regulative standards of knowledge and generate well-warranted claims. These are crucial ethical questions for the researcher on conflict-related crimes. For example, the GoJ project analyses patterns of conflict-related sexual violence. Research in this area frequently uses ICTY statistics as the basis for an analysis of prosecutions.[1] On this basis, the ICTY appears to prosecute high numbers of individuals for crimes of sexual violence. However, the ICTY does not provide the methodology or methods used to generate these statistics. Nevertheless, it is clear that this analysis does not distinguish between charges, cases, and convicted accused, or identify the gender of victims or perpetrators. If this distinction is made, then lower numbers and patterns of prosecutions emerge. There are significantly fewer cases of sexual violence prosecuted, and the number of these cases significantly decline over time. If we identify gender of victims and perpetrators in these earlier cases, then significant difference in patterns of prosecution of sexual violence, with 'an overrepresentation of counts of sexual violence against male compared to female victims, and a differential distribution of the categories of offences being charged between genders' (Campbell 2007: 426–7). These issues show the necessity of engaging with epistemic practice as an ethical practice. What are the appropriate epistemic norms for evaluating these (and other) knowledge claims? How do we include the ethical values of responsibility and reflexivity in the methodologies and methods that we use? Finally, how can commitments to social justice inform the epistemic practices we use?

Evaluating data: values and valuation

The problem of the ICTY 'in numbers' typifies the field of research on conflict-related crimes, in which there are few empirical studies, and insufficient reflection on methods or methodologies. Recently, there have been increasing calls to address these gaps in knowledge. For example there are growing demands for more empirical data and quantitative or large-scale data on conflict-related sexual violence (see e.g. Cohen and Nordås 2014). This also includes demands for more evidence that can be used as a basis for policy development and criminal prosecutions (see. e.g. Foreign and Commonwealth Office 2014). However, Ní Aoláin points out that this 'data demand culture' does not 'point the way towards *data quality* (what standards should be applied and to what ends the data will be used)' (2014: 10–11). Questions of data quality require reflection upon our epistemic practice and norms, as well as upon the purposes for which we generate that data. This is particularly true of data concerning conflict-related crimes. For example, how do we measure conflict-related sexual violence in quantitative empirical studies? What counts as 'evidence' for policy or prosecutorial purposes?

The ethical challenge is that epistemic judgements (what and how we know) always involve normative judgements (what and how we should know). Knowledge-claims are epistemic practices that are regulated by communities of knowers, in which those practices reflect the values of that epistemic community concerning the most appropriate methods of inquiry and justification of knowledge. Helen Longino argues that '[t]he complete set of regulative standards, inclusive of theoretical virtues, guiding a community's epistemic practices could be called its epistemology'. These regulative standards are the normative criteria by which members of the community of inquiry determine which practices 'will advance our cognitive aims' and political goals (1997: 33–34). These are the epistemic values of the research field. Accordingly, developing data quality involves 'knowing well', as it requires reflexivity about, and responsibility for, our epistemic values.

Ethical strategy three: epistemic practice as ethical practice

The third ethical strategy is epistemic accountability. This develops a model of epistemic practice as ethical practice. Epistemic accountability involves asking how the transformative values of social justice shape which normative epistemic standards research will use. It also asks how the knowledge that is generated will be applied. To answer these questions requires considering the values that inform our theory of how research should proceed (methodology), and our choice of techniques of evidence gathering (method) (Harding 1986: 2). So, for example, Helen Longino identifies 'feminist cognitive values' as including 'empirical adequacy, novelty, ontological heterogeneity, mutuality of interaction, applicability to human needs, and decentralization of power or universal empowerment' (Longino 1997: 21). This is a model of reflexive and responsible epistemic practice. For example, the GoJ project employs a strategy of epistemic accountability to choose its methodology and methods. It uses a feminist methodological framework for studying conflict-related sexual violence. This critical framework focuses on the social constitution of masculinity and femininity in the violence of armed conflict. The GoJ project also seeks not to reproduce those power relations in the methods it chose to use. For this reason, an important part of this strategy is to use feminist participatory research. This enables the researchers to reflexively engage with the perspectives of victims and activists seeking to change current models and practices of gender justice, while also aiming to contribute to that process of social change.

The ethical issue of accepted epistemic practices in the study of conflict-related crimes is still to be properly explored. Given that there is little consensus within this emerging field on how to engage with values in methodologies and methods, developing epistemic accountability has become a key task for researchers. This fundamental challenge of ethical knowledge production is as much a collective as an individual engagement.

Summary

This chapter has explored key ethical challenges and strategies for ethical accountability when researching conflict-related crime. It identifies three key sets of challenges and strategies for engaging with these issues. The first challenge is how to conceptualize the object of inquiry. This involves two key problems of the concept of criminalization, and the visible and invisible values in the research field. The first ethical strategy is theoretical accountability, which requires an explicit and reflexive engagement with values in a process of concept building. The second challenge arises because of the research context of conflict. This crystallises around issues of conflicting data, and the situation of the researcher and researched. The second ethical strategy is situated ethics. This involves the evaluation of ethical practice in terms of accountability to others, and to transformative social change in our research. The third challenge concerns values in methodology and method, which is evident in the problem of evaluation of data. The third ethical strategy is epistemic accountability, which develops normative criteria for evaluating our research practices. Because this is the least examined area of research on conflict-related crimes, it is also arguably the most challenging area of ethical engagement.

Review questions

1. What values inform your concept of conflict-related crime, and your intervention in the research field?
2. What is your position as researcher in the context of the conflict? What values inform your research relationship to the persons and societies you are seeking to study?
3. What values inform your choice of methodology and methods?
4. How do the strategies of theoretical accountability, situated ethics, and epistemic accountability change how you undertake this research?

Guide to further reading

Ní Aoláin (2014) and Buss, D. (2014): these two papers provide important analyses the ethics of research practices and fields, focusing on conflict-related sexual violence.

Smyth, M. and Robinson, G., eds., (2001) *Researching Violently Divided Societies: Ethical and methodological issues*. (London: Pluto Press): a wide-ranging and careful discussion of ethical research around societies in conflict.

Sriram, C., King, J., Mertus, J., Martin-Ortega, O. and Herman, J. eds., (2009) *Surviving field research: Working in violent and difficult situations*. (London: Routledge): an excellent discussion of the range of ethical issues raised by research in conflict settings.

Campbell, K. (2004): Chapter One sets out key approaches in feminist theories of value and knowledge.

Note

1 'In Numbers', http://www.icty.org/sid/10586, ICTY, accessed 7 April 2015.

References

Adetoun, B. (2005). 'The Role And Function Of Research In A Divided Society', in E. Porter, C. Robinson, M. Smyth, A. Schnabel and E. Osaghae, eds., *Researching Conflict in Africa: Insights and Experiences*, New York: United Nations University.

Bassiouni, C. M. (1994). 'Final Report of the Commission of Experts', UN Doc. S/1994/674.

Bassiouni, C. M. (1996). *The Law of the International Criminal Tribunal for the Former Yugoslavia*. New York: Transnational.

Boose, L. E. (2002). 'Crossing the River Drina', *Signs* 8(1): 71–96.

Buss, D. (2014). 'Seeing Sexual Violence in Conflict and Post-Conflict Societies' in D. Buss, J. Lebert, B. Rutherford, D. Sharkey and O. Aginam, eds., *Sexual Violence in Conflict and Post-Conflict Societies,* New York: Routledge, pp. 3–27.

Campbell, K. (2002). 'Legal Memories', *Signs* 28(1): 149–178.

Campbell, K. (2004). *Jacques Lacan and Feminist Epistemology*. London: Routledge.

Campbell, K. (2007). 'The Gender of Transitional Justice', *The International Journal of Transitional Justice*, 1(3): 411–432.

Campbell, K. (2011). 'Victims and Perpetrators of International Crimes', *International Humanitarian Legal Studies*, 2: 325–351.

Code, L. (1987). *Epistemic Responsibility*. Hanover, NH: Brown University Press.

Cohen, D. and Nordås, R. (2014). 'Sexual Violence in Armed Conflict', *Journal of Peace Research,* 51(3): 418–428.

Cohen, D. K., Hoover Green, A. and Wood, J. (2013). *Wartime Sexual Violence*. Washington: United States Institute of Peace.

Downes, J., Kelly, L, and Westmarland, N. (2014). 'Ethics in Violence and Abuse'. *Sociological Research Online*, 19(1): 2, http://www.socresonline.org.uk/19/1/2.html.

Foreign and Commonwealth Office (2014). *International Protocol on the Documentation and Investigation of Sexual Violence in Conflict*. London: United Kingdom Foreign and Commonwealth Office.

Gagnon, C. and Brown, K. (2014). 'The Fog of Peace', in C. Gagnon and K. Brown, eds., *Post-Conflict Studies*, New York: Routledge.

Garland, D. (2002). 'Of Crime and Criminals', in M. Maguire, R. Morgan and R. Reiner, eds., *The Oxford Handbook of Criminology*, 2nd edn, Oxford: Oxford University Press.

Hansen, L. (2000). 'Gender, Nation, Rape', *International Feminist Journal of Politics*, 3(1): 55–75.

Haraway, D. (1991). *Simians, Cyborgs, and Women*. Abingdon: Routledge.

Harding, S. (1986). *The Science Question in Feminism*. Ithaca and London: Cornell University Press.

Hay, I. and Israel, M. (2006). *Research Ethics for Social Scientists*. London: Sage.

Helms, E. (2013). *Innocence and Victimhood*. Madison: University of Wisconsin Press.

Kesić, V. (2002). 'Muslim Women, Croatian Women, Serbian Women, Albanian Women', in D. Bjelić and O. Savić, eds., *Balkan as Metaphor*, Cambridge, MA: MIT.

Lacey, N. (2002). 'Legal Constructions of Crime', in M. Maguire, R. Morgan and R. Reiner, eds., *Oxford Handbook of Criminology*, 2nd edn, Oxford: Oxford University Press.

Lee, R. M. (1993). *Doing Research on Sensitive Topics*. London: Sage.

Liamputtong, P. (2007). *Researching the Vulnerable*. London: Sage.

Longino, H. (1997). 'Feminist Epistemology as a Local Epistemology', *The Aristotelian Society*, 71: 19–35.

MacKenzie, C., McDowell, C., and Pittaway, E. (2007). 'Beyond "Do No Harm"', *Journal of Refugee Studies*, 20(2): 300–319.

Mehring, S. (2014). *First Do No Harm*. Leiden and Boston: Brill.

Mischkowski, G. and Mlinarevic, G. (2009). *And That It Does Not Happen to Anyone Anywhere in the World*. Cologne: Medica Mondiale.

Mullins, C. and Rothe, D. (2008). 'A Supranational Criminology', in J. Ross, ed., *Cutting The Edge*, New Brunswick, NJ: Transaction Publishers.

Ní Aoláin, F. D. (2014). *The Gender Politics of Fact-Finding in the Context of the Women, Peace and Security Agenda*, Minnesota Legal Studies Research Paper No. 14–31.

Niarchos, C. (1995). 'Women, War and Rape,' *Human Rights Quarterly*, 17(4): 649–690.

O'Reilly, M. (2015). 'Researching Sensitive Topics and Ethics of War Crimes Research', *Gender of Justice Working Paper*.

Oosterhoff P., Zwanikken, P. and Ketting, E. (2004). 'Sexual Torture of Men in Croatia and Other Conflict Situations', *Reproductive Health Matters*, 12(23): 68–77.

Pittaway, E., Bartolomei, L., and Hugman, R. (2010). 'Stop Stealing Our Stories', *Journal of Human Rights Practice*, 2: 229–251.

Renzetti, C. and Lee, R., eds. (1993). *Researching Sensitive Topics*. Newbury Park, CA: Sage.

Sjoberg, L. (2014). *Gender, War, And Conflict*. Cambridge: Polity.

Smyth, M. and Robinson G., eds. (2001). *Researching Violently Divided Societies*. London: Pluto Press.

Sriram, C. L. (2009). 'Maintenance of Standards of Protection during Write Up and Publication', in C. L. Sriram, J. C. King, J. A. Mertus, O. Martin-Ortega, J. Herman, eds., *Surviving Field Research*, London and New York: Routledge.

Treadwell, J. (2012). *Criminology: The Essentials*. London: Sage.

Vojdik, V. (2014). 'Sexual Violence Against Men and Women in War', *Nevada Law Journal*, 14(3): 15.

Wood, E. (2006). 'The Ethical Challenges of Field Research in Conflict Zones', *Qualitative Sociology*, 29: 373–386.

World Health Organisation (2007). 'WHO Ethical And Safety Recommendations For Researching, Documenting And Monitoring Sexual Violence In Emergencies', Geneva: World Health Organisation.

10

METHODOLOGICAL INNOVATIONS AND ETHICAL CHALLENGES IN GREEN CRIMINOLOGY

Avi Brisman and Nigel South

This chapter defines the field of 'green criminology', noting the breadth of issues of concern and the challenges facing their investigation. Methods can be diverse, from analysis of epidemiological and large data sets to localised anthropological and visual analysis.

This chapter contemplates challenges to research on topics that can be sensitive and protected by gatekeepers, including issues of access, power imbalances, and understanding cultural barriers or conflicts. Particular ethical and political issues may arise for an area of criminology that may be critical of state and corporate systems, yet make calls for more rigorous regulatory and legal interventions.

Key definitions

Environmental crime: Environmental harms proscribed by law (e.g., acts or omissions relating to the illegal taking of flora and fauna, pollution offences, transportation of banned substances). Environmental crime that crosses the borders of nation-states is often referred to as *transnational environmental crime* and includes the illegal trade in wildlife, the international transfer of toxic waste, and the black market in ozone-depleting substances.

Environmental harm: Refers to a wide range of injuries to and degradations of the natural environment (e.g., forests, deserts, oceans, rivers) due to human use, misuse and poor management, including logging, pollution and the killing of nonhuman animals and plants. Unlike environmental *crime*, environmental *harm* includes both acts and omissions that are *legal* and those that are *illegal*.

Green criminology: The study by criminologists of environmental crimes, harms, laws and regulations.

Various writers across a range of academic disciplines (and at points of overlap and convergence) have exposed political inertia, failures of regulation, and avoidance of corporate, state, and personal responsibility regarding environmental harms and threats, and preservation of the environment. While criminology has much to contribute to debates about the numerous harms and threats resulting from or presented by climate change, natural resource depletion, loss of biodiversity, pollution, and the like, for too long, the subject sat passively, leaving the study of environmental damage and its regulation to researchers in other fields. But over the past twenty-five years, a (now substantial and growing) body of work concerned with environmental crime, harm and risk has emerged.

While there is something of a debate about the appropriate name or label for this sub-field or perspective within criminology (see, e.g., Ellefsen et al., 2012; Eman et al., 2009; Gibbs et al., 2010; Halsey, 2004; Herbig and Joubert, 2006; Lynch, 1990; South, 1998a; Walters, 2010, 2011; White, 2008, 2010b, 2011), 'green criminology' is the term that criminologists most frequently employ to describe the study of environmental crimes and harms, laws and regulation (South et al., 2013). The range of issues covered is broad and can incorporate violations of existing environmental law and regulations designed to protect the health, safety and vitality of humans and non-human species, natural resources and ecosystems, as well as harms that may not be statutorily proscribed (Brisman, 2008a; Lynch and Stretesky, 2003; Sollund, 2008; South, 2014; South and Brisman, 2013; South et al., 2014; Walters et al., 2013; White, 2010a; White and Heckenberg, 2014). Thus, for green criminologists, it is important that 'environment' is not conceived in a narrow sense and 'harm' is defined in both ecological and legal terms. As Skinnider (2013: 1) notes, harms and damages can be felt immediately or only in the long-term and may be 'direct or indirect', their causes may arise in many different ways, their origins may be 'point source or diffuse', their effects may be 'individual or cumulative', 'local, trans-boundary or global', and those responsible might be individuals, groups, corporations, governments or criminal enterprises.

Topics of research within green criminology include:

- climate change (e.g., harm caused by human contributions to global warming; criminality associated with the aftermath of natural disasters);
- economy, consumption and waste (e.g., harm caused by the hazardous transport of e-waste and the illegal disposal of toxic substances by organized crime syndicates);
- pollution of air, land and water by state-corporate entities;
- environmental justice and environmental victims/victimization;
- food (including the negative ecological consequences of the use of genetically modified organisms);
- abuse of nonhuman species and cruelty to nonhuman animals; and
- poaching, trafficking and trading (e.g., illegal trade in endangered species; illegal harvesting of 'natural resources', such as forests and fisheries, as well as

harms associated with legal activities, such as logging old-growth forests – see South et al., 2014 for general discussion).

As with any social scientific inquiry, the *methodology* that the green criminologist employs – 'the overall approach to the research process including the theoretical approach that influences the way the research is designed and conducted, and the lens through which the researcher views the social world' (White and Heckenberg, 2014: 79), and the *method* or *technique* used to gather and analyze the research data – all depend on the types of questions the green criminologist wishes to ask and the kind of issues he/she would like to examine.

Typically, green criminologists have considered the following:

*   How and in what ways does environmental harm occur? (And why?).
*   Who or what is responsible for the environmental harm? (Technology? Capitalism? Humans – and, if so, are these individuals? Groups/cultures? Corporations? Nation-states?).
*   Where are the environmental harms occurring? Where geographically is the harm manifest (e.g., locally, globally)? What is the main site in which the harm is apparent (e.g., built environment, natural environment)?
*   Who is being harmed? (Are the victims humans? Nonhuman animals? Both?).
*   What is the scope and extent of the environmental harm (e.g., contained, cumulative, dispersed)?
*   What is the timeframe in which the environmental harm has occurred and within which its consequences can be analyzed (e.g., before it occurs; as it evolves or unfolds; after the fact; a number of years in the past or the future)?
*   What is to be done about the environmental harm? (What are the challenges of regulating environmentally damaging practices in a globalized world? What are the problems besetting criminal justice system responses to environmental harms?).
*   What is the potential of – and what are the challenges for – criminal law and/or administrative regulations in preventing or intervening in various practices and processes in order to limit harms to the environment and nonhuman animals? What does such environmental harm mean and how has it been represented?

In approaching these questions, green criminologists have drawn on a variety of research designs to collect their data, including surveys, observation, experiments (although this is uncommon), and existing sources (see, e.g., Heckenberg and White, 2013; White and Heckenberg, 2014).

A green criminological study is usually concerned with an issue in order to argue about its significance. In most circumstances, such argument may be strengthened by evidence, and green criminologists have employed a range of methods and orientations appropriate to the gathering of empirical data (e.g., Lynch and Stretesky, 2001; Stretesky and Lynch, 2001, 2004). Lynch and Stretesky (2014: 68) argue that:

drawing on the scientific knowledge base of green sciences [i.e. natural sciences concerned with environmental matters] to enhance the examination of green crime and justice issues … is important because it illustrates the extent to which green criminology can be linked to scientific values and principles. By making that link green criminology can demonstrate that its objectives are not simply a reflection of moral principles or philosophies or of preferences, but that at its base green criminology involves a reliance on objective, scientific standards for its views about environmental harms, crimes and justice.

But of course, not all research questions and issues of interest yield readily accessible or easily observable data. In many cases, environmental crimes or harms are hidden and pose challenges related to access, examination and health and safety. As in similar studies, the task of researching sensitive and/or hidden forms of harm, which may, for example, be legal but not something to draw attention to or illegal and therefore certainly clandestine, may require adoption of particular research methods. Ethnographic and qualitative methods are most frequently chosen in such cases and can generate rich and deep information, although the task of interpretation, analysis and representation is then not without its own challenges. Immersion in the field generates numerous well-known methodological and ethical dilemmas (see, e.g., Scarce, 1990[2006], 1994, 2005). In analyzing the material arising from close, sustained and in–depth experience, the researcher may also find that the implications and messages that can be drawn from the mass of material gathered may resemble a maze rather than a linear narrative. It can be hard, as Geertz (1973: 16) noted, to distinguish between 'winks' and 'twitches'. Qualitative approaches can range from, for example, visual analysis (Natali, 2010, 2013), in–depth ethnography (Cianchi, 2015; Kane 2012, 2013), through grounded theory as used in human ecology and other approaches (McIntosh, 2012: 248) to action research as a 'participatory paradigm', defined by Wilding, (2012: 375) as 'research *with* people, not *on* them', being 'more about facilitating communities of learning, and less about individual researchers gathering *data* from research *subjects*. Central to action research is extending the forms of knowledge that are acceptable as evidence'.

In many cases, a mixed methods approach sensitive to history and place is necessary or may be appropriate because of the variety of research opportunities and sources that are available. In some situations, official data may be accessible but as is often the case with invisible crimes (Davies et al., 2014) or crimes of the powerful (Barak, 2015), may be partial, deliberately rendered weak or insufficient, may be implausible, or appears to show 'only the tip of the iceberg' being investigated. In her study of the illegal trade in tropical timber, stretching between Europe and points of origin such as Africa and Brazil, Bisschop (2012: 6) used document analysis from various primary and secondary sources (governments, international bodies, corporations and civic-society organizations), semi-structured interviews, and location visits which provided context – in essence, a range of sources, methods and theoretical orientations that were combined or 'triangulated' to provide a comprehensive picture of global illicit-trade flows between different geographical hubs.

In examining other cases that may represent either existing trends or new developments, it may be necessary to think about *future* risks, harms and precautions. Indeed, because many threats and opportunities are at present poorly recognized, *horizon-scanning* can 'provide insight into risks (potential problems) and harms (actual problems)' and can offer 'a mechanism to discern where emerging threats (and positive opportunities) may arise and potential ways to mitigate or adapt to these' (White and Heckenberg, 2014: 40).

Whatever methods are employed, an approach based on research 'good practice' and professional ethical standards will be encouraged and expected. To some extent, this is a matter of personal ethical behaviour as well as sound research training but it is also often the prerogative of academic institutions, nongovernmental organizations and funders to require adherence to particular codes of ethics or rules of research. Professional bodies promote such codes and these will usually set out the ways in which commonly shared ethical standards apply to research across the social sciences, and hence also to green criminology. According to the ideal standards of such codes, green criminologists, like environmental sociologists, political ecologists and others studying environmental crimes and harms, should endeavor to maintain objectivity and integrity, respect the research subject's right to privacy and dignity, protect subjects from personal harm, preserve confidentiality, seek informed consent when data are collected from research participants or when observed behavior occurs in a private context or setting, acknowledge research collaboration and assistance, and disclose all sources of financial support. When seeking data or information about crimes and harms of a hidden nature or when it is in the interests of powerful groups to restrict such material, however, then abiding by the letter of such research principles and codes can be restrictive and even make some research endeavours impossible. Thus, it has become a legitimate debate in relation to criminological and sociological methodology to ask: How certain kinds of research can be carried out when ethical codes seem to protect offenders and the powerful and restrict researchers and critics?

As Carrabine and colleagues (2014: 40) ask, 'Is a criminologist working within tight ethical codes still able to conduct effective research into 'closed' worlds of different kinds, such as the 'closed' worlds of child sexual abuse, people trafficking or corporate crime' – or, we add, environmental crime? Or, to continue:

> Is it always possible or desirable for research aims to be 'transparent' and equally open to all parties? Could excessive risk assessment mean that researchers no longer take risks and, if so, what might be the effects of that? These kinds of questions are in part connected to the question of taking sides in criminological research.

This matter of 'who the research is for?' and 'whether sides are taken?' has a significant literature attached to it (Carrabine et al., 2014: 41–42) and need not be explored further here. It does, however, have very direct relevance to one factor that can greatly help or hinder research – the support or absence of funding. Although funding on critical criminological projects is not impossible to obtain it is not easily won and this is true for a number of fairly unsurprising reasons. First, government or commercial sponsors are probably most interested in evaluations that are concerned with efficiency and effectiveness or with policy and practice outcomes. Second, they will generally be interested in research that is supportive of their values and aims rather than work that is likely to be sceptical or critical.

Having noted these various approaches and issues, we do not intend in the rest of this chapter to provide simply a comprehensive review of research methodologies and methods easily obtainable elsewhere (for guides to researching sensitive subjects and the crimes of the powerful see Crowther-Dowey and Fussey, 2013; King and Wincup, 2007; Pitts and Smith, 2007; Tombs and Whyte, 2003). There *is*, however, something distinctive about research and intellectual engagement with the subject of the environment that we inhabit and the other species with which we share the planet. This relates to the philosophical and hence ethical position we adopt in valuing nature and other species.

A green perspective will, at the very least, be informed by a critique of anthropocentrism, and this raises some particular ethical issues. The *anthropocentric* view of nature sees the environment in utilitarian terms – as existing 'to be appropriated, processed, consumed and disposed of in a manner which best suits the immediate interests of human beings' (Halsey and White, 1998: 349). Anthropocentrism emphasizes human superiority over other living creatures and decisions regarding the environment are often made on economic grounds (usually at the expense of long-term stability of ecological systems). Although an anthropocentric view can be stretched to embrace the 'long-term' in a way that includes human individuals or communities of future generations, thereby acknowledging the principle of intergenerational equity (Skinnider, 2013: 7), anthropocentrism tends to be a present-oriented human-centered approach that regards humans as separate from and above nature.

Biocentrism, in constrast, recognizes non-human species as having intrinsic value and considers human beings as 'simply 'another species' to be attributed the *same* moral worth as such organisms as, for example, whales, wolves and birds' (Halsey and White, 1998: 352). This species-centered approach views all beings as possessing an equal right to live and blossom and to reach their own forms of self-realization, and thus would see 'any human activity that disrupts a biotic system as environmental crime' (Skinnider, 2013: 7–8). Because biocentrism regards all organisms as equal in intrinsic worth, '[d]ecisions concerning the environment would…be made according to which outcomes are most likely to foster the widest possible diversity of life, both non-human and human' (Halsey and White, 1998: 353). As such, more radical proponents of biocentrism have insisted that war, mass starvation, widespread disease, entrenched poverty and other forms of social injustice should be met with policies of *non*-intervention on the grounds that the planet is overpopulated and that 'such measures are Gaia's method of 'dealing with the problem' (Halsey and White, 1998: 354).

An *ecocentric* perspective, in turn, regards humans and their activities as inextricably intertwined with the rest of the natural world. While ecocentrism is based on the belief that human beings are 'merely one component of complex ecosystems that should be preserved for their own sake' (White, 2011: 34, 2013: 14, 31), it

> attempts to strike a balance between the instrumental and intrinsic conceptions of non-human nature espoused by anthropocentrists and biocentrists respectively. That is, while there is an explicit recognition that human beings – as living, breathing components of the natural world – need to impact upon or utlize non-human nature in order to survive, there also exists the realization that human beings need – in the interests of future human generations and the well-being of non-human nature – to develop ecologically sustainable ways of satisfying their basic needs.
>
> *(Halsey and White, 1998: 356)*

In other words, ecocentrism neither places humanity 'above' or 'below' the rest of non-human nature, but recognizes that damage to non-human nature can destroy that which sustains humans and human nature; humans have the unique capacity to develop and deploy methods of production that have global consequences and thus humans have a responsibility to ensure that such methods do not exceed the ecospheric limits of the planet.

Such categories are well established in philosophical debate and have stimulated important discussion in green criminology. Put starkly, ethical questions (and hence methodological problems) might arise when research is designed in support of the needs of one group (whether human or non-human) but has negative implications for another group or species (see, e.g., Kraul, 2014). For example, wildlife poaching, human interference with habitats and other influences have threatened the sustainability of some species. A response might be designed that aims to reduce poaching and also minimize loss of threatened species to predator species but in trying to put conservation into practice is it right that some animals need to be killed or culled? (Bekoff, 2010: 24).

To move beyond simply introducing methods and raising ethical conundrums, our aim in the rest of this chapter is to offer a handful of case examples to highlight some of the tensions that can arise when conducting research on environmental crime and harm – research that may expose different values, worldviews, notions of justice and positions of power. The tensions and dilemmas here are significant in public policy terms but also pose a very difficult set of challenges to the green criminological or environmental researcher.

Case examples

Individual-level environmental harm

Green criminologists often focus their analytical gaze on "acts of the powerful' in causing widespread and long-term environmental damage' (Walters, 2010: 314) – on the state, corporations or state-corporate actors – rather than on micro-/individual-level environmental crimes and harms (e.g., Kauzlarich and Friedrichs, 2003). One exception is Agnew (2013: 58), who explores 'the ordinary acts that contribute to ecocide – or the contamination and destruction of the natural environment in ways that reduce its ability to support life' (citing South 2009: 41). Such ordinary acts, which include regularly consuming meat, driving automobiles with poor fuel efficiency for most transportation, and living in a large, suburban home cooled and heated to comfortable levels, possess several characteristics: 'they are widely and regularly performed by individuals as part of their routine activities; they are generally viewed as acceptable, even desirable; and they collectively have a substantial impact on environmental problems' (Agnew, 2013: 58). Agnew's work notwithstanding, the preponderance of green criminological scholarship has been more concerned with environmental degradation perpetrated by states, corporations and state-corporate entities – despoliation that is frequently systemic and/or larger in scale than harm brought about by individual actors. That said, individuals *do* contribute to environmental destruction through certain habitual, quotidian behaviors and consumption practices (Brisman, 2013). The challenge for green criminologists is to analyze and critique these patterns and activities, while recognizing that they may reflect 'a particular philosophical stance on the appropriate relationship between human beings and nature (i.e., human-centered, nature-centered, balanced)' (Gibbs et al., 2010: 125). Moreover, while humans are to blame, not all humans are equally blameworthy (White, 2013; White and Heckenberg, 2014). Thus, another task of green criminologists in researching individual-level environmental harm is to be sensitive to various socio-economic realities that affect environmental decision-making (Brisman, 2009a, 2009b).

Punishing environmental crime: the ethics and policies of prosecution versus shaming

Public perceptions of, and punitive attitudes towards, environmental crime and harm vary over place and time (Shelley and Hogan, 2013). While environmental harms can and often do have violent consequences (Lynch, 2013), in the United States at least, environmental issues often rank near the bottom when people are asked to list the most pressing problems faced by individuals or society (Agnew, 2012a, 2012b; Dietz and Shwon, 2007; Hayward, 2010). In other cultures and countries, there is much greater and much more widespread support for holding responsible those people who endanger the public health of communities (Nader, 1980, 2003; RT, 2013).

The extent to which laws against environmental crime can and should be enforced and result in punishment, presents challenges and reveals tensions for green criminologists to negotiate. For example, the U.S. Environmental Protection Agency's 'most wanted' list names 'fugitives' at-large for various environmental crimes (http://www2.epa.gov/enforcement/epa-fugitives). As Walters (2010: 310) observes '[m]any on the list include corporate entrepreneurs who have owned and operated installations that have deliberately released toxic waste into the atmosphere'. But as Kaufman (2010: A17) reports, the list also includes 'people wanted for crimes ranging from dumping oil or contaminated soil to importing vehicles that fail to meet United States emissions standards'. In the United States, the enforcement of corporate environmental law remains extremely rare – fewer that one-half of one per cent of violations of federal environmental laws trigger criminal investigations and 'the vast majority of corporate environmental lawbreakers…escape prosecution' (Kates, 2014; see also Burns et al., 2008) – so listing small scale offenders and bringing cases against individuals and small businesses raises questions about whether the federal government is really pursuing the United States' worst environmental offenders.

Animal-abuse registries, to offer another example, require persons convicted of felonies involving animal cruelty to register with the police and provide a range of personal information and a current photograph, which are posted online, along with information on the person's offense – something akin to registries for sex offenders (as well as California's online registry for arsonists). Proponents consider it a way to notify the public and provide an early warning system for other crimes on the grounds that animal abuse is an indicator for future violent behavior (McKinley, 2010; Urbina, 2010). Such registries can serve a shaming function – and there is some support, more generally, for approaching environmental harm through shaming (Mares, 2010; Roug, 2014) – but as with all shaming, there are disintegrative and reintegrative forms. Green criminologists must consider not simply the relative effectiveness but also the ethics and politics of questions about whether environmental offender 'wanted lists' and animal-abuse registries and similar types of shaming help prevent future offending or whether they label, stigmatize and isolate guilty parties (Braithwaite, 1989).

When crime prevention and punishment causes problems: Wildlife conservation and green corrections

Some activities are or become so widely accepted in a particular context or setting that their commission is essentially deemed normal, rather than deviant (Brisman, 2015). For example, as Duffy (2010: 11), in her account of wildlife conservation, points out: 'When wildlife reserves are established, local communities can suddenly find that their everyday subsistence activities have been outlawed and that they have been redefined as criminals'. It seems almost a contradiction that some of the 'world's best-known pristine wilderness areas are, in fact, engineered environments. Creating a national park means drawing up new conservation rules which outlaw the everyday subsistence activities of local communities, such as hunting for food and collecting wood' (Duffy, 2010: 11; see also Hall, 2013: 229; Hill, 2010; White, 2013: 102, 135, 155). In addition, White (2013: 155) notes that the creation of roads to facilitate wildlife tourism can lead to habitat destruction and loss of biodiversity: 'The construction of wildlife parks can distort local species distributions, involve relocating animals across vast distances, and present a narrow view of which animals ought to be protected and how'. This raises questions as to '[w]hose interests and whose rights ought to be protected, and under what conditions?' (White, 2013: 155).

In a different vein, 'green corrections' can be defined as the adoption of 'environmentally friendly business practices' in the redevelopment of existing facilities and in the planning and construction of future facilities, as well as an increased environmental awareness in the field of corrections, more generally. In addition 'green corrections' encapsulates attempts to develop and integrate programs that make penal industries and correctional agencies 'more environmentally friendly and self-sustaining' and that prepare participants for green-collar jobs upon release (United States Department of Justice, National Institute of Corrections, 2008). On the one hand, given 'the adverse environmental impact of overloaded and undermaintained prison and jail wastewater treatment systems' and given that 'rural prison building taps the precious water reserves of poor, dry, sparsely populated western and southwestern counties in the United States' (Brisman, 2008a: 730 n.10), many green criminologists might support jails and prisons that have or are developing environmentally friendly practices and might back the construction of new facilities with lesser ecological footprints. In addition, given the collateral consequences of conviction and imprisonment (Brisman, 2004, 2007) – especially the barriers to employment – many green criminologists might endorse efforts by prisons and jails to train inmates in green collar jobs (Brisman, 2008a, 2008b), which are less restrictive in licensing or other employment history requirements than some blue collar positions, thereby increasing the potential for ex-offenders to secure gainful employment upon release (Pinderhughes, 2007). There is also good evidence that exposure to a green environment if it includes hands-on experience, can be beneficial for offenders and contribute to crime prevention goals (Brisman, 2009a; Carter and Pycroft, 2010; Pretty et al., 2013). On the other hand, green criminology's roots lie in critical criminology (Lynch, 1990; South, 1998a, 1998b, 2014) – an orientation or approach that includes abolitionist perspectives (see, e.g., Bianchi and van Swaaningen, 1986; Cohen, 1988; de Haan, 1990; Matthiesen, 1974). Green criminologists may need to ask whether conducting research that is favourable to 'green corrections' does, in essence, constitute support for practices and policies that will make jails and prisons more energy efficient, therefore cheaper to run and with enhanced 'green credentials' that may assist with the rejection of some criticism of the dehumanizing atmosphere of penal regimes. Ethically and in terms of values there is potential conflict here with the critical criminology that undergirds much of green criminology.

Social harms and negative impacts of industrial contraction

Davies (2014) draws attention to the ethical and philosophical conflicts that can arise in cases of success in the implementation and enforcement of environmental regulations but which then lead to social damage and community hardship, as measured in terms of resulting unemployment, reduction in income and hence, in some associated indicators, of personal wellbeing. Davies presents a case study describing an aluminium plant that constituted 'an industrial giant' at the heart of a local and regional community in Northumberland, in the North-East of England. The case described reveals the difficult tensions that arise when equally just or socially worthwhile objectives come into conflict.

The owners of the plant argued it could not survive as a viable economic business if the costs of compliance with European and UK environmental standards were to be met and if compliance were to be enforced; the only commercial response could be closure of the plant. As Davies (2014: 301) explains, 'The closure of this plant was a success in green terms', however, the case also 'illustrates how social and environmental justices appear to collide and be jointly and equally unsustainable'. So, suggests Davies, 'When green/brown (environmental) concerns appear to be prioritized, they engender further social harms and impact negatively on local and regional communities'. Davies explores the case presented with a view to highlighting the 'nuances of what constitutes harm and victimization in such scenarios' and to lead to a suggestion 'for a green dialogue on these issues and for a green victimological research agenda to draw attention to such trading of costs'. Ethical and methodological issues arise in the fine balance between two arenas of 'justice' that have compelling value and attraction for many researchers in this field, and this is emphasized particularly starkly by Davies's (2014: 312) point that environmental policies and justice may be regressive and discriminatory in their impacts. While there has been much research that shows how it is the poor and lower class population groups that disproportionately suffer the health consequences of having dirty industries located near to them (Pellow, 2004; Pinderhughes, 1996; Saha and Mohai, 2005), the corollary is that these communities often depend economically on these companies, and the loss of the company is also a loss of jobs and income and hence of lifeblood for the community.

Summary

One of the most fundamental challenges for a researcher concerned with highlighting environmental harms or exploring corporate crimes of pollution or similar offences, arises from the confrontation between a professional ethical value base that defends honesty, transparency and care, and actors and behaviours that embody the opposite of these. Conducting research on crime and harm is always difficult but while some sites of research may seem remote to us, we all have experience of environmental 'goods' and 'bads' – whether, with respect to the former, enjoying the sight of a sunset by the beach or the first birds of spring, or, with respect to the latter, complaining of city traffic pollution or waste dumped in a stream. Thus, there is something immediate about the topic. By the same token, this may also mean that while some wish to protect the environment from excessive or indeed *any* exploitation and abuse, others take the environment for granted, believe it is intended for human consumption, has a natural resilience and will always be there, and hence will go to great lengths to secure the profitability of commercial use of environmental resources. When faced with the latter point of view, research on environmental issues may be very difficult.

In this chapter, we have referred to methods typically used and have flagged ethical matters that are commonly encountered. There are no easy ways to do this kind of research and there are no easy answers to ethical problems. Our hope, however, is that some assistance in thinking through these matters of methods and ethics will have been furnished by the small selection of case examples we have provided and that these have been useful in highlighting some of the tensions that may arise when conducting research on environmental crime and harm.

Review questions

1. Does green criminology limit itself to the study of environmental *crimes* or does it consider environmental *harms* not proscribed by law? Why or why not? Please provide examples.
2. In what ways does green criminology implicate questions of ecophilosophy – of the relationship of humans to (the/their) environment? How do such questions arise in the study of environmental crimes and harms?
3. Are efforts to protect the environment always beneficial? In what ways, might environmental protection create or produce other/social harms?
4. What kinds of methodologies have green criminologists used to study environmental crime and harm? Why might one particular methodology be more appropriate in a particular context than in another?

Guide to further reading

Beirne, P., and South, N. (eds.) 2007. *Issues in Green Criminology: Confronting harms against environments, humanity and other animals.* Cullompton, Devon, UK: Willan.
South, N., and Brisman, A. (eds.) 2013. *Routledge International Handbook of Green Criminology.* Abingdon, UK: Routledge.
White, R. (ed.) 2009. *Environmental Crime: A Reader.* Cullompton, Devon, UK: Willan Publishing.
White, R., and Heckenberg, D. 2014. *Green Criminology: An Introduction to the Study of Environmental Harm.* London and New York: Routledge.

References

Agnew, R. (2012a). Dire forecast: a theoretical model of the impact of climate change on crime. *Theoretical Criminology* 16(1): 21–42.

Agnew, R. (2012b). 'It's the end of the world as we know it: the advance of climate change from a criminological perspective'. In *Climate Change from a Criminological Perspective*. New York: Springer, pp. 13–25.

Agnew, R. (2013). 'The ordinary acts that contribute to ecocide: a criminological analysis'. In N. South and A. Brisman (eds.), *Routledge International Handbook of Green Criminology*. London and New York: Routledge, pp. 58–72.

Barak, G. (ed.) (2015). *The Routledge International Handbook of the Crimes of the Powerful*. London: Routledge.

Bekoff, M. (2010). 'First do no harm', *New Scientist*, 28 August: 24–25.

Bianchi, H. and van Swaaningen, R. (eds.) (1986). *Abolitionism: Towards a Non-Repressive Approach to Crime*. Amsterdam: Free University Press.

Bisschop, L. (2012). Is it all going to waste? Illegal transports of e-waste in a European trade hub. *Crime, Law and Social Change* 58(3): 221–249.

Braithwaite, J. (1989). *Crime, Shame and Reintegration*. Oxford: Oxford University Press.

Brisman, A. (2004). Double whammy: collateral consequences of conviction and imprisonment for sustainable communities and the environment. *William & Mary Environmental Law & Policy Review* 28(2): 423–475.

Brisman, A. (2007). Toward a more elaborate typology of environmental values: liberalizing criminal disenfranchisement laws and policies. *New England Journal on Criminal & Civil Confinement* 33(2): 283–457.

Brisman, A. (2008a). Crime-environment relationships and environmental justice. *Seattle Journal for Social Justice* 6(2), 727–817.

Brisman, A. (2008b). Fair fare? Food as contested terrain in U.S. prisons and jails. *Georgetown Journal on Poverty Law & Policy* 15(1): 49–93.

Brisman, A. (2009a). Food justice as crime prevention. *Journal of Food Law & Policy* 5(1): 1–44.

Brisman, A. (2009b). It takes green to be green: environmental elitism, 'ritual displays,' and conspicuous non-consumption. *North Dakota Law Review* 85(2), 329–370.

Brisman, A. (2013). Not a bedtime story: climate change, neoliberalism, and the future of the arctic. *Michigan State International Law Review* 22(1): 241–289.

Brisman, A. (2015). 'Environmental harm as deviance and crime'. In E. Goode (ed.) *Wiley Handbook on Deviance*, Hoboken, NJ: Wiley.

Burns, R.G., Lynch, M.J. and Stretesky, P. (2008). *Environmental Law, Crime, and Justice*. New York: LFB Scholarly Publishing.

Carrabine, E., Cox, P., Fussey, P., Hobbs, D., South, N., Thiel, D. and Turton, J. (2014). *Criminology: A Sociological Introduction*, London: Routledge.

Carter, C., and Pycroft, A. (2010). 'Getting out: offenders in forestry and conservation work settings'. In J. Brayford, F. Cowe, and J. Deering (eds.) *What Else Works? Creative Work with Offenders*, Cullompton, Devon: Willan, pp. 211–235.

Cianchi, J. (2015). *Radical Environmentalism: Nature, Identity and More-than-Human Agency*. Basingstoke: Palgrave.

Cohen, S. (1988). *Against Criminology*. New Brunswick, NJ: Transaction.

Crowther-Downey, C. and Fussey, P. (2013). *Researching Crime: Approaches, Methods and Application*. London: Palgrave.

Davies, P. (2014). Green crime and victimization: tensions between social and environmental justice. *Theoretical Criminology* 18(3): 300–316.

de Haan, W. (1990). *The Politics of Redress: Crime, Punishment and Penal Abolition*. London: Unwin Hyman.

Dietz, T. D. A., and Shwon, R. (2007). Support for climate change policy: social psychological and social structural influences. *Rural Sociology* 72: 185–214.

Duffy, R. (2010). *Nature Crime: How We're Getting Conservation Wrong*. New Haven and London: Yale University Press.

Ellefsen, R., Sollund, R. and Larsen, G. (eds.) (2012). *Eco-Global Crimes: Contemporary Problems and Future Challenges*, Surrey: Ashgate.

Eman, K., Meško, G. and Fields, C.B. (2009). Crimes against the Environment: Green Criminology and Research Challenges in Slovenia, *Varstvoslovje* 11(4): 574–592.

Geertz, C. (1973). *The Interpretation of Cultures: Selected Essays*, New York: Basic Books.

Gibbs, C., Gore, M. L., McCarrell, M. F. and Louie Rivers III. (2010). Introducing conservation criminology: towards interdisciplinary scholarship on environmental crimes and risk. *British Journal of Criminology* 50(1): 124–144.

Hall, M. (2013). 'Victims of environmental harms and their role in national and international justice'. In Westerhuis, D., Walters, R., and Wyatt, T. (eds.) *Emerging Issues in Green Criminology: Exploring Power, Justice and Harm*. Basingstoke: Palgrave Macmillan, pp. 218–241.

Halsey, M. (2004). Against 'green' criminology, *British Journal of Criminology* 44(6): 833–853.

Halsey, M. and White, R. (1998). Crime, ecophilosophy and environmental harm. *Theoretical Criminology* 2(3): 345–371.

Hayward, S .F. (2010). Public opinion about the environment: notable shifts in recent years. *Environmental Trends*, November 2. Available at: http://www.environmentaltrends.org/single/article/public-opinion-about-the-environment-notable-shifts-in-recent-years.html.

Heckenberg, D. and White, R. (2013). 'Innovative approaches to researching environmental crime'. In N. South and A. Brisman, (eds.) *Routledge International Handbook of Green Criminology*. London and New York: Routledge, pp. 85–103.

Herbig, F. J. W. and Joubert, S. J. (2006). Criminological semantics: conservation criminology: vision or vagary? *Acta criminologica* 19(3): 88–103.

Hill, A. (2010). 'Wildlife Conservation Projects Do More Harm than Good, Says Expert', *The Guardian*, 29 July. Available at: http://www.theguardian.com/environment/2010/jul/29/wildlife-conservation-projects-more-harm.

Hogan M. J. and O'Connor, S. T. (2013). 'Public perceptions of corporate environmental crime: Assessing the impact of economic insecurity on willingness to impose punishment for pollution'. In N. South and A. Brisman, (eds.) *Routledge International Handbook of Green Criminology*. London and New York: Routledge, pp. 282–289.

Kane, S. C. (2012). *Where Rivers Meet the Sea: The Political Ecology of Water*. Philadelphia: Temple University Press.

Kane, S. C. (2013). 'Coastline conflict: implementing environmental law in Salvador da Bahia, Brazil'. In N. South and A. Brisman (eds.) *Routledge International Handbook of Green Criminology*. London and New York: Routledge, pp. 379–393.

Kates, G. (2014). Environmental crime: the prosecution gap. *The Crime Report*. July 14. Available at: http://www.thecrimereport.org/news/inside-criminal-justice/2014-07-environmental-crime-the-prosecution-gap.

Kaufman, L. (2010). Woman wanted by E.P.A. is arrested. *The New York Times*. November 3: A17.

Kauzlarich, D. and Friedrichs, D. O. (2003). 'Crimes of the state'. In M. D. Schwartz and S. E. Hatty (eds.) *Controversies in Critical Criminology*. Cincinnati, OH: Anderson, pp. 109–120.

King, R. D. and Wincup, E. (eds.) (2007). *Doing Research on Crime and Justice,* 2nd edn. Oxford: Oxford University Press.

Kraul, C. (2014). Primate rights vs research: battle in Colombian rainforest. July 21. *Yale Environment 360*. Available at: http://e360.yale.edu/feature/primate_rights_vs_research__battle_in_colombian_rainforest/2788/.

Lynch, M. (1990). The greening of criminology: a perspective on the 1990s. *The Critical Criminologist* 2(3): 1–4, 11–12.

Lynch, M. (2013). 'Reflections on green criminology and its boundaries: comparing environmental and criminal victimization and considering crime from an eco-city perspective'. In N. South and A. Brisman, (eds.) *Routledge International Handbook of Green Criminology*. London and New York: Routledge, pp. 43–57.

Lynch, M. and Stretesky, P. (2001). Toxic crimes: examining corporate victimization of the general public employing medical and epidemiological evidence, *Critical Criminology* 10(3): 153–172.

Lynch, M. and Stretesky, P. (2003). The meaning of green: contrasting criminological perspectives. *Theoretical Criminology* 7(2): 217–238.

Lynch, M. and Stretesky, P. (2014). *Exploring Green Criminology: Toward a Green Criminological Revolution*. Farnham: Ashgate.

Mares, D. (2010). Criminalizing ecological harm: crimes against carrying capacity and the criminalization of eco-sinners. *Critical Criminology* 18(4): 279–293.

Matthiesen, T. (1974). *The Politics of Abolition*. London: Martin Robertson.

McIntosh, A. (2012). 'Teaching radical human ecology in the Academy'. In L. Williams, R. Roberts and A. McIntosh (eds.) *Radical Human Ecology: Intercultural and Indigenous Approaches*. Farnham: Ashgate.

McKinley, J. (2010). California lawmakers consider creating an online registry for animal abusers. *The New York Times*. February 22. A10.

Nader, L. (1980). 'Preface'. In L. Nader (ed.) *No Access to Law: Alternatives to the American Judicial System*. New York: Academic Press, pp. xv–xix.

Nader, L. (2003). 'Crime as a category – domestic and globalized'. In P. C. Parnell and S. C. Kane (eds.) *Crime's Power: Anthropologists and the Ethnography of Crime*. New York: Palgrave Macmillan, pp. 55–76.

Natali, L. (2010). 'The big grey elephants in the backyard of Huelva, Spain'. In R. White (ed.) *Global Environmental Harm: Criminological Perspectives*. Cullompton, Devon: Willan, pp. 193–209.

Natali, L. (2013). Exploring environmental activism: a visual qualitative approach from an eco-global and green-cultural criminological perspective. *CRIMSOC: the Journal of Social Criminology*, Green Criminology Issue, Autumn 2013: 64–100. Available at: http://socialcriminology.webs.com/CRIMSOC%202013%20Green%20Criminology.pdf.

Pellow, D. N. (2004). The politics of illegal dumping: an environmental justice network. *Qualitative Sociology* 27(4): 511–525.

Pinderhughes, R. (1996). The impact of race on environmental quality: an empirical and theoretical discussion. *Sociological Perspectives* 39(2): 231–48.

Pinderhughes, R. (2007). Green Collar Jobs: An Analysis of the Capacity of Green Business to Provide High Quality Jobs for Men and Women with Barriers to Employment. A Case Study of Berkeley, California: A Report for the City of Berkeley: Funded by The City of Berkeley Office of Energy and Sustainable Development. Available at: http://community-wealth.org/sites/clone.community-wealth.org/files/downloads/report-pinderhughes.pdf.

Pitts, M. and Smith, A. (2007). *Researching the Margins: Strategies for Ethical and Rigorous Research With Marginalised Communities*. London: Palgrave.

Pretty, J., Wood, C., Bragg, R. and Barton, J. (2013). 'Nature for rehabilitating offenders and facilitating therapeutic outcomes for youth at risk'. In N. South and A. Brisman (eds.) *Routledge International Handbook of Green Criminology*. London and New York: Routledge, pp. 184–196.

Roug, L. (2014). 7 People who stand in the way of progress on climate change. *Mashable*. Sept. 22. Available at: http://mashable.com/2014/09/22/a-rogues-gallery-7-people/.

RT. (2013). 'Polluting to death: China introduces execution for environmental offenders'. *RT*. June 20. Accessed at: http://rt.com/news/china-execution-environmental-offenders-967/.

Saha, R. and Mohai, P. (2005). Historical context and hazardous waste facility siting: understanding temporal patterns in Michigan. *Social Problems* 52(4), 618–648.

Scarce, R. (1990). *Eco-Warriors: Understanding the Radical Environmental Movement*. Chicago: Noble Press. [2006. *Eco-Warriors: Understanding the Radical Environmental Movement* Updated Edition. Walnut Creek, California: Left Coast Press.]

Scarce, R. (1994). (No) trial (but) tribulations: when courts and ethnography conflict. *Journal of Contemporary Ethnography* 23(2): 123–149.

Scarce, R. (2005). *Contempt of Court: A Scholar's Struggle for Free Speech from Behind Bars*. Walnut Creek, California: Alta Mira Press.

Shelley, T. O'C. and Hogan M. J. (2013). 'Public perceptions of corporate environmental crime: Assessing the impact of economic insecurity on willingness to impose punishment for pollution'. In N. South and A. Brisman, (eds.) *Routledge International Handbook of Green Criminology*. London and New York: Routledge, pp. 282–289.

Skinnider, E. (2013). Effect, issues and challenges for victims of crimes that have a significant impact on the environment. Vancouver: International Centre for Criminal Law Reform and Criminal Justice Policy. Available at: http://icclr.law.ubc.ca/sites/icclr.law.ubc.ca/files/publications/pdfs/Final%20Paper%20-%20Effect%20Issues%20and%20Challenges%20for%20victims%20of%20Environmental%20Crime.pdf.

Sollund, R. (ed.) (2008). *Global Harms: Ecological Crime and Speciesism*. New York: Nova Science.

South, N. (1998a). A green field for criminology? A proposal for a perspective. *Theoretical Criminology* 2(2): 211–234.

South, N. (1998b). Corporate and state crimes against the environment: foundations for a green perspective in European criminology. In V. Ruggiero, N. South and I. Taylor (eds.) *The New European Criminology*. London: Routledge, pp. 443–461.

South, N. (2009). 'Ecocide, conflict and climate change: challenges for criminology and the research agenda in the 21st century'. In K. Kangaspunta and I. H. Marshall (eds.) *Eco-Crime and Justice: Essays on Environmental Crime*. Turin, Italy: UNICRI, pp. 37–54.

South, N. (2014). Green criminology: reflections, connections, horizons. *International Journal for Crime, Justice and Social Democracy* 3(2): 5–20.

South, N. and Brisman, A. (eds.) (2013). *Routledge International Handbook of Green Criminology*. London and New York: Routledge.

South, N., Brisman, A. and Beirne. P. (2013). 'A guide to a green criminology'. In N. South and A. Brisman (eds.) *Routledge International Handbook of Green Criminology*. London and New York: Routledge. pp. 27–42.

South, N., Brisman, A. and McClanahan, B. (2014). Green criminology. *Oxford Bibliographies Online: Criminology*. 28 April 2014. DOI: 10.1093/OBO/9780195396607-0161. Available at: http://www.oxfordbibliographies.com/view/document/obo-9780195396607/obo-9780195396607-0161.xml.

Stretesky, P. and Lynch, M. (2001). The relationship between lead and homicide, *Archives of Pediatric and Adolescent Medicine* 155(5): 579–582.

Stretesky, P. and Lynch. M. (2004). The relationship between lead and crime, *Journal of Health and Social Behavior*, 45(2): 214–229.

Tombs, S. and Whyte, D. (2003). *Unmasking the crimes of the powerful: scrutinizing states and corporations*. Oxford: Peter Lang.

United States Department of Justice, National Institute of Corrections. (2008). Green corrections. *Corrections Community*. December 17. Available at: http://community.nicic. gov/blogs/green_corrections/archive/2008/12/17/green-corrections.aspx.

Urbina, I. (2010). Animal abuse as clue to additional cruelties. *The New York Times*. March 18: A16.

Walters, R. (2010). Toxic atmospheres air pollution, trade and the politics of regulation. *Critical Criminology* 18(4): 307–323.

Walters, R. (2011). *Eco Crime and Genetically Modified Food*. Abingdon: Routledge.

Walters, R., Westerhuis, D. S. and Wyatt, T. (eds.) (2013). *Emerging Issues in Green Criminology: Exploring Power, Justice and Harm*. Basingstoke: Palgrave Macmillan.

White, R. (2008). *Crimes Against Nature: Environmental Criminology and Ecological Justice*. Cullompton: Willan.

White, R., ed. (2010a). *Global Environmental Harm: Criminological Perspectives*. Cullompton: Willan.

White, R. (2010b). 'Globalisation and Environmental Harm'. In R. White (ed.) *Global Environmental Harm: Criminological Perspectives*. Cullompton: Willan, pp. 3–19.

White, R. (2011). *Transnational Environmental Crime: Toward an Eco-global Criminology*. London and New York: Routledge.

White, R. (2013). *Environmental Harm: An Eco-Justice Perspective*. Bristol: Policy Press.

White, R., and Heckenberg, D. (2014). *Green Criminology: An Introduction to the Study of Environmental Harm*. London and New York: Routledge.

Wilding, N. (2012). 'Experiments in action-research and human ecology: developing a community of practice for rural resilience pioneers'. In L. Williams, R. Roberts and A. McIntosh (eds.) *Radical Human Ecology: Intercultural and indigenous approaches*. Farnham: Ashgate.

PART III
The changing face of governance
Issues, dilemmas and practical solutions

Introduction to Part III

The final part of the book considers issues of governance and pragmatism; governance is concerned with ensuring that researchers are accountable for the nature and conduct of their projects. Accountability lies beyond the immediate parameters of the project and may link to University ethics committees, other external ethics committees (for example linked to criminal justice or health institutions) or funding bodies. Mark Israel and Loraine Gelsthorpe highlight conflicting perspectives on the operation of research governance bodies – on the one hand they may be an independent means for protecting research participants from over-ambitious or insensitive research programmes; on the other hand they may be groups of people divorced from the context of research and concerned only with protecting institutional reputation. They go on to describe how positive practices of ethics ideally merge the strengths of both perspectives and can inform research and teaching agendas in criminology. Simon Winlow and Fiona Measham, however take an adversarial position in relation to the role of institutional ethics committees, which they suggest are closely tied to market forces that seek to shape particular forms of knowledge. Commercial demands, they suggest, exert powerful influence on the decisions made by University ethics committees, and within this is the imperative to avoid litigation and reputational damage which may adversely affect the University's ability to generate income (from recruiting students and securing research funding). They suggest that ethnography and social science research should be protected from the distorting demands of market forces.

11

ETHICS IN CRIMINOLOGICAL RESEARCH

A powerful force, or a force for the powerful?

Mark Israel and Loraine Gelsthorpe

Research ethics and integrity governance arrangements grounded in principlism might be seen as operating to protect the interests of relatively vulnerable groups. Alternatively, they might be allowing ethical decision-making to be divorced from context, protecting powerful agencies from scrutiny by independent researchers by over-generalising understandings developed within bioethics. Drawing on the experiences of criminologists in engaging with national regulations and local review processes, we explore how the practices of ethics and integrity might shape research agendas and teaching practices within our discipline in the United Kingdom.

Key definitions

Principlism: It is widely accepted that 'principlism' is a system of ethics based on the four moral principles of:

- **autonomy** – free-will or agency;
- **beneficence** – do good;
- **non-maleficence** – do no harm, and
- **justice** – social distribution of benefits and burdens.

Advocates for principlism argue that from the beginning of recorded history most moral decision-makers descriptively and prescriptively have used these four moral principles, and that they are part of or compatible with most intellectual, religious, and cultural beliefs.

Introduction

Research ethics and integrity governance arrangements grounded in the principlist ideals of respect for persons, beneficence and justice might be seen as operating to protect the interests of relatively vulnerable groups from harmful research carried out by more powerful organisations. Alternatively, they might allow ethical decision-making to be divorced from a critical analysis of context. As a result, they may be protecting powerful agencies from scrutiny by independent researchers by over-generalising understandings developed within bioethics of matters such as informed consent, confidentiality, non-maleficence, risk, conflict of interest and research merit. Drawing on the experiences of criminologists in engaging with national regulations and local review processes, we explore how the practices of ethics and integrity might be shaping the research agendas of and teaching practices within the discipline of criminology in the United Kingdom.

Reflection on such issues is of paramount importance. As the recent experience in the United States suggests, it is also not straightforward. In 2015, the American Society of Criminology (ASC) proposed the adoption of code of ethics. This came three decades after its Ethical Issues Committee first started submitting drafts to the Society's governing board. Once again, the 2015 draft has prompted a mixture of support and consternation. Major criticisms have revolved around the extent to which the code would seek to control behaviour. The Code employs broad language such as 'oppression' and 'dignity' that remains undefined; critics argue that holding anyone accountable for behaviour that cannot be specified is itself potentially unethical. The Code also includes reference to ASC members having 'an obligation not to recreate forms of social injustice such as discrimination, oppression, or harassment in their own work' (General Principle 5). Might this impact on scholarship that, though scientifically true, be interpreted by some scholars as 'recreating social injustice' by attributing inequality to individual differences and not structural factors? It might be objected that this is not really what the Code of Ethics had in mind. But broad general principles are open to wide interpretation and application. Other concerns reflect the notion that when producing codes of ethics scholars have in mind 'others' to whom the codes would apply, not recognising their own vulnerability to the uses and abuses of criminological knowledge. Moreover, there are concerns about lack of attention to enforcement (with potential risks of legal liability whether there is enforcement or not). Thus the issue of research ethics regulation is very much a live one.

Growth in the ambit of research ethics regulation

Criminologists in Australasia, North America and the United Kingdom have expressed serious concerns about the increasing impact of research ethics review requirements on their work (Lowman and Palys, 2000; Haggerty, 2004; Israel, 2004; Winlow and Hall, 2012). They have complained that the codes that govern research and the local bodies that review research projects have failed to understand the methodologies, political agendas and power relations that constitute the field of criminology. As a result, it is possible that important work, work that is both ethically and methodologically sound, is being hindered or even stigmatised by research ethics bureaucracies. In some countries and institutions, the end result has been a system where regulators and the regulated view each other as responsible for an antagonistic relationship (Israel et al., 2016).

Most British criminologists were not subject to research ethics review until far later than their colleagues in the United States, Canada or Australia. However, the United Kingdom has not learned much from the problems caused by poorly conceived research ethics governance elsewhere and has ended up with a poorly connected range of regulatory requirements. This has not helped the discipline in the long run.

While the United States, Canada or Australia were establishing national systems and extending these to criminology, the United Kingdom focussed on the needs of the health and social services sectors. The debates and heated arguments in these other countries seemed quite alien, as research ethics regulation in the United Kingdom was largely limited to medical research and, for several decades, there was little encroachment on criminology. In the United Kingdom, medical research was subject to review by committees from 1968. Local Research Ethics Committees and Multi-Research Ethics Committees were established by the Department of Health for research activity in the National Health Service. A specialist committee for social sciences was set up in 2009 to enable review of research in social care contexts. Several social researchers claimed these health and social services committees were hostile to the social sciences (Burr and Reynolds, 2010), although others identified more thoughtful behaviour (Hedgecoe, 2008; Jennings, 2012).

However, this growing culture of regulation which might be seen as a concomitant result of an emerging 'culture of blame' now has an impact on criminologists, particularly those working in higher education institutions (Wilcox, 2009). Over the same time, universities established codes of practice, set up ethics committees, or offered ethical guidance via other institutional structures. About 80 per cent of British universities had created committees by 2003 (Tinker and Coomber, 2004). Initially aimed at health research, their mission extended slowly and unevenly to the social sciences. Apparently concerned about the seemingly inevitable extension of bioethics-based regulation, the Economic and Social Research Council (ESRC) stepped in to provide a framework for institutions that accepted its funding. In doing so, the ESRC shifted the locus of power in research ethics governance 'from being endogenously controlled by communities of disciplinary practice to exogenously determined regimes of control in the form of new ethical bureaucracies' (Boden et al., 2009, p. 736). However, for many social scientists even these guidelines, like those used by the Department of Health, still bear the hallmarks of bioethics.

The ESRC released its first *Research Ethics Framework* (REF) in 2005; this was subsequently replaced by the *Framework for Research Ethics* (FRE) in 2010, revised in 2012 and then replaced in 2015. The successive Frameworks set out the ESRC's expectations for work it is asked to fund, and identifies good practice for all social science research. The first Framework claimed to: preserve researchers' disciplinary affiliations; emphasize their ethical reflexivity and responsibilities; and seek a thoughtful, consistent structure for social science ethics scrutiny. To its credit, the Framework followed the lead of the first and second Canadian Tri-Council Policy Statements (1998, 2010) in recognising that research undertaken in the social sciences may quite deliberately and legitimately work to the detriment of research participants by revealing and critiquing their role in causing 'fundamental economic, political or cultural disadvantage or exploitation' (Economic and Social Research Council, 2012, p. 28). However, the initial 2005 REF was criticized for being wrong both in principle and in practice by fashioning narrow and overly prescriptive requirements more concerned with institutional risk and reputation than with fostering an ethical research culture (Dingwall, 2012; Hammersley, 2009; Roberts and Lewis, 2009).

The 2010 Framework extended the remit of research ethics committees and specified minimum requirements for their composition. It made review mandatory for those researchers seeking ESRC funding, removing exemption for those researchers engaging in arguably routine methods of research, and requiring full review for a broad range of 'sensitive topics' that included matters of gender and ethnicity or elite status, and for research occurring outside the United Kingdom or involving the internet or data sharing. Critics of the 2005 Framework found even less comfort in the new version, with Stanley and Wise (2010) describing the new document as 'bad in its entirety' (para. 1.4), based on an inadequate and, within its own terms, 'unethical' (para. 6.2) consultation process.

British research institutions responded to ESRC requirements and, by 2012, Jennings described a:

> revolution in ethics review in universities, with any university with a substantial research profile now having some sort of ethics review process. The quality of these reviews is likely to be patchy, but more problematically, there is no national system in place for evaluating the quality of consideration generated by such RECs.
>
> *(Jennings, 2012: 94)*

While there was a short lull in direct activity, after 2012 the ESRC co-sponsored symposia and a working group of social scientists circulated a draft set of generic principles, values and standards for social science research (Academy of Social Sciences Working Group, 2014). In 2015, the ESRC issued a new Framework.

The 2015 FRE rehearsed many points made in earlier frameworks:

> The Economic and Social Research Council (ESRC), in facilitating innovative and high quality research, expects that any research supported will be carried out to a high ethical standard. By establishing the Framework for Research Ethics (FRE) we confirm commitment to a process of regular

review through consultation with the research community and stakeholders, to ensure ethical standards reflect changing scientific agendas and policy developments.

(ESRC, 2015: 1)

The 2015 version also established key principles and minimum requirements and confirmed what the ESRC regarded as good practice for all social science research. And, it identified requirements for ethics review for the research the ESRC is asked to support. Importantly:

> whilst adherence to these requirements is mandatory for ESRC-funded research, the guidance is also a useful tool to other audiences including other funders, research organisations (ROs), Research Ethics Committees (RECs), individual researchers, research teams (including teams with non-academic researchers) and research participants.
>
> *(ESRC, 2015, p. 1)*

The 2015 REF placed far more emphasis than earlier versions on the need for researchers to think ethically when conducting research and consider ethical issues *throughout* the research lifecycle. The research lifecycle includes the planning stage, the period of funding for the project and all activities that relate to the project once funding has ended. These encompass knowledge exchange and impact realisation activities, the dissemination process and archiving, future use, sharing and linking of data.

It stipulated that all parties involved with research should aim to maximise the benefit of the research and minimize harm to participants. The ESRC's principles were revised to emphasise the need for researchers to consider the balance and proportionality of individual rights (such as respect, trust and privacy), as well as the public benefits of research. Further, the REF required researchers and research organisations to abide with the UUK *Concordat to Support Research Integrity* (Universities UK, 2012) and RCUK *Guidelines on Governance of Good Research Conduct*.[1] As a result of harmonization of policy across the Research Councils, the ESRC no longer required written confirmation of ethics approval prior to the release of funds on funded proposals. However it expected that an appropriate ethics review would be carried out before research is conducted.

Finally, in order to facilitate thinking around ethics issues throughout the lifecycle of the research project, the ESRC website included ethics case studies of ESRC-funded projects. The FRE was also updated in relation to other requirements. For instance, the FRE reflected the establishment of the Health Research Authority (HRA).[2] The HRA was established as a Special Health Authority by Government in response to a review of research regulation by the Academy of Medical Sciences. The Care Bill established the HRA as a Non-Departmental Public Body (NDPB) on 1 January 2015 with responsibility for the UK-wide Research Governance Framework.

This growth in the ambit of ethics regulation has had clear effects on British criminology. Criminologists seeking access to data from criminal justice agencies were routed through the National Offender Management Service Integrated Research Application System (IRAS).[3] This system stipulated that ethics approval must be given by an organisation (institutional or learned society or professional association) before access will be granted. These developments are interesting in their own right. Our focus, however, is on how far ethical considerations merge into research regulation.

During this period, various professional associations, such as those associated with sociologists, psychologists and criminologists, developed their own ethical guidelines or codes. The British Society of Criminology first established an Ethics Committee in the early 1990s; this later became the Professional Affairs and Ethics Sub-Committee, of which both authors were members. The first *Code of Ethics for Researchers in the Field of Criminology* emerged in 1991; the Code was substantially revised in 1996, again in 2006 and 2015.

The 2015 revision of the *Statement of Ethics for Researchers* partly reflected the changing landscape within which regulation and other codes of practice transgressed geographical and disciplinary boundaries. Interestingly, *Code* has been changed to *Statement* – perhaps reflecting the symbolic value of the input and limitation in terms of having 'teeth', since one can be in breach of a code and sanctions might be assumed. The 2015 Statement did not seek to impose a single model of ethical practice, but rather offered a frame of reference to encourage and support reflective and responsible ethical practice in criminological research. In keeping with the aims of the Society, the statement sought to challenge questionable practice, and promote broad principles, values and standards to ensure that ethical standards in criminological research were maintained. The Statement was intended to make members aware of the ethical issues that may arise throughout the research process and to encourage members to take responsibility for their own ethical approaches by promoting and supporting good practice. It was written as an aspirational document, not a prescriptive one. Members of the British sub-committee have continued to offer an advisory service to all members of the Society regarding ethical issues and reviews and comments on research proposals.

Protecting the vulnerable?

A central feature of codes, guidelines or statements of ethics is that they have the protection of potentially vulnerable research participants as a primary focus, and all participants may be potentially vulnerable. The general principles of *beneficence, nonmaleficence, autonomy and fidelity* arguably go some way to indicate how participants might be protected. The quest to protect participants ranges from the need to protect people against self-incrimination to ensuring, more generally, that people know what they have let themselves in for in agreeing to participate in the research and that they will offer their views and information on a voluntary basis. It is now widely recognised that 'consent' is not simply a one-off decision, but in ethnographic approaches, for example, is ongoing and has to be renegotiated between research and researched throughout the research process. Moreover, 'consent from the top' (say from a prison governor) cannot be taken to mean that everyone in the organisation gives consent (see Israel, 2016).

Autonomy and the need for individual 'consent' of course assumes capacity to give consent, when personal trauma and language difficulties make it difficult to know whether consent is being given (even with interpreters). In research conducted by Hales and Gelsthorpe (2012) on the criminalisation of migrant women who found themselves in prison for criminal offences (including the possession of a false passport or working on a cannabis farm), the interpreters were individually chosen by the researchers via trusted networks and no one who had previously worked for the government interpretation services was included because of the service's poor reputation and because the researchers felt they could not trust the interpreters to negotiate consent or interpret accurately.

Where there are particular concerns about intellectual disability or cognitive impairment, measures have to be taken to ensure that a 'responsible person' is able to communicate with the potential participant as best they can in ways which they are most likely to understand (a carer, for example). Those with severe intellectual disability are considered particularly vulnerable to exploitation in research (Roberts and Roberts, 1999). Notwithstanding the fact that the lives and experiences of people with learning disabilities were for a long time considered antithetical to academic life, there is relatively little research which has involved them within the research process. As Kiernan (1999) noted, it was not until the 1980s that people with learning disabilities were involved even as interviewees in social research that was about them. Discovery of exploitative practices in recent history has motivated the development of guidelines for informed consent and proxy decision-making when involving these individuals in research. The Social Care Institute for Excellence has produced guidance on different types of abuse and it is clear that 'failure to respect privacy' and 'preventing the expression of choice and opinion' would count as psychological or emotional abuse.[4] Similarly, the Medical Research Council has produced guidance on protecting patients.[5] Steps must be taken to identify severe vulnerability, and the multi-faceted and complex nature of consent must be considered on an individual project basis.

The ESRC's own guidance revolves around the fact that researchers working with vulnerable people will need to secure *Disclosure and Barring Service* (DBS) clearance.[6] The service offers organisations a means to check the criminal record of researchers to ensure they do not have a history that would make them unsuitable for research involving children and vulnerable adults. Responsibility for ensuring that applicants are suitable to work with such groups ultimately rests with individual employers. In some cases other individuals (such as a head teacher or social services manager) may be better placed to provide information on necessary disclosures.[7]

Proxy consent can be obtained by a person authorised to act on behalf of a vulnerable person. Where proxy consent for research participants is necessary, the best interests of the vulnerable person should be of the highest importance.

Importantly, 'proxy consent should only be used when participants are unable to consent themselves or where it is legally necessary' (ESRC, 2015: 24). When proxy consent is used, agreed criteria should be provided to confirm that participants fully understand what they are participating in, and identify signs of participants' unwillingness to take part or wish to terminate the research interaction.

In terms of beneficence (acting to enhance participants' well-being), it is hard to say whether the research will enhance anything; researchers in the criminological field generally include a statement to indicate that the research may not benefit individuals, but future generations of people subject to criminal justice policy. Non-maleficence is arguably more straightforward, but even here there are stories of research where people have been persuaded to participate with disastrous results. Arguably 'no pressure' was put on HMP Wormwood Scrubs sex offenders to participate in an experiment involving hormonal treatment, but the results (loss of facial hair and the development of breasts) made subsequent social contact more difficult for them (Scott and Codd, 2010). Another point here relates to delayed harm. Interviews with those who have experienced childhood sexual abuse or domestic violence may be approached sensitively, but the impact of the interview won't always be known at the time. Similarly, fidelity, treating participants in a fair and just manner *seems* as if it is a principle which will naturally protect research participants, but no two interviews are the same. We might anticipate interviews being exactly the same length, but sometimes, in practice, one has little control. Even when it comes to asking questions in a consistent manner, participants may anticipate some questions and unintentionally subvert the ordering. Certainly, there have been cases where research participants have been disappointed not to be able to engage with restorative justice processes, having been randomly selected for the group destined for court within a randomised control trial.[8]

At a general level, 'protection' for research participants is seen to reside in a three-pronged strategy: appropriate research design; informed consent and, maintaining confidentiality. But what is meant by appropriate research design? For a very long time it was assumed that interviews would be the most appropriate – and sensitive – method of approaching those who have experienced childhood sexual abuse. But questionnaires (where there is more distance between the researcher and the researched) may be better, allowing research participants to indicate something of their experiences without having to face anyone (Martin et al., 1993). But 'best for whom'? Researchers concerned with reliability might have a different take on matters than research participants themselves (Bernstein et al., 1994).

Some of the complexities of 'informed consent' have been discussed above especially in relation to there being different degrees of consent at different levels and in relation to capacity to give consent; there are additional points to make. 'Consent' assumes that people know what they are consenting to, but how far can or should researchers disclose what they are interested in? One might imagine research with magistrates on what informs their decision-making when it comes to sentencing, for example. But should the researcher disclose that they are interested in racial and sexual bias, or merely mention 'factors which influence decision-making'? The issue of confidentiality also 'appears' to offer protection for research participants, but sometimes even where data are anonymised, research participants can recognize themselves in the data and, in identifying who they are, unwittingly reveal who other participants are. Malcolm Cowburn (2005 and this volume), for example, raises some important questions about confidentiality and interview-based research with adult sex offenders and whether they are deserving of confidentiality. All of this simply serves to highlight that although there is need for the protection of vulnerable research participants, none of it is as straightforward as it may seem.

Protecting the powerful?

The dominant discourses in research ethics literature are based on the Belmont Report's principles of respect for persons, beneficence and justice (National Commission for the Protection of Human Subjects of Biomedical and Behavioral Research, 1979). Developed by American bioethicists, Tom Beauchamp and James Childress, principlism argued research should be based on the prima facie obligations do good or, at least, minimize harm, allow individuals to make their own decisions, and ensure that risks and potential benefits were fairly distributed (Israel, 2015). While there have been many critiques of principlism, two areas of weakness are particularly relevant to a criminology concerned with the critical analysis of power and inequality through an investigation of the relationship between crime and the state, corporations, gender, class, ethnicity or global inequalities. The first issue is that principlism presupposes individual autonomy. The second, is that it privileges a Western bioethics-derived model as a universalist approach to ethics.

Principlism rests on a philosophical tradition that envisaged a world of autonomous individual decision-makers – invariably code for people who were white, adult, male and from the Global North. Criminology has come a long way since claims to generalisability from that population were left uncontested. In addition, scholars associated with a wide variety of criminological approaches have rejected the idea that individuals can be considered in isolation. Instead, interactions between researchers and research participants are grounded in the broader structural relationships within society. So, a society stratified according to race, gender or class will replay these relationships of domination and subordination through research. This has implications for the role of the researcher, for the consent process, for an assessment of harm and benefits, and for an analysis of research ethics governance.

Zachary Schrag (2010) described the extension of the regulation of biomedical research to social sciences in the United States as a form of ethical imperialism. The intervention of the ESRC in the United Kingdom has meant that there are clear differences between the history of regulation in the United States and the United Kingdom, however the earlier ad-hoc development of NHS- and university-based reviews do bear the hallmarks of the mission creep across disciplines that so concerned Schrag. As we have noted, the FRE also rests on the language and assumptions of bioethics.

We argue that research ethics policies may have a disciplining effect on criminology within the United Kingdom by failing to protect the more vulnerable and by protecting the more powerful parts of our society from critical scrutiny. We suggest that this bias may operate through use of the apparently neutral language of informed consent, confidentiality, harm-minimisation and researcher safety as well as through a failure to address conflicts of interest in our discipline.

The regulation of informed consent could operate in such a way that it protects the interests of vulnerable groups such as prisoners from harmful research carried out by government agencies. Alternatively, it could protect powerful agencies from scrutiny by independent researchers by robbing researchers of one of their most powerful methodologies, covert research. Deception could compromise both the informed and voluntary nature of consent but some researchers have argued that consent need not be obtained where any harm caused by lack of consent might be outweighed by the public benefit obtained. In addition, it might be impossible to gain access to some participants if other people were not deceived.

Covert research has been justified on the basis of utilitarianism in limited circumstances where it is necessary for the research to remain secret in order to maintain access to the research setting, perhaps in the face of the desire of 'powerful or secretive interests' (British Sociological Association, 2002; Socio Legal Studies Association, 2009) to block external scrutiny. Without covert research, Geoff Pearson (2009) argued, some aspects of society, including harms and injustices will remain 'hidden or misunderstood' (p. 252) and the images that powerful groups wish to project may go unchallenged. Researchers have defended partially covert research when they found it difficult to negotiate their presence as researchers because of the institutional, physical or virtual setting or the numbers of people that would be involved.

The European Commission's (2010) draft Guidance Note for social science researchers counselled against allowing powerful figures or organisations the right to withdraw or withhold consent for fear of leaving social scientists 'without even the most basic rights to make enquiries by other social groups, such as investigative journalists, or even ordinary citizens who might confront such figures at public meetings' (p. 11). The value of covert studies has been accepted by the FRE in exceptional circumstances 'if important issues are being addressed and if matters of social significance which cannot be uncovered in other ways are likely to be discovered' (p. 30). Similarly, the British Society of Criminology's 2006 Code of Ethics allowed departure from a requirement to obtain informed consent where this might be necessitated by 'exceptional importance of the topic' (p. 3). Such provisions might include the possibility of using covert research in institutions to expose, for example, state violence or corporate misconduct. However, the FRE hardly offered strong endorsement for covert investigations.

In Canada, the Tri-Council Policy Statement (2010) suggested institutions should not be protected by requirements for consent. The Canadian Statement recognised that 'social science research that critically probes the inner workings of publicly accountable institutions might never be conducted without limited recourse to partial disclosure' (p. 37). As a result, researchers were not required to obtain consent from those corporate or government organisations that they were researching, nor were such institutions entitled to veto projects, though private organisations might refuse researchers access to records or create rules governing the conduct of their employees that might make it difficult for those employees to cooperate with researchers. However, even in these situations, the research could not involve more than minimal risk to participants (Article 3.7(a)), which might make it difficult for researchers to work with whistleblowers in some jurisdictions. Not surprisingly, the use of covert methodologies is in serious decline, even in Canada (van den Hoonaard, 2011). While there is little, if any, concrete evidence of such methodological dieback in the United Kingdom, there are anecdotal stories of scholars having to argue their way through institutional ethics committees, especially when proposing covert research in the street, or at football matches, or in refugee camps.

As criminologists, we may find ourselves asking participants to reveal information in exchange for little direct benefit. Most researchers go to significant lengths to preserve the confidentiality of their data. However, some researchers offer limited assurances of confidentiality because they believe they have an obligation to a third party. For example, several British researchers have indicated that they would breach confidentiality to protect vulnerable groups such as children (Barter and Renold, 2003; Cowburn, 2005; Harne, 2005; Tisdall, 2003). The FRE, rather unhelpfully, required that 'In projects collecting data on criminal behaviour, it may be necessary to explain to participants that confidentiality will be preserved as far as the law permits' (ESRC, 2015: p. 24). In doing so, it failed to identify whether or the degree to which researchers have a responsibility to contest attempts through the legal system to obtain confidential information. Two recent examples suggest that information collected by British researchers may be vulnerable to court orders, even if they archive the data outside the United Kingdom.

In August 2012, Bradley Garrett, an urban ethnographer was arrested at Heathrow airport. Four years earlier he had started doctoral research on 'urban explorers' or 'place hackers' in London and elsewhere. Underground tube stations proved to be particularly attractive for the research and in due course the British Transport Police (BTP) took note. Following his arrest, the BTP seized field notes and related research materials. Garrett and eight of his research participants were subsequently charged with 'conspiracy to commit criminal damage' – a charge which carries a ten year prison sentence. The BTP also alleged that the amount of material which they had collected from Garrett's home indicated that he must have been the instigator of the crimes.

Bradley Garrett's exploration of British urban space which involved trespass onto land owned by the public transport authority raised a number of concerns for social research. The prosecution argued Garrett's law-breaking was both unethical and unnecessary since he could have completed the work legally. They might also have pointed to the possibility that repeated trespass would have required the authority to spend more on security, a cost that would have been passed on to passengers. In turn, the defence drew on a range of experts (including members of the British Society of Criminology). Jeff Ferrell in particular, indicated that if ethnography were to be 'deep and full' it might well require engagement in interactions and situation that are illegal (Ferrell et al., 2015). Garrett himself argued that it was 'deeply problematic' to block research by people simply because they lived close to 'legal boundaries'. He also argued that participant observation with such groups might entail breaking the law. Similar arguments have been made by those researching football hooliganism and the night-time economy (Pearson, 2009; Winlow et al., 2001). The case ended with Garrett (2014) receiving a conditional discharge. One might interpret the result as signifying successful defence of the principles of ethnography and the fact that research can sometimes take people beyond the boundaries of the law. A more prosaic and realistic interpretation might be that Garrett acknowledged trespass and very limited criminal damage but was not found guilty of conspiracy to commit criminal damage.

In another example, 2011, the British government sought a federal court order in the United States requiring Boston College to surrender oral history interview data relating to the 1972 murder in Belfast of Jean McConville, suspected by the Provisional IRA of acting as a British informant (Schmidt, 2012). The researchers obtained political and media support and sought to protect the data they had deposited with the College. However, the College initially turned over some material. It later attempted to hold on to data provided by an interviewee who was still alive (Palys and Lowman, 2012). In April 2013, The First Circuit Court of Appeals reduced the amount of material to be handed over from 85 interviews to segments of 11 interviews. Apparently, on the basis of this information, Sinn Féin leaders Gerry Adams and Bobby Storey were arrested in Belfast in 2014. Following Adams' release, the Police Service of Northern Ireland indicated its intention to obtain further data from Boston College. In turn, the College offered to return tapes to interviewees rather than face further claims on the material.

Recognising that full confidentiality may not be assured, the ESRC has required researchers to offer only limited assurances of confidentiality indicating to participants that they could be forced to hand data over to courts (Economic and Social Research Council, 2015). The British Society of Criminology's Statement of Ethics has a similar requirement (s.4(12)). This practice could undermine the relationship of trust between researcher and participant, making it far more likely that participants will be reluctant to divulge information for fear their revelations might be used against them or their friends, colleagues, or family members. For criminologists, this can be particularly serious if the failure to uncover information is seen as endorsing particular institutional practices. Ivan Zinger, a Canadian psychologist, told prisoners who participated in his doctoral research on administrative segregation that he was obliged to disclose information that related to the safety of prisoners or the institution (Zinger, 1999, quoted in Lowman and

Palys, 2001). Ted Palys and John Lowman (2001) argued Zinger's approach privileged institutional loyalties over the interests of research participants. They also claimed that as areas excluded from confidentiality were central to the research study, the 'eyes wide shut' limited assurance compromised the research to the point of rendering data obtained invalid.

Researchers may find they have little choice but to take physical and emotional risks in their work. This might be a consequence of the location of their work, the nature of participants, the sensitivity of the topic, underfunding, or even professional pressures to venture into new settings. We have very little idea about how widespread risks to researchers are. We do know that a small number of researchers have lost their lives as a direct result of their research activities, while others have been harassed by security forces or offenders (Israel, 2015).

Responsibility for ensuring the safety of the scholar does not simply fall upon the individual researcher, and it seems reasonable that funders, employing institutions and research managers should all play some role in managing risk (Dickson-Swift et al., 2007). However, some institutions lack the skills to handle researcher safety and may allow over-protective, paternalist and ill-informed risk assessment to enter the ethics review process. For example, Konstantin Belousov and his British colleagues (Belousov et al., 2007) were forced to reassess the risk posed to their fieldworkers in St Petersburg following the murder of the Captain of the Port. They found professional international risk assessors were always likely to identify fieldworkers conducting criminological research in environments where social order was breaking down in the face of weakened state control as being 'at risk'. The problem for criminologists is that the focus of our research often refuses to be confined to safe environments.

Research agendas and projects are vulnerable to pressure from financial, political, social, cultural or religious interests. These can influence the topics, methodologies, researchers and institutions likely to be funded, and the way research might be reported. Large pharmaceutical companies have been found to write journal articles and pay academics to publish them under their own names. They have also held back research results that might harm their profitability. It is harder to see opportunities for corporations to exert such influence on criminology, but not impossible. Geis et al. (1999) were particularly concerned by a criminologist from the University of Florida who they concluded had received research funding and private income from private corrections in direct conflict with the contractual requirements of his consultancy work for the state regulator, and his apparent independence as a public commentator. A few NGOs have continued to question the funding of university research by operators of private prisons, research that is then used to legitimate the funders' practices (Takei, 2014). Hedgecoe (2015) has suggested that the machinery of research ethics review has been used by some universities to block or censor activities that might have been less than flattering to the researchers' own institutions, citing one example of a Kingston University research project that sought to investigate student involvement in the sex industry and another of a review by a research ethics committee of the teaching materials of a politics lecturer at the University of Nottingham who had protested at the treatment of a postgraduate student and administrator.

In the United Kingdom in 2012, Universities UK brokered a Concordat to Support Research Integrity with the support of the higher education funding and research councils and the NHS. The Concordat committed signatories to 'Transparency and open communication in declaring conflicts of interest' (p. 11) and identified 'failure to declare competing interests' (p. 17) as a form of research misconduct. However, it contained little detailed advice, devolving responsibility to institutions to decide how they might best achieve this and to professional associations and funding agencies to guide researchers. Having rejected an earlier draft, the Academy of Social Sciences (2013) eventually supported the Concordat, though the Academy remained wary the agreement might turn into a cumbersome, risk-averse, bureaucratic exercise that did little to encourage scholars to grapple with issues of professional integrity. The British Society of Criminology's Statement of Ethics remained silent on conflicts of interest. In 2014, the American Association of University Professors (AAUP) was more forthright in its approach and published Recommended Principles and Practices to Guide Academy–Industry Relationships. The AAUP urged universities to require academics and administrators to disclose financial conflicts of interest on publicly accessible websites (Principle 31). While such guidelines are increasingly common in biomedical journals, they are less frequently found among criminology journals which tend, like the *British Journal of Criminology*, to focus specifically and somewhat unhelpfully on funding sources.

Summary: shaping the discipline?

There is no doubt that ethical regulation of criminological and social research has become big business in recent years. The impetus for more regulation has come from a number of different directions. Codes and statements of ethics have proliferated both within professional circles and within institutions. Thus it is important to question the helpfulness of such codes and whether ethics committees can really make sound judgments about research practice. Indeed, one key issue is whether such regulation is legitimate; another is whether it will necessarily raise standards.

The import of the chapter is to encourage critical reflection on guidelines, codes and statements of ethics and frameworks for research ethics and to challenge regulatory bodies which seemingly restrict scholarly enquiry. If we do not do this, we run the risk of reshaping the discipline – excluding research 'at the edge' which is arguably fundamental to the health of the discipline, and providing yet another way of reducing the accountability of criminal justice agencies. There is obviously need to encourage consideration of what the law requires, what codes require and also what personal ethics require – as different and sometimes competing matters. But we should not allow questions about ethics to merge into regulations regarding safety or security. They are different if related issues. Moreover, codes of ethics encourage reflexivity, but do not provide solutions; indeed they sometimes confuse matters, and researchers are required to develop their ethical imaginations so that they can justify their actions when they need to challenge current practices. Of course, there is need to protect vulnerable research participants, but this need not stultify and restrict research. History indicates our incapacity to develop and balance regulations regarding research in criminology (and other social science disciplines) that are simultaneously unambiguous, meaningful and justifiable, leaving aside enforceable. As a result, we call for constant vigilance in regard to regulation and committed reflexivity.

Review questions

1. What are the strengths and limitations of codes or statements of ethics of ethics?
2. How has the institutional ethical regulation that you know about changed over recent years? What are the challenges of these changes?
3. How best can institutional regulation of research be challenged?

Guide to further reading

Adorjan, M. and Ricciardelli, R. (eds) (2016) *Engaging with Ethics in International Criminological Research*. London: Routledge.

Israel, M. (2015) *Research Ethics and Integrity for Social Scientists: Beyond Regulatory Compliance*. London: Sage.

Mertens, D. and Ginsberg, P. (eds) (2009) *The Handbook of Social Research Ethics*. London: Sage. See Section III in particular 'Perspectives on Ethical Regulation'.

Acknowledgments

Some of the material in this chapter is drawn from Israel (2015) and Israel (2016).

Notes

1   http://www.rcuk.ac.uk/publications/researchers/grc/
2   http://www.hra.nhs.uk/
3   See: https://www.myresearchproject.org.uk
4   http://www.scie.org.uk/adults/safeguarding/
5   http://www.mrc.ac.uk/research/research-policy-ethics/guidance-on-patient-consent/.
6   https://www.gov.uk/government/organisations/disclosure-and-barring-service.
7   See the Safeguarding Vulnerable Groups Act 2006 (http://www.legislation.gov.uk/ukpga/2006/47/contents); Rehabilitation of Offenders Act 1974 (http://www.legislation.gov.uk/ukpga/1974/53); the Rehabilitation of Offenders Act 1974 (Exceptions Order 1975) (http://www.legislation.gov.uk/uksi/2013/1198/contents/made).
8   Personal communication with Heather Strang regarding London Metropolitan Police research on restorative justice.

References

Academy of Social Sciences (2013). Academy of Social Sciences Response to the HEFCE Consultation on the Research Integrity Concordat. Available at: http://acss.wpengine. com/wp-content/uploads/2014/01/Concordat-Final1-March-2013.pdf (accessed 11 June 2014).

Academy of Social Sciences Working Group (2014). Towards common principles for social science research ethics? A discussion document. In: *Finding Common Ground?* Academy of Social Sciences conference, London, UK, 10 January 2014.

American Society of Criminology (2015). *Proposed Code of Ethics.* Available at: https:// www.asc41.com/ASC_code_of_ethics.pdf (accessed 3 April 2016).

Barter, C. and Renold, E. (2003). Dilemmas of control: methodological implications and reflections of foregrounding children's perspectives on violence. In: R.M. Lee and E.A. Stanko (eds.) *Researching Violence: Essays on Methodology and Measurement.* London: Routledge, pp. 88–106.

Belousov, K., Horlick-Jones, T., Bloor, M., Gilinsky, Y., Golbert, V., Kostikovsky, Y., Levi, M. and Pentsov, D. (2007). Any port in a storm: fieldwork difficulties in dangerous and crisis-ridden settings. *Qualitative Research* 7(2): 155–175.

Bernstein, D., Fink, L., Handelsman, L., Foote, J., Lovejoy, M., Wnezel, K., Sapareto, E. and Ruggerio, J. (1994). Initial reliability and validity of a new retrospective measure of child abuse and neglect. *The American Journal of Psychiatry,* 151(8): 1132–1136.

Boden, R., Epstein, D. and Latimer, J. (2009) 'Accounting for ethos or programmes for conducting research in the brave new world of research ethics committees', *The Sociological Review* 57(4): 727–749.

British Sociological Association (2002). *Statement of Ethical Practice for the British Sociological Association.* Available at: http://www.britsoc.co.uk (accessed 23 December 2013).

Burr, J. and Reynolds, P. (2010). The wrong paradigm? Social research and the predicates of ethical scrutiny. *Research Ethics Review* 6(4):128–133.

Cowburn, M. (2005). Confidentiality and public protection: ethical dilemmas in qualitative research with adult male sex offenders. *Journal of Sexual Aggression,* 11: 49–63.

Dickson-Swift, V., James, E., Kippen, S. and Liamputtong, P. (2007). Doing sensitive research: what challenges do qualitative researchers face? *Qualitative Research* 7(3): 327–353.

Dingwall, R. (2012). How did we ever get into this mess? The rise of ethical regulation in the social sciences. In: Love, K. (ed.) *Ethics in Social Research.* Bingley: Emerald, pp. 3–26.

Economic and Social Research Council (ESRC) (United Kingdom) (2005). *Research Ethics Framework.* Swindon: Economic and Social Research Council.

Economic and Social Research Council (ESRC) (United Kingdom) (2010, revised 2012). Framework for Research Ethics. Swindon: Economic and Social Research Council. Available at: http://www.esrc.ac.uk/_images/framework-for-research-ethics-09-12_tcm8-4586.pdf (accessed 20 June 2014).

Economic and Social Research Council (ESRC) (United Kingdom (2015). *Framework for Research Ethics.* Swindon: Economic and Social Research Council. http://www.esrc. ac.uk/funding/guidance-for-applicants/research-ethics/

European Commission (2010). Guidance Note for Researchers and Evaluators of Social Sciences and Humanities Research. Available at: http://ec.europa.eu/research/ participants/data/ref/fp7/89867/social-sciences-humanities_en.pdf (accessed 15 August 2016).

Ferrell, J., Hayward, K. and Young, J. (2015). *Cultural Criminology: An Invitation,* second edition. London: Sage.

Garrett, B. (2014). Place-hacker Bradley Garrett: research at the edge of the law. *Times Higher Education*, 5 June. Available at: http://www.timeshighereducation.co.uk/story. aspx?storyCode=2013717 (accessed 9 June 2014).

Geis, G. Mobley, A. and Schichor, D. (1999). Private prisons, criminological research, and conflict of interest: a case study. *Crime & Delinquency* 45: 372–388.

Haggerty, K. (2004). Ethics creep: governing social science research in the name of ethics. *Qualitative Sociology* 27(4): 391–414.

Hales, L. and Gelsthorpe, L. (2012). *The Criminalisation of Migrant Women*. University of Cambridge: Institute of Criminology.

Hammersley, M. (2009). Against the ethicists: on the evils of ethical regulation. *International Journal of Social Research Methodology*, 12(3): 211–225.

Harne, L. (2005). 'Researching violent fathers'. In T. Skinner, M. Hester and E. Malos (eds.), *Researching Gender Violence: Feminist Methodology in Action*. Devon: Willan, pp. 167–189.

Hedgecoe, A. (2008). Research ethics review and the sociological research relationship. *Sociology* 42: 873–886.

Hedgecoe, A. (2015). Reputational risk, academic freedom and research ethics review. *Sociology*, doi:10.1177/0038038515590756.

Israel, M. (2004) 'Strictly confidential? Integrity and the disclosure of criminological and socio-legal research', *British Journal of Criminology* 44(5): 715–740.

Israel, M. (2015). *Research Ethics and Integrity for Social Scientists: Beyond Regulatory Compliance*. London: Sage.

Israel, M. (2016). A short history of coercive practices: the abuse of consent in research involving prisoners and prisons in the United States. In: M. Adorjan and R. Ricciardelli (eds.) *Engaging with Ethics in International Criminological Research*. London: Routledge, pp.69–86.

Israel, M., Allen, G. and Thomson, C. (2016). Australian research ethics governance: plotting the demise of the adversarial culture. In: W. van den Hoonaard and A. Hamilton (eds.) *The Ethics Rupture: Exploring Alternatives to Formal Research-Ethics Review*. Toronto: University of Toronto Press, pp.285–316.

Jennings S. (2012). Response to Schrag: What are ethics committees for anyway? A defence of social science research ethics review. *Research Ethics* 8(2): 87–96.

Lowman, J. and Palys, T. (2000). The research confidentiality controversy at Simon Fraser University. Available at: www.sfu.ca/~palys/Controversy.htm (accessed 15 August 2016).

Kiernan, C. (1999). Participation in research by people with learning difficulties: origins and issues. *British Journal of Learning Disabilities*, 27(2): 43–47.

Martin, J., Anderson, J., Romans, S., Mullen, P. and O'Shea, M. (1993). Asking about child sexual abuse: methodological implications of a two stage survey. *Child Abuse & Neglect*, 17(3): 383–392.

National Commission for the Protection of Human Subjects of Biomedical and Behavioral Research (NCPHSBBR) (1979). *Belmont Report: Ethical Principles and Guidelines for the Protection of Human Subjects of Research*. Report, Department of Health, Education and Welfare, Office of the Secretary, Protection of Human Subjects, Michigan. Available at: http://www.hhs.gov/ohrp/humansubjects/guidance/belmont.html (accessed 28 January 2014).

Palys, T. and Lowman, J. (2001). Social research with eyes wide shut: the limited confidentiality dilemma. *Canadian Journal of Criminology*, 43(2): 255–267.

Palys, T. and Lowman, J. (2012). Defending research confidentiality 'to the extent the law allows': lessons from the Boston College subpoenas. *Journal of Academic Ethics*, 10: 271–297.

Pearson, G. (2009). The researcher as hooligan: where 'participant' observation means breaking the law. *International Journal of Social Research Methodology*, 12(3): 243–255.

Roberts, C. and Lewis, J. (2009). *ESRC Consultation Document – Review of the ESRC Research Ethics Framework*, Submission to the ESRC on behalf of the Academy of Social Sciences.

Roberts, L. and Roberts, B. (1999). Psychiatric research ethics: an overview of evolving guidelines and current ethical issues in the study of mental illness. *Biological Psychiatry*, 48(8): 1025–1038.

Schmidt, P. (2012). Boston College case shows weakness of researchers' confidentiality pledges. *Chronicle of Higher Education*, 58(19): A13.

Schrag, Z. (2010). *Ethical Imperialism: Institutional Review Boards and the Social Sciences, 1965–2009*. Baltimore: Johns Hopkins University Press.

Scott, D. and Codd, H. (2010). *Controversial Issues in Prisons*. Maidenhead: Open University Press/McGraw-Hill Education.

Socio-Legal Studies Association (2009). *Statement of Principles of Ethical Research Practice*. Available at: http://www.slsa.ac.uk/index.php/ethics-statement (accessed 10 June 2014).

Stanley, L. and Wise, S. (2010). The ESRC's 2010 Framework for Research Ethics: Fit for research purpose? *Sociological Research Online* 15(4): 12. Available at: http://www.socresonline.org.uk/15/4/12.html (accessed 28 January 2014).

Takei, C. (2014). Karma: Private Prison Company Throws Shade and Fails, Badly. *Blog of Rights* https://www.aclu.org/blog/prisoners-rights/karma-private-prison-company-throws-shade-and-fails-badly.

Tinker, A. and Coomber, V. (2004). University research ethics committees: their role, remit and conduct. In: M. Smyth and E. Williamson (eds.) (2004) *Researchers and their 'Subjects': Ethics, Power, Knowledge and Consent*. Bristol: The Policy Press.

Tisdall, E. (2003). The rising tide of female violence? Researching girls' own understandings and experiences of violent behaviour. In: R. Lee and E. Stanko (eds.), *Researching Violence: Essays on Methodology and Measurement*. London: Routledge, pp.137–152.

Tri-Council (Canadian Institutes of Health Research, National Science and Engineering Research Council of Canada, Social Sciences and Humanities Research Council of Canada) (2010). *Tri-Council Policy Statement: Ethical Conduct for Research Involving Humans. Ottawa: Public Works and Government Services*. Available at: http://www.pre.ethics.gc.ca/pdf/eng/tcps2/TCPS_2_FINAL_Web.pdf (accessed 23 December 2013).

Tri-Council (Medical Research Council of Canada, National Science and Engineering Research Council of Canada, Social Sciences and Humanities Research Council of Canada) (1998). *Tri-Council Policy Statement: Ethical Conduct for Research Involving Humans*. Ottawa: Public Works and Government Services. Available at: http://www.pre.ethics.gc.ca/eng/archives/tcps-eptc/Default/ (accessed 28 January 2014).

Universities UK (2012). *The Concordat to support research integrity*. Available at: http://www.universitiesuk.ac.uk/highereducation/Documents/2012/TheConcordatToSupport ResearchIntegrity.pdf (accessed 20 June 2014).

van den Hoonaard, W. (2011). *The Seduction of Ethics: Transforming the Social Sciences*. Toronto: University of Toronto Press.

Wilcox, C. (2009). *Scapegoat: Targeted for Blame*. Denver, CO: Outskirts Press.

Winlow, S. and Hall, S. (2012). What is an 'ethics committee'? Academic governance in an epoch of belief and incredulity. *British Journal of Criminology*, 52: 400–416.

Winlow, S. Hobbs, D. Lister, S. and Hadfield, P. (2001). Get ready to duck. Bouncers and the realities of ethnographic research on violent groups. *British Journal of Criminology*, 41: 536–548.

Zinger, I. (1999). *The psychological effects of 60 days in administrative segregation*. Unpublished doctoral dissertation. Ottawa, ON: Department of Psychology, Carleton University.

12

DOING THE RIGHT THING

Some notes on the control of research in British criminology

Simon Winlow and Fiona Measham

In this chapter we discuss some of the problems associated with developing forms of ethical oversight in the field of criminology and criminal justice. We argue that the core concerns of institutional ethics committees are inextricably bound up with the logic of the market. The ongoing marketisation of the university is, quite clearly, affecting the production of knowledge, and institutional ethics committees now possess an unstated and unacknowledged desire to defend the institution from litigation and reputational damage. This desire now exhorts a subtle but powerful influence upon the deliberations of institutional ethics committees. Using our own research backgrounds and engagement with institutional ethics committees as a foundation for our critique, we argue that ethnography and *in situ* social research must be protected from those forces that would seek to formalise, sanitise and control it.

Key points

1. Institutional ethics committees now function to defend the institution from litigation and reputational damage.
2. The consideration of 'ethics' – properly defined – actually plays a marginal role in the deliberations of ethics committees.
3. This situation is dissuading, or actively preventing, some social scientists from utilising their preferred research methodologies.
4. The transformation of the ethics committee, and its role in dissuading some forms of social research, is already affecting the production of criminological knowledge.

Introduction: context

Criminology has grown enormously in recent years. In Britain the discipline has also recently undergone a benchmarking exercise that sought to apply some order and rigor to the materials covered within the country's undergraduate criminology programmes. Criminology, once a rag-tag discipline populated by academics with a general interest in crime who had migrated to this new shared space from a broad variety of fields – often bringing with them concepts and methodologies from across the social sciences and humanities – has become more organised and institutionalised, and its once porous and hazily defined boundaries appear to have hardened. In Britain, of course, undergraduate criminology degrees have been around for some time, and many younger professional criminologists have passed through undergraduate criminology programmes. Their educational experience is often quite specific to this field. It is clear that we have already passed through a period in which our disciplinary history has been codified and reified. It is now endlessly reproduced in textbooks, and no longer argued about to any great extent. We might also suggest that with every passing year the discipline of criminology displays less and less interest in theory-building and a growing preoccupation with empirical data collection, criminal justice practice, crime prevention and the management of offenders (Hall et al., 2008). Thorough-going critical accounts of criminal motivations and the background to crime certainly form a smaller part of the discipline than they once did (Hall, 2012). Political and theoretical truth projects have also declined quite markedly (Winlow, 2012), and we might tentatively suggest this decline is closely connected to a growth in careerism in the academy generally and the ubiquity of abstract empiricism within our discipline specifically (Currie, 2007; Matthews, 2009).

At first glance the discipline appears to be splitting apart into competing factions. However, the surface factionalism of criminology is not all it seems. There remains a good deal of accord, even between factions that have historically displayed a degree of hostility towards each other. There may be brief skirmishes here and there but a genuine clash of ideologies no longer takes place in the field of criminology. This is a shame, because without ideological commitment there can be no genuine dialectical movement. British criminology has instead adopted something of a bunker mentality. Critical criminologists fire the odd salvo at administrative criminologists but they cause no damage and nothing changes. Instead, each sub-field of criminology appears strangely self-sufficient and there is less and less intellectual engagement between them. Those on the left complain about the power and privilege of those on the right, but in fact only a tiny number of British criminologists can be identified as being adherents of right-wing politics or philosophy. In our times it is the philosophy of liberalism that has triumphed, and the monumental scale of its triumph has ensured that liberalism has lost much of its original philosophical substance (see Bell, 2014; Hall, 2012). It now stretches from the hard-core Randian libertarianism of the right to the interventionist social liberalism of the left, and criticism of the overbearing state is as common of criminology's left wing as it is on its right (Matthews, 2015; Winlow et al, 2015). It seems that, for the time being, all intellectual skirmishes in criminology will take place on this rather strange and inhospitable 'post-ideological' landscape (see Horsley, 2014). This stark fact should encourage us to acknowledge that beneath our discipline's surface discord lie a range of shared, if often disavowed, political and philosophical commitments that bond the discipline together and inform its present condition.

It is entirely possible that the reader will disagree with this brief and partial assessment – indeed, we believe that such disagreements should now be aired quite openly in the hope of prompting a productive interchange about the future of our discipline – but what we can say without fear of contradiction is that criminology is at a crossroads. In our institutions we remain locked into hectic schedules of teaching, research and administration. We tend to focus on impending deadlines and the range of tasks that structure our working week. As space for quiet contemplation and abstract thought diminishes, we tend not to be greatly preoccupied with the present trajectory of our discipline or its intellectual health and vitality. However, despite the growing gap between the institutional lives of criminologists and the broader national and international academic discipline of criminology, there appears to be a growing recognition that all is not well and that the future of our discipline may not be as rosy as we once imagined.

The drive to generate research income and the considerable pressures of the Research Excellence Framework are transforming the working lives of criminologists across Britain. The 'publish or perish' ethos may have contributed to the expansion of criminology, especially in terms of the breadth of topics covered and the mass of data produced, but it has also meant that criminologists have less and less time to keep abreast of new developments in the field. We are writing more and reading less it seems. There is now a huge variety of journals on the market and there has been a staggering growth in the number of criminology books published each year. However, there is little sense that a growth in quantity has led to a growth in quality, or that, as the discipline steps gingerly into the twenty-first century, new truths are being revealed to us.

Throwing out the baby with the bath water

We want to focus upon one small aspect of this general disciplinary inertia. It is clear that empirical research has edged out theory to occupy the core of our discipline. Criminology is now teeming with data, and almost all of the bespoke subfields that make up our disciplinary mosaic have benefitted from the turn towards empirical research. But despite the considerable successes of our empirical research projects, there is a growing sense among social scientists – and those orientated to qualitative research in particular – that their work is now being impeded by institutional systems of ethical governance. What, we must ask, has changed in research governance, and why is there a growing antagonism among researchers towards ethics committees?

We should note that, as our discipline began to establish itself during the final third of the twentieth century, it rather thoughtlessly followed other social science disciplines in adopting models of methodological rigor that owe a great deal to the core methodological concerns of the hard sciences (Smart, 2003). Research practice since those days has changed hardly at all, but ethical oversight of research practice now seems far tougher and more demanding. Perhaps we should conclude that this is no bad thing if problematic research projects are no longer slipping through the net, and rigorous oversight is keeping the harms of the research process to an absolute minimum. However, despite the nature of our discipline, criminology has not proven to be any more ethically problematic than other disciplines in the social sciences. Our history is not littered with cases of unethical research practice, and it is not immediately clear that the toughening of ethical governance has been a necessary measure that has prevented problematic research conduct in criminology (Winlow and Hall, 2012).

It makes sense to conclude that forces external to the discipline have prompted this toughening. Under the standard rubric of 'professionalisation', the market imperatives that have quickly moved to the very heart of the British university system appear, in a very subtle and indirect manner, to have prompted our ethics committees to tighten the net in order to protect our institutions from litigation and reputational damage. A dull bureaucratised pragmatism has taken over and the positive substance that must be retained is seeping out of the system at an alarming rate, leaving only a creaking and often alienating administrative process that frequently blocks important, challenging or cutting edge research, or places significant impediments in front of researchers keen to engage with criminals, deviants or marginalised populations in a reasonably naturalistic manner (see Smith, 2014; Ancrum, 2012). And this is not just a system that impedes working criminologists. Postgraduate and undergraduate students are also affected. Often our most talented and intellectually engaged undergraduate students are very keen to leave behind the confines of the university and head out into the world to gather their own data for their final year dissertation. In many cases this proves to be impossible. The risk averse nature of the institutional ethics committee increasingly leads talented students to opt for library-based study or, at the very most, empirical research on 'safe' fellow students, which in turn makes the emphasis that is placed on research methods teaching all the more mystifying. All too rarely do students get a chance to conduct their own research outside of the university, and even those who progress to postgraduate study quickly discover that it is now very difficult to gain approval for research projects that involve actually meeting and talking to criminals and 'deviants' in non-institutional settings.

Let us be clear: we are not claiming that ethnography, qualitative research and social research conducted *in situ* with offenders is on the verge of extinction, or that they will play an increasingly marginal role in the production and reproduction of criminological knowledge as the discipline moves forward. Rather, we are claiming that these methodologies are increasingly deprived of their traditional substance. To us, and other social researchers we have consulted, it seems that something is missing, and it seems to be missing because ethics committees appear dedicated to minimising risk and sanitising research processes that, in truth, do not need to be sanitised. Many field researchers complain about the ethics committee's drive to control interaction and engagement between the researcher and the researched, and its drive to set firm limits on how such interactions are brought into being and how they develop over time. All researchers who place themselves in what might appear, to the ethics committee, to be 'risky settings' that might precipitate 'risky encounters' – are increasingly over-policed, and researchers are understandably keen to avoid breaching the rules handed down by ethics committees, and increasingly cautious about their engagement with populations considered in some way 'deviant'. The ethics committee's drive to professionalise research practice, monitor interaction and protect against harm has led to the erection of unnecessary barriers between the researcher and the research subject. Quite clearly, these barriers can be negotiated and valuable research can still be done, but we should not dismiss the possibility that the intimacies that existed between the researcher and the research subject in earlier epochs are a good deal harder to construct and maintain these days. The drive to rid the discipline of unethical research practice needs to be placed in an appropriate context, and we must avoid meekly accepting ethical governance in its present form as a necessary intervention that will eventually lead to beneficial outcomes. Instead we should be bold enough to contemplate a more disturbing reality in which we appear to be throwing out the baby with the bathwater.

The practice of ethics committees

Within our discipline there is a broad agreement that steps should be taken to ensure that our research practice does not harm participants and that researchers are not exposed to unnecessary danger (see, for example, the British Society of Criminology, 2006), but many criminologists also feel these important considerations are no longer of paramount importance to our institutional ethics committees. Other concerns that appear to have little to do with 'ethics' have begun to sneak in and progressively work their way closer to the centre, and the traditional activities associated with ethical oversight have been marginalised or forgotten entirely. When presenting our own work to institutional ethics committees, we have encountered there what might be termed a lawyer's mentality that appears to operate within an essentially administrative and managerialist culture that encourages the various academics who gather under its auspices to grind their way through the agenda while sifting and sorting research proposals into piles of 'the approved' and 'the disapproved'; the consideration of ethics, properly understood, nowhere to be seen. Can the committee envisage a situation in which the researcher witnesses or becomes aware of criminal acts? Is there any possibility that the research might threaten an individual's legal entitlements or those of a business entity or organisation? If there is a chance that research might be conducted in or on privately-owned property, have the necessary permissions been sought? Is there any chance that this research might threaten the reputation of the university? These are the questions that appear most often to inform the committee's deliberations.

In our view, the rubric of 'informed consent' appears to have become something of a panacea for ethics committees, or at least those forced to engage with the thorny problems that accompany qualitative and *in situ* research proposals in the field of criminology. Forms outlining the aims and outcomes of the research project, and the rights of the research participant in relation to it, must be signed by each contact before data-gathering can commence. On the surface of things we might, with some justification, claim that the increased focus upon 'informed consent' reflects a growing concern for the rights of research participants. However, some researchers we have spoken to doubt that the requirements of 'informed consent' are truly altruistic and reflect a genuine desire to ensure that no harm comes to research participants. Instead, they take the view that beneath this surface positivity lies a darker motivation. This motivation is never fully revealed, but its influence can be detected across the new terrain of research management. The pragmatism of the market, and its concern with the bottom line, is subtly working its magic, disturbing traditional cultures and enforcing new logics of managerialism, professionalisation and oversight. Beneath the surface of concern for participants lies a powerful desire to ensure that nothing returns to harm the interests of the institution.

What are the institutional and ideological roles of ethics committees, and how are ethics committees shaping the research produced within our discipline? How might the new rigors of ethical oversight be affecting the production of criminological knowledge? How do ethics committees reach their decisions, and do forthright discussions of ethics – properly understood – play any role at all in these deliberations? Who sits on ethics committees, and how might the background, fieldwork experience and social identities of members inform the practice of these committees? Are members 'socialised' into the committee's normative practice, and, as they become inured to this new reality, might the bonds that connect committee members to more esoteric – but hugely important – questions about what is good and right begin to loosen? Does the ethics committee member, keen to get out of another boring meeting as quickly as possible, simply reapply an already-in-place logic rooted in expediency, compliance with the law and protecting the institution from any kind of negative attention? Has the contemplation of ethics been formalised and bureaucratised or has the contemplation of ethics been entirely withdrawn, replaced only with a malign institutional pragmatism?

What concerns us most is that 'ethics', and 'ethical governance', have gradually become a system of external control that enforces a prescribed set of rules that relate to research practice. Inevitably, when 'ethics' exists as an external – rather than an internal – system of governance, the researcher is forced to engage with it as such. Submitting a research proposal to an ethics committee is relegated to the status of a mere administrative task, a hurdle we must overcome before the researcher is allowed to get on with the real work. This gradual transformation is far more important and negativistic than we might imagine. The ethics committee as a system of governance, a regulator that determines what is and is not allowed, encourages researchers to engage with it in an essentially sociopathic manner. The researcher is encouraged to say the right things and tick the right boxes, to acknowledge the rules and promise to abide by them. The researcher must ask, what will the ethics committee make of this or that? Does my proposal break the rules in any way? What should I write in my research proposal that might encourage the committee to look favourably upon it? Of course, there has always been a clear division between the initial research proposal and the actual lived research project, but as the researcher becomes increasingly conversant with the demands of the ethics committee, and learns how to 'play the game', this division becomes increasingly stark. The research proposal is simply an administrative task that must be completed, and the researcher knows that it is in his or her best interests to present research plans in a particular way. Like the stereotypical sociopath, the researcher knows the rules, and knows that it is in his or her interests to live by them. However, like the sociopath, these rules remain only external rules that are imposed upon and seek to regulate the subject. They are not absorbed or used as a determining structure in our mental life, forming part of what we call our conscience, the 'voice in our heads' that constantly reminds us to abide by the rules of our community. When our postgraduate students contact us about ethical matters, they often pitch their questions in this rather disconcerting manner. What will the ethics committee say about this or that? What are the 'rules' when faced with this particular kind of ethical problem? Of course, during research, when one is faced with challenging events, the proper response is to think and respond in relation to one's own conscience and embodied ethics. One should ask, is such a thing right or wrong, rather than, what are the rules that govern research practice when faced with such a dilemma? Of course, in the well-adjusted individual, all of this should happen immediately. We should respond morally to the world as we encounter it. We should think, what is the right thing to do, and then do it, rather than suspending judgement until one has had an opportunity to consult the rules and regulations. A worrying gap is opening up between the ethics committee, which acts as a regulatory agency, and our own research practice, which of course should be constantly monitored by our own embodied ethics, our own independent sense of what is right and wrong. In order to advance this argument, it seems necessary to step back a little and consider other issues connected to the governance of research practice in criminology.

Ethnography must be defended

Criminology is a discipline that exists at the forefront of ethical condemnation. Our subject matter is inherently contentious as it references some kind of rupture in the moral, ethical or regulatory foundations of our world. Because our discipline proceeds from this base, there exists a powerful imperative to ensure that our research sticks rigidly to established ethics frameworks. Of course, in order to remain faithful to the concerns upon which the discipline was founded, we must engage with criminals of all kinds: we must speak to individuals involved in drug use and supply, sexual violence and child abuse, rioting and terrorism, fraud and racial violence, and many other criminal or deviant activities, and, if we remain committed to working through the complexities of motivation, drive and causation, it is beneficial to talk with our respondents *in situ*, in non-custodial settings and in places where they feel sufficiently relaxed, safe and willing to open up to a researcher. We must also note that the vast majority of criminals actively attempt to conceal their crimes. Even when criminals are caught and incarcerated they may continue to disguise the reality of their deeds to interested academics. Observing deviant populations in action and talking to criminals who are actively engaged in criminal markets is therefore of huge value. We should be fighting hard to resuscitate the dying art of ethnography, especially those forms of ethnography that seek to capture the realities of culture in action. The ethics committee's drive to regulate research practice means that increasingly only those forms of ethnography go ahead that can work in accordance with its rules. Can the ethnographer conduct informed consent procedures? Will every research participant be equipped with the knowledge to make informed decisions? Of course, conducting research with criminals and deviants *in situ* opens up a host of methodological and ethical dilemmas, but rather than address these in a reasonably considered manner, the clear ideological orientation of the ethics committee is to construct hard boundaries on what is and isn't allowed, and then force researchers to live with its decisions.

Certainly, many ethnographic accounts of deviant populations operate within an essentially *appreciative* ideological frame (see for example, Becker, 1963; Young 1971) that encourages readers to reconsider the role of power in the construction of law and order and in social conceptions of deviance and normalcy. Perhaps we could do more to move beyond cultural appreciation and develop more realistic ethnographic accounts of criminal and deviant cultures (Hall and Winlow, 2015), but the benefits of ethnography as a method should be quite clear. Forthright, truth-seeking qualitative research is integral to the health of our discipline. The attempts made by ethics committees to regulate ethnographic research practice inevitably impact upon the data we gather. Some populations of great interest to criminologists are quite unwilling to talk honestly and openly to a researcher brandishing a recording device and official-looking documents, and this is especially true when the researcher asks for a signature and hopes to discuss the involvement of that population in crime and deviance. However, a talented and generally unencumbered ethnographer who presents herself as a fully human presence, possessed of her own identity and views and willing to engage in open-ended discussion, might just manage to elicit genuinely illuminating information from hard-to-reach research populations. This requires time and effort and a willingness to leave the world of the university behind. It requires the researcher to respond to the world as she encounters it rather than constantly worrying whether she has transgressed the rules. Here, the requirements handed down by the ethics committee act as a significant impediment to those forms of ethnographic research practice that used to be quite common in sociological criminology. Ethnography continues of course, but, we claim, it is vital that we wrestle with the possibility that it does so *despite* new regulatory measures. The ethics committee's drive to regulate research practice in order to mitigate harm brings with it a general reduction in the human intimacy that makes ethnography such a vital research methodology for the social sciences.

Criminology at a crossroads

If we are to prevent criminology's gradual slide into 'controlology' (Ditton, 1979), it seems to us important to reconnect criminology to its principle objects of crime and harm. We need to know what they are and why they occur. Already too much of our discipline is concerned with the aftermath of crime: the response of the media, the response of the police and the criminal justice system, the response of the victim and the victim's community, and so on. These things are of considerable importance, but with every passing year British criminology appears marginally less interested in the actual causes of crime, deviance and harm, as if all that can be said about such things has already been said, and so the discipline can leave behind its traditional objects in order to construct research-informed demands for a more comprehensive system of human rights and a more civilised criminal justice system (see Hall and Winlow, 2015). We should be doing all we can to encourage ambitious and energetic postgraduate students to engage with real life as it is lived by populations of interest to criminology. Instead we tend to treat institutional ethics committees as a regrettable inevitability. Researchers across the land complain in private but tend to go along with the process of applying for ethical clearance, despite the fact that they have little or no faith in the ethics committee to form reasonable judgements. Tales of the staggering naivety and the breath-taking stupidity of ethics committees are quite common when one broaches the topic of ethical governance with active field researchers. Almost all of the social researchers we've talked to had a tale to tell. In the pages that follow we will report upon our own research experiences among criminal and deviant populations of various kinds.

Both of the authors of this paper, when about to undertake research with deviants and law-breakers, have been repeatedly asked by members of institutional ethics committees if they intended to inform the police of any illegality they may encounter during their studies. Winlow (2001) was encouraged to use consent forms in a project that involved interviewing young men involved in the sale and distribution of cocaine and ecstasy (see also Winlow and Hall, 2006), and Measham was encouraged to use consent forms when observing clubbers consuming dance drugs (see Measham et al,. 2011). Amazingly, Measham was asked by her institutional ethics committee to inform the police if she saw any actual drug consumption in nightclubs populated almost entirely by people who had taken drugs. This request was particularly mindboggling, given that the police themselves were fully aware that the venue was frequented by drug users. Indeed, the police knew about and actively supported the research, and were forward-thinking enough to see the value of research that was geared towards identifying opportunities to prevent harm. Don't cases such as this indicate that the principal concern of ethics committees is simply to enforce the rules rather than engage with individual research proposals in a reasonably intelligent fashion? Quite clearly, there often exists a huge disconnect between the world of the criminologist and the institutional work of the ethics committee. This gap is important and revealing. At least part of the problem stems from the multi-disciplinary nature of ethics committees and the lack of knowledge or understanding academics working in other disciplines often have of criminology. Of course, many foundational works in criminology and the sociology of deviance evolved in a naturalistic and unruly manner and yet still managed to produce illuminating data and transformative theory. These researchers were not required to inform the police if they happened to witness a crime, and nor were they encouraged to conduct elaborate consent procedures before engaging with research participants (consider, for example, Thrasher, 1927; Polsky, 1967; Young, 1971). Somehow they managed to muddle through, and the results were positive. To the best of our knowledge no great harms accrued. The past of our discipline is not a barbarous past we should attempt to leave behind as we make our way inexorably to a civilizational ideal in which all the foibles and risks of human relationships have been removed. Qualitative social research forms an important part of our shared disciplinary past and we should do all we can to maintain a connection to it and ensure that it is not policed out of existence.

When conducting covert work as a nightclub doorman, it was imperative for Winlow (see Winlow, 2001; Winlow et al., 2001; Hobbs et al., 2003) to actively assume that identity and become involved in all of the incidents that fall within the remit of nightclub doormen. Of course, doormen, landlords and private security firms have nothing to gain by allowing a criminologist to assume such a role within their cultures. We can, of course, interview doormen and ask them about their occupational culture and their involvement in violent incidents, but becoming immersed in their culture, witnessing and reporting upon the actuality of violent incidents, and, essentially, 'seeing the world as they see it' (Berger, 1972), produces data of an entirely different order. Of course, things that are mundane and uninteresting to a nightclub doorman can be illuminating for a social researcher. Such events are often missing from interview data as foreground action tends to dominate conversation. Being there in the flesh can provide the observer with insights that would be unforthcoming if other methodologies were used. In interviews, for example, one might ask a doorman what happened on a particular evening at work. Often doormen will reply with 'nothing much', or 'it was another boring night'. Of course, their assessment is based upon their own experience of their work and the environment in which they conduct their work. However, when the bouncer says 'nothing happened', he is in fact quite wrong. 'Something' did happen, even if, from the bouncer's point of view, it was not particularly interesting (see Hobbs et al., 2003). For social researchers keen to accurately capture the social scene, accessing this hidden reality means that one must go deeper into the researched community.

Measham recently undertook 200 hours of ethnographic observation in Soho, London, between the hours of 6pm to 4am, across twenty consecutive nights. The study, funded by Westminster Council (Hadfield et al., 2015), sought to investigate the benefits and costs of the night time economy in Soho. Her presence on the street from dusk till dawn in all weathers allowed her the opportunity to get to know the characters who inhabited the area after dark – the touts, dealers, sex workers, homeless drinkers, beggars, taxi drivers, rickshaw cyclists, pickpockets and flower sellers – those who lingered long after the customers had left the theatres, bars and nightclubs. Over the course of the fieldwork, seeing the same characters night after night, she was able to build up a rapport with these various street inhabitants and begin to hear their stories. These various nocturnal habitués grew to trust her and gradually became willing to confide in her. Measham exposed herself to significant personal risks, and she witnessed or became aware of a wide range of sometimes very serious crimes. However, it is only by taking on these challenges that we can access the rich data that *in situ* research can yield. It is only by developing personal relationships with groups of interest to criminologists that we can begin to refine our understanding of complex issues that lie beneath mere verbal recollections of the social scene. And, of course, if Measham had informed the police every time she witnessed or heard about a crime, her research project would have been over just as it was beginning to get underway. Conducting research projects of this kind takes time, and they are not without risk. However, there is no 'ethical' reason why we should effectively close off participant observation to researchers keen to take on the challenges of engaging with the world in this way (see Ancrum, 2012).

Of course many criminal groups remain almost totally inaccessible to criminological researchers. In such instances it may be necessary to use covert methods to generate data, and it is at this point that we need the thoughtful and considered judgement of our peers to determine how far the researcher can or should go in search of criminological knowledge. It is quite obviously counter-productive to deny ourselves knowledge of reality because researching that reality may necessitate the use of covert methods. We completely refute the suggestion that covert methods are necessarily unethical and in every instance harm the researched community. Of course, by demanding that all ethnographers utilise consent procedures the ethics committee is engaged in a subtle process of eradicating covert ethnography. When used judiciously, covert ethnography has great utility for criminology. It is only in the current context of panoramic liberalism – in which we assume that denying individuals all available information is necessarily 'unethical' – that we have formed the view that covert research is fundamentally wrong and must be dispensed with. Perhaps more than any other methodology covert ethnography has the capacity to reveal hidden worlds. It enables the criminological community to leave behind the confines of the campus and become conversant with the lifeworlds of our most marginalised communities. However, in British criminology it has almost disappeared.

Other forms of qualitative research are also under pressure. Today virtually all researchers who engage with human subjects are required to use consent forms.

These forms usually outline the research project, describe how the words of the interviewee will be used, indicate that the interviewee can withdraw from the interview at any time, and provide the interviewee with contact information for a supervisor working at the university who they can contact if they feel uncomfortable about what has taken place. In many respects this process is unproblematic, but we should also note that such formalities immediately disturb social behaviour and deprive it of a degree of authenticity. If we are interviewing probation officers, an occupational group with direct experience of bureaucracy and with little to lose when engaging with academic researchers, then it's likely that their commentary will not be hugely affected by the presence of consent forms. However, if we are interviewing violent criminals in a non-custodial setting, and if we intend to ask them about their own involvement in violent crime (see for example Winlow, 2014), then the consent procedure quite clearly has the potential to disrupt and potentially ruin the research project. Of course, some research contacts cannot read and write and feel ill-at-ease in the presence of such forms. They are uncomfortable with 'authority' as most of their encounters with it have been negative. They have encountered forms in police stations and prisons, and associate such formalities with those settings. What chance does the researcher have of getting a violent criminal to talk honestly and openly about his crimes in such circumstances?

In the example alluded to above, Measham applied for ethical approval for annual surveys, ethnographic observations and stakeholder interviews in South London gay clubs as part of her broader portfolio of research on dance drug use in dance music venues. The project hinged on a decision by a university ethics committee to demand the written informed consent of every customer in a nightclub (which often held around one thousand people) before the project could be granted ethical approval and data collection could go ahead. Of course, the management of the nightclub would have immediately withdrawn its support for the research if such a strategy was adopted, and the research project would then have had to be abandoned. It would be almost impossible to go through a consent procedure with one thousand clubbers in the space of one night, and totally impossible to do this before moving on to the actual business of researching drug-users and club-goers. And, of course, those attending the venue had no interest in such matters. They wanted to get into the club as quickly as possible so that they could enjoy their night out. Forcing clubbers to go through this procedure would have ensured many club-goers simply disengaged and went elsewhere. To complicate matters further still, this was a nightclub popular with men who have sex with men. Understandably, many of the club's patrons would have been unwilling to leave a record that they had been in attendance. An absurd judgement by an ethics committee keen to enforce the rules almost destroyed a research project that held great promise. Edicts such as this indicate quite clearly just how detached some ethics committees are from the actual business of social scientific research.

Ethics committees with a little more experience in dealing with research proposals put forward by criminologists often accept that, in such circumstances, a verbal consent procedure can be used instead of the usual forms. In verbal consent procedures the researcher simply talks through the content of the consent form and outlines for the interviewee key points of note. Again, this can work, but it can also alienate respondents and encourage them to withdraw. When conducting ethnographic work with violent offenders (Winlow), or with customers in the night time economy (Measham), a huge amount of effort is needed simply to get the respondent into a position where it is possible to ask research-based questions. The researcher needs respondents to feel comfortable with his or her presence. If the researcher then pulls out a recording device and adopts the formal language of the university, events can quickly take a turn for the worse. And further, we should not simply assume that it will be easy to come across another research contact of this type. Many ethnographers conduct interviews as part of their broader projects, and snowball sampling is often used to develop a workable sample. The ethnographer needs gatekeepers. He or she needs to develop and maintain workable relationships with key contacts. Even verbal consent procedures have the potential to impede data gathering and disrupt budding research relationships.

Understandably enough, many active criminals distrust those who carry forms and ask for signatures. They have learnt to clam up when faced with individuals from an alien culture who talk about research projects, outputs and complaints procedures. It is not that the interviewee's initial reticence cannot be overcome, but considerable effort needs to be applied to maintain affective research relationships in the presence of such formalities, and inevitably some research contacts will find the process too off-putting and decide to withdraw or otherwise withhold information. Our claim is not that research that fully subscribes to the logic of informed consent has little value. Such research can be of considerable use. However, we must accept that covert participant observation, or research that bypasses the formalities of informed consent procedures, is better suited to capturing something approaching authenticity, or at least a reality less disturbed by the presence of a researcher.

Conclusion: towards an embodied professional ethics

To us it seems obvious that criminologists must mount a determined campaign to defend ourselves against forces that have the potential to curtail the production of criminological knowledge. We must defend qualitative and *in situ* research methodologies and fight for the right to engage with the world as we find it. We must do all we can to ensure that, as much as possible, market pragmatism is dispensed with and proper ethical consideration of research problems becomes the focus of attention.

Research questions

1. According to the authors, how has the institutional ethics committee changed in recent years?

2. How might informed consent procedures, both written and verbal, disrupt ethnographic research encounters?

Case example

> Gordon… begins to kick the man and is joined in this by Frankie and Matty. They aim kicks at the man's head, the way you would shape up to strike a football with utmost force. Frankie is swearing, calling the man a bastard. I see the man role into the foetus position and cover his head with his hands. Matty… is also swearing and is now raising his foot to stamp on the man's head. Frankie and Matty, and now Kevin, kick the man for a while longer and then ease up for a moment. The wounded man, lying on the ground, has stopped moving and I consider seriously the possibility that they've killed him. However, he then sparks back into life, rolls onto his other side, re-covers his head and the kicking recommences. Against all instinct I tell the men to stop. I don't want to, but I feel compelled. I know what doing this can mean. I am not naïve about what these men can do. My stomach is turning as I say, leave him alone, he's had enough… The Monday following this incident I was in the more comfortable confines of Durham University. I spoke to my supervisor and we agreed it was time to start negotiating my withdrawal from the field.
>
> *(Winlow, 2001: 157–159)*

Questions

1. For the researcher, what was the most ethical course of action in this case?
2. Can there ever be a reasonable justification for conducting covert research among criminal groups of this sort?
3. If covert research is judged fundamentally 'unethical', how will this judgement affect the production of criminological knowledge?

Summary

In this chapter we have argued that institutional ethics committees are now less concerned with 'ethics' than they are with defending the institution from possible litigation, reputational damage and negative attention. The infiltration of market concerns into the realm of ethical deliberation has the potential to shift the trajectory of British criminology and deprive generations of scholars forms of knowledge that spring from participant observation, covert ethnography and other forms of qualitative and *in situ* social research.

Guide to further reading

Measham, F., Wood, D., Dargan, P. and Moore, K. (2011), 'The Rise in Legal Highs: Prevalence and patterns in the use of illegal drugs and first and second generation "legal highs" in south London gay dance clubs', *Journal of Substance Use*, 16 (4): 263–272. In this article Measham and colleagues discuss their work in south London dance clubs and reflect upon some of the problems associated with generating data in such a setting.

Winlow, S. and Hall, S. (2012) 'What is an "Ethics Committee"? Academic Governance in an Epic of Belief and Incredulity', *British Journal of Criminology*, 52 (2): 400–416. In this article, using Lacanian psychoanalysis, Winlow and Hall offer a critique of postmodernism, the marketisation of the university and contemporary institutional ethics committees.

References

Ancrum, C. (2012). 'Stalking the Margins of Legality: Ethnography, Participant Observation and the Postmodern Underworld' in S. Winlow and R. Atkinson (eds) *New Directions in Crime and Deviancy*, London: Routledge.

Becker, H. (1963). *Outsiders*, New York: The Free Press.

Bell, D. (2014). 'What is Liberalism?', *Political Theory*, DOI: 10.1177/0090591714535103.

Berger, J. (1972). *Ways of Seeing*, Harmondsworth: Penguin.

British Society of Criminology (2006). *Code of Ethics for Researchers in the Field of Criminology*, http://www.britsoccrim.org/docs/CodeofEthics.pdf.

Currie, E. (2007). 'Against Marginality: Arguments for a Public Criminology', *Theoretical Criminology*, 11(2): 175–90.

Ditton, J. (1979). *Contrology: Beyond the New Criminology*, London: Macmillan.

Hadfield, P., Measham, F., Sharples, S. and Bevan, T. (2015). The Evening and Night-time Economy in London's West End: A Behavioural Audit and Case Studies in 10 Locations, Final Report to the City of Westminster, www.philhadfield.co.uk.

Hall, S. (2012). *Theorizing Crime and Deviance: A New Perspective*, London: Sage.

Hall, S. and Winlow, S. (2015). *Revitalizing Criminological Theory: Towards a New Ultra-Realism*, London: Routledge.

Hall, S., Winlow, S. and Ancrum, C. (2008). *Criminal Identities and Consumer Culture: Crime, Exclusion and the New Culture of Narcissism*, Cullompton: Willan.

Hobbs, D., Hadfield, P. Lister, S. and Winlow, S. (2003). *Bouncers: Violence and Governance in the Night-time Economy*, Oxford: Oxford University Press.

Horsley, M. (2014). 'The Death of the Deviance and the Stagnation of 20th Century Criminology' in M. Dellwing, J. Kotarba and N. Pino (eds) *The Death and Resurrection of Deviance*, London: Palgrave Macmillan.

Matthews, R. (2009). 'Beyond 'so what?' Criminology: Rediscovering Realism', *Theoretical Criminology* 13(3): 341–362.

Matthews, R. (2015). *Realist Criminology*, London: Palgrave Macmillan.

Measham, F., Wood, D., Dargan, P. and Moore, K. (2011). 'The Rise in Legal Highs: Prevalence and Patterns in the Use of Illegal Drugs and First and Second Generation "Legal Highs" in South London Gay Dance Clubs', *Journal of Substance Use*, 16 (4): 263–272.

Polsky, N. (1967). *Hustlers, Beats and Others*, New York: Anchor.

Smart, C. (2003). 'Feminist Approaches to Criminology or Postmodern Woman meets Atavistic Man', *Crime: Critical Concepts in Sociology*, London: Routledge, pp. 153–169.

First published in 1991 in Feminist Perspectives in Criminology edited by Gelsthorpe, L. and Morris, A. (Milton Keynes: Open University Press).

Smith, O. (2014). *Contemporary Adulthood and the Night-Time Leisure Economy*, London: Palgrave Macmillan.

Thrasher, F. (1927). *The Gang*, Chicago: University of Chicago Press.

Winlow, S. (2001). *Badfellas: Crime, Tradition and New Masculinities*, Oxford: Berg.

Winlow, S. (2012). 'Is it OK to Talk about Capitalism Again? Or, Why Criminology Must Take a Leap of Faith' in S. Winlow and R. Atkinson (eds) *New Directions in Crime and Deviancy*, London: Routledge.

Winlow, S. (2014). 'Trauma, Guilt and the Unconscious: Some Theoretical Notes on Violent Subjectivity' in J. Kilby and L. Ray (eds) *Violence and Society: Towards a New Sociology*, Sociological Review Monograph Series, *The Sociological Review*, Volume 62, Issue Supplement S2, pages 32–49, December 2014, Oxford: Wiley-Blackwell.

Winlow, S. and Hall, S. (2006). Violent Night: Urban Leisure and Contemporary Culture, Oxford: Berg.

Winlow, S. and Hall, S. (2012). 'What is an "Ethics Committee"? Academic Governance in an Epic of Belief and Incredulity', *British Journal of Criminology*, 52 (2): 400–416.

Winlow, S., Hall, S., Briggs, D. and Treadwell, J. (2015). *Riots and Political Protest: Notes from the Post-Political Present*, London: Routledge.

Winlow, S., Hobbs, D., Lister, S., and Hadfield, P. (2001). 'Get Ready to Duck: Bouncers and the Realities of Ethnographic Research on Violent Groups', *British Journal of Criminology*, 41 (3): 536–548.

Young, J. (1971). *The Drugtakers*, London: Paladin.

13

CRITICAL REFLECTIONS

Creating, curtailing and communicating academic freedoms

Malcolm Cowburn, Loraine Gelsthorpe and Azrini Wahidin

This collection of essays demonstrates that criminological research is diverse both in the subjects it considers, the methods it uses and its approach to ethical issues. However, in looking back at the various contributions we are struck by the thematic links across the three separate parts of the book. Each of the chapters explores issues related to recognition, responding and reflection, all of which are concerned with the tensions in developing new knowledge, sustaining academic freedom whilst ensuring that research does not cause harm. All of the chapters indicate issues to be addressed but do not point to the simple clear cut solutions, often sought by students, colleagues and ourselves. In this final chapter we highlight some issues related to the three 'Rs' highlighted above – recognition, response and reflection.

Recognition

Recognition is an ongoing process that incorporates both epistemological and practical issues. Epistemology points to both what is known and *how* it is known. It involves identifying and refining relevant knowledge of the area to be researched. Conventionally this may start with an area of interest and move on to developing a research question; the research question points to relevant literatures to be identified, explored and critiqued. The process of identifying sources also involves rejecting material and in this activity of refinement the researcher's standpoint towards her/his area of inquiry emerges. Standpoint (re)emerges through processes of review and the inevitable reframing of the research areas. However, this does not merely identify personal and political preferences in relation to the subject matter and the construction of knowledge. As Winlow and Measham, in their chapter suggest, choices of subject and epistemological orientation are also shaped by more practical issues – for example, the preferences of funding bodies, and funding bodies make decisions based on many criteria, including political priorities (e.g ESRC sponsorship of a seminar series on Right Wing Extremism in Contemporary Europe, ESRC 2016). However, political priorities are not the only factors that determine what is recognised as being worthy of research(ing). Concerns with methodological rigour and ethical imperatives also shape the knowledge that is constructed by research. Fox points to the problems in evidence based policy research, where the quantitative paradigm is (politically) deemed to produce the only 'valid' form of knowledge. Whilst quantitative approaches are very important in identifying wide social issues (e.g. demographic patterns of crime etc.) they largely ignore personal experiences of people who are affected by crimes, either as perpetrators, as victims, or people working within the criminal justice system. Methodological approaches that involve qualitative approaches engage with the complexities of personal experience and sensitive data whether or not this involves personal contacts (see Knepper's chapter).

To recognise the sensitive nature of some criminological research is not necessarily to constrain or curtail exploring a subject, it does, however, present challenges which, when thought through, can produce richer data (see for example Girling and also Hackett on researching children and young people). Recognition entails an awareness of the shortcomings of research data and finding ways to redress this – listening to children's contemporaneous accounts of being victims of sex crimes greatly adds to previous knowledge based on retrospective studies with adults. Neyroud describes both the strengths and problems with 'insider' research of the police; the insider may recognise issues that are invisible to the outsider researcher, but the insider may also be subject to suspicion that s/he is betraying her/his colleagues. One way of addressing this (and many other) issue(s) is to clarify how researchers will *respond* to what they hear.

However before we move on to consider *responding* there are more practical issues to address in relation to *recognition*. These involve the ability to see and recognise issues prior to and during the process of research that require ethical consideration and practical response. We mentioned above that, ideally, researchers would like a 'how to' guide to recognising problematic situations in empirical research; this chapter cannot offer this.

In recognising that epistemological assumptions and research design shape the data that emerges from a project, it is not possible to ignore how practical constraints may also inhibit or curtail the knowledge created. Smith and Cowburn, amongst others, discuss the parameters of confidentiality on criminological research, and propose 'limited confidentiality' in most circumstances. However recognising situations where confidentiality may need to be broken is not always easy. In focus groups and in semi-structured interviews disclosure of sensitive material may happen very quickly before researchers are aware of it. Of course, research has the potential to be harmful – to participants, to researchers and in certain cases to previous or potential victims. If we accept that researchers have a responsibility to aim to 'do no harm' then they also have responsibility to recognise *where* their research may cause harm or trigger harms to occur. There is also the potential harm of offering confidentiality and then breaching it.

We also have to recognise that criminologists work in a changing landscape, this means that new ethical dilemmas are constantly emerging. The chapters on research on evidence-based policy (Fox), archives (Knepper), with children (Girling), prisons (Moore and Wahidin), police (Neyroud), social work in criminal justice (Smith), sex offenders (Cowburn), child sexual assault (Hackett), war crimes (Campbell) and green criminology (Brisman and South) all point to new areas of research and new ethical challenges. Looking forwards, we might add to this by mentioning for instance, the emergence of the digital age means new research methods, new possibilities and new ethical challenges.

Indeed, an increasing number of people access the internet, often through their mobile phones. The development of Web technology has led to what has been described as the 'Participative Web' – an evolution from mainly information seeking behaviour to more interactive behaviour including user-generated content (ugc) (OECD, 2007). UGC has been defined as 'i) content made publicly available over the internet, ii) which reflects a certain amount of creative effort, and iii) which is created outside of professional routines and practices' (OECD, 2007: 4). User-generated content of course can include postings to chatrooms, newsgroups or forums as well as blogs and multi-media uploads (OECD, 2007: 10). Online activity and UGC provide a rich arena for both interactive research as well as unobtrusive research which is easy to access and gives unique insights into everyday life in contemporary society (Garcia et al., 2009; Kozinets, 2015).

As Kozinets (2015) has pointed out, there are a number of challenges in the relative freedom of undertaking internet-based research. While it seems that many of the ethical issues raised by internet research are similar to those in conventional research, internet research raises some unique ethical questions (McKee and Porter, 2009, Wood and Griffiths, 2007). Over the past fifteen years many researchers have debated the adequacy of applying traditional ethics to internet research without reaching consensus (Buchanan, 2010; Berry, 2004). Of course, netnographic incursions have potential to be as invasive as any other forms of research and just thinking about the issue of 'informed consent' raises particular challenges. Firstly, since the research does not involve direct meetings with people, does it count as 'human subjects research' where consent is needed? It seems that there is also lack of agreement about the need for informed consent – even when the authors agree that it is human subjects research. Some commentators have suggested that it is good practice to secure informed consent unless there is good reason not to. Hoser and Nitschke (2010: 183), for instance, argue that online postings should only be used for the 'intended audience' unless informed consent has been secured. Reasons for not seeking informed consent on publicly accessible sites include not wanting to disrupt the online community especially if the data collection is to be anonymised (Hudson and Bruckman, 2004). At the same time, the practical difficulties involved in securing consent from the entire population of an online forum may warrant a waiver of informed consent (Hudson and Bruckman, 2004). From a copyright perspective, it may be suggested that if the material is for research and 'fair use' then it is exempt from requiring informed consent (Hookway, 2008). Where consent is considered necessary, alternative approaches to seeking informed consent from the whole community include contacting the site moderator for 'negotiated consent' to study the site or contacting individual participants for their permission if quotes are to be used in the study. Those posting online may be unaware that their communication may be subject to covert research, perhaps due to the relative anonymity that the internet appears to offer. Yet when considering whether to refer or quote directly from online material that is publicly available, it is important to consider the impact of this on the participants. There is certainly indication that people post personal information online without awareness of the informational traces that they leave behind and which may later cause concern about privacy (Hoser and Nitschke, 2010: 181). It is also important to consider the impact of the study on the community if informed consent is not sought. As Elgesem (2002: 202) has put it:

> Indeed, the climate of trust in a self-defined community ... can be threatened if information is disseminated without the consent of those concerned. Not only can this be harmful to the people whose words are quoted, but it can also potentially be a threat to the social dynamics that made the group an interesting object of study in the first place.

Interestingly, Pollock (2009) suggests that remote research, in some cases, may be safer for researchers and we should remind ourselves that users of 'chat-rooms' tend to use pseudonyms in their interactions.

Concerns about informed consent and privacy have a long history which pre-date the rise of digital culture, and which have been expressed in a range of different forms, from dystopian novels and films, legal judgments and political leaks and scandals. The problems of consent and privacy have to be reconfigured with the arrival of new technologies of writing, reading and communication. We simply want to remind readers of this.

We cannot pursue matters further here, but we hope that we have given sufficient lead for such matters to be considered in thinking about ethics and research in Criminology. As indicated, there must be alertness to the changing research landscape and to changing notions of consent and privacy. But let us now turn to 'Responding'.

There are two major journals largely dedicated to research on the internet. *Ethics and Information Technology* and *International Journal of Internet Research Ethics*. There is also an Association of Internet Researchers (http://aoir.org) and a number of helpful texts are available (see, for example, Boellstorff et al., 2012; McKee and Porter, 2009).

Responding

So how should researchers respond to ethical dilemmas. One of our aspirations for this book is to make readers aware of the need to practise exercising what we might call 'ethical muscles'. As indicated, notwithstanding common areas of concern relating to 'harm' and 'consent', there are perhaps no absolute blueprints for action or guides or off the shelf solutions for researchers because all research situations contain elements which are unique. Researchers need to know when to record things, when not to, when to intervene, and when not to. Some years ago, the BSC Ethics Committee received indication that a young researcher in prisons had witnessed an officer 'stealing' an item which belonged to an inmate. He was concerned to know what to do since his first instinct was to go and tell a prison governor. Further exploration with the student concerned revealed that he did not know whether the officer had 'stolen' the property or merely 'removed' property which the prisoner was not meant to have in his cell. But in the course of considering his case the BSC Ethics Committee suggested that an immediate recourse to a prison governor may not have helped the research; indeed, it may well have exacerbated an already tense situation with prison staff since the research followed hot on the heels of a management review of working practices and there was already some suspicion that further research simply meant 'time and motion' monitoring. Further discussion with the student led to a realisation that the observation itself might lead to new enquiry itself and that in the overall analysis of the research, focused on how new prison officers 'learn on the job', he might have posed the question as to how the prison authorities ensure that officers do not 'steal' items or behave in any other fashion that would be disreputable. In other words, how were new recruits, fresh on the wing, inculcated with the required professional standards? But would this decision to approach the issue 'sideways' rather than confrontationally work as well in a case of observations of police brutality, for example. There, any decision would be shaped by perceptions of immediate harm and an action to inform a senior police officer might well be justified.

Neyroud's research on the police raises related questions about insider research and role conflict. This is a more common problem than we might first imagine, given the proliferation of courses where students are professionals within the criminal justice system and where they are required to submit a research-based dissertation as part of the course. Such researchers may well observe things that they know are not good practice and wish to intervene, there and then, but have to think through the possibility that the research will be all the more effective if 'research distance' is maintained and whatever is observed used in research findings rather than the basis of immediate action. The exceptions, here of course, as with all research, might be where immediate risk of harm (invariably a subjective judgement) is exposed. But 'biding one's time' and approaching the matter side ways on can be important on occasion.

David Smith challenges us to consider related issues where commitment to anonymity and confidentiality may have to be limited. He poses questions as to whether confidentiality can be offered where research participants reveal past criminal acts or future acts which they are contemplating. A pragmatic response (and seemingly ethically sound response) is for the researcher to acknowledge that some topics may be off limits. But, as Smith reflects, what counts as a serious criminal offence? It is hard to assume moral consensus here; consultation may be important to check that one's own moral compass is in line with others' sense, bearing in mind that there may be different perceptions of the same behaviour. For the most part, there will be others to consult, supervisors, advisors, colleagues, learned societies and so on. But there will also be situations where one has to make decisions in the moment, notwithstanding preparation and the adoption of protocols. The prisoner who shows you a shard of glass with which s/he intends to harm himself/herself may well be asking for help, even if s/he says don't tell anyone and the research will have to work with this, possibly by informing a senior officer, possibly by seeking out a sympathetic officer or saying very clearly to the prisoner that you are so concerned that you see no alternative than to abandon the research interview and to tell someone who will be able to help (and then you have to hope that there will be someone who can help…but there may be a Listening Scheme within the prison or the number of the Samaritans on display and one can direct the prison, if not accompany the prisoner, to those potential sources of help). This example goes to the core of anticipating and recognising potential ethical issues before the research starts. The participant information sheet outlines how researchers should behave in such circumstances, but such protocols should not take the place of ethical engagement. Protocols can provide a structure that is known to both researcher and research participant that enable an ethical and non-harmful outcome.

Reflection

Following Schön (1983: 76–104) who identifies two types of reflection – 'on action' and 'in action', the previous section encouraged reflection *on* action. In this section we start by encouraging reflection *in* action. The terms reflective and reflexive are concerned with thinking; in connection with research they point to *thoughtful* practice from initial conception to publication of findings. Throughout this book both types of reflection are found. Reflection 'on action' begins with identifying, designing and planning the research project. Apart from the consideration of practical issues it involves focus on epistemological and ethical issues (see for example the chapters by Girling, Moore and Wahidin, Brisman and South, and Smith). As these chapters, and many others in this collection show, it is an ethical obligation to interrogate and explore epistemologies and previous knowledge of areas under consideration. Knowledge of any area is not homogenous, and whilst there may be a dominant/orthodox way of looking at things, this is always open to challenge (for example consider the challenges posed to hegemonic knowledge by various forms of feminism, green criminology and post-colonial thought). It is an ethical obligation of a researcher to justify her/his relationship to pre-existing literature.

Schön (1983) also points to a more dynamic form of reflection – 'in action'. This is sometimes also referred to as 'reflexivity'. This requires of researchers self-awareness, particularly in considering how personal values influence research practice, and in turn how these impact on research participants. Fook and Gardner

(2007: 29), discussing social work practice, describe reflexivity that is also key to ethical research:

> Being reflexive … means being aware of what methods we are using, the setting and purpose of the information being gathered, the effects this has on the information obtained, and, of course, making an assessment about whether they are mutually appropriate.

Thus, in ethically conducted research we suggest that there needs to be a constant interplay between three elements: theoretical frameworks that shape the knowledge of the area being explored; ethics to monitor that the research is not harmful and is respectful of human rights; and reflexive attention to the detail of what is happening in the total research project. Fook and Gardner (2007: 30) neatly summarise the provisional nature of a reflexive approach:

> Being reflexive from this perspective means understanding how any knowledge may in fact represent only limited perspectives, from the particular point in time or a particular standpoint. This means being open to the possibility of other perspectives.

More broadly, the aim of this book has been to encourage reflexivity in relation to the changing landscape of criminological topics, and in relation to the changing patterns of control and regulation. The questions and exercises provided with each chapter provide vehicles for critical reflection in specific areas of criminological research.

References

Berry, D. (2004). Internet research: privacy, ethics, and alienation: an open source approach. *Internet Research* 14(4): 323–32.

Boellstorff, T., Nardi, B., Pearce, C. and Taylor, T. (2012). *Ethnography and Virtual Worlds: A Handbook of Methods*. Princeton, NJ: Princeton University Press.

Buchanan, E. (2010). Internet research ethics: past, present, and future. In Burnett, R. Consalvo, M. Ess, C. (Eds.) *The handbook of internet studies*. Malden, MA: Wiley-Blackwell.

Elgesem, D. (2002). What is special about the ethical issues in online research? *Ethics and Information Technology* 4: 195–203.

ESRC (2016). 'Right Wing Extremism in Contemporary Europe' http://gtr.rcuk.ac.uk/project/96219EA5-F9B6-4BEC-9B72-095EC78E8210 (Accessed 7th May 2016).

Fook, J. and Gardner, F. (2007). *Practising critical reflection: a resource handbook*. Maidenhead: Open University Press.

Garcia, A., Standlee, A., Bechkoff, J. and Cui, Y. (2009). Ethnographic approaches to the internet and computer-mediated communication. *Journal of Contemporary Ethnography* 38(1): 52–84.

Hookway, N. (2008). Entering the blogosphere: some strategies for using blogs in social research. *Qualitative Research* 8(1): 91–113.

Hoser, B., and Nitschke, T. (2010). Questions on ethics for research in the virtually connected world. *Social Networks* 32(3): 180–6.

Hudson, J. and Bruckman, A. (2004). 'Go away': participant objections to being studied and the ethics of chatroom research. *The Information Society* 20: 127–39.

Kozinets, R. (2015). *Netnography: redefined*. London: Sage.

McKee, H. and Porter, J. (2009). *The ethics of internet research: a rhetorical, case-based process.* New York: Peter Lang Publishing.

OECD. (2007). *Participative web and user-created content: Web 2.0, Wikis and social networking.* Paris: OECD Publishing.

Pollock, E. (2009). Researching white supremacists on-line: methodological concerns of researching 'speech', *Internet Journal of Criminology*: 1–19. www. internetjournalofcriminology.com.

Schön, D. A. (1983). *The reflective practitioner*. London: Temple Smith.

Wood, R. and Griffiths, M. (2007). Online data collection from gamblers: methodological issues. *International Journal of Mental Health and Addiction* 5: 151–63.

INDEX

Note: Page numbers in *italic* type refer to *tables*; page numbers followed by 'n' refer to notes